CUT AND ENGRAVED GLASS
1771–1905

CUT
AND ENGRAVED
GLASS
1771-1905

*The Collectors' Guide
to American Wares*

BY DOROTHY DANIEL

*DRAWINGS BY
SIGISMUND VIDBERGS*

Sixth Edition

M. BARROWS AND COMPANY, INC.
NEW YORK

TO ROYAL

FOR REASONS TOO OBVIOUS
TO MENTION

CONTENTS

ILLUSTRATIONS

[9]

ILLUSTRATIONS

ILLUSTRATIONS

ILLUSTRATIONS

Mankind resemble glass; they are, like it,
For use or fashion, show or service fit;
Some bright and fair, some dull and more obscure,
These prized as good, those, estimed poor;
To grace a kitchen, or a parlour made,
As use is most consulted, or parade;
But all as various; and eke they are,
As frail, as brittle, and as keen a ware.

Their bases differ, as our chemists say,
This made of sand, that fashioned out of clay
Yet shall we, in both compositions find,
Similitude in beauty, use and kind.
To man, 'tis true, some small objections lie
In point of texture and transparency,
But though we grant him, in material blind,
Yet lacks he not transparency of mind,
And we no surer faults in each detect
By rays of light, than rays of intellect.

So nice the processes the art requires,
So pure th' ingredients, so intense the fires,
. . . .
Such just connection links the several parts,
That let one fail, and vain are vitric arts.
Hence faults arise—such faults in glass there be.
And all perfection is but in degree.
So men are good, or evil, just and wise,
Compared to devils or to deities,
And this a good and pious man we call,
Opposed to that, who lacks the virtues all
None are quite perfect, and the best I wot,
Heav'n mend them! may display a flaw or spot
And the whole question, talk it o'er and o'er,
Is who has fewest foibles to deplore.

GLASS, *a poem by* HENRY ROWE SCHOOLCRAFT,
Lake Dunmore, 1814, from a manuscript in the
Library of Congress

PREFACE

I N THE years that this book was in preparation, and since, the question asked me most frequently has been, "How did you become interested in cut glass?" And often the inflection is much the same as though I had taken up sword swallowing or bee keeping.

The answer is very simple. I was born interested in cut glass.

My grandmother, whose tastes were molded and pretty well fixed in the last quarter of the nineteenth century, lived in a large and very ugly house in a small and very pretty town in Iowa. In her dining room was a china cupboard about six feet high with curved glass sides and door. On the bottom shelf was the fish-and-game set. On the next shelf was the hand-painted china, including the mayonnaise bowl with the purple grapes and gold border that my mother painted for Grandmother one Christmas. This belongs to me now and it pleases me to notice, whenever I use it, that Mother must have got a little bored with the whole thing before she finished because the saucer has the gold border but only the outline of the grapes.

On the three shelves above the hand-painted china was the cut glass. There were plates and bowls, bottles and tumblers, salts and butters, cruets and nappies, goblets and water pitchers—but no decanters. Grandmother had inherited some nice decanters from her mother, but they had been sold at the Methodist rummage sale the year Granddaddy unexpectedly was elected an honorary member of the W.C.T.U.

My grandfather was a lawyer. And Grandmother was a very good cook. Sometimes when court was in session, Granddaddy in a burst of generosity would invite the visiting judge home for dinner, which we had in the middle of the day.

The day that Granddaddy chose to bring the Judge home would be the day that Grandmother had spent the morning with her quilt scraps and was not prepared for company. All we would have on such a day were boiled limabeans (the dry kind), country sausage (seasoned highly with sage and red pepper and a lot of other things people have forgotten the use of), johnnycake, baked apples, crisp fried mush, and a dried peach pie, hot out of the oven with the juice bubbling out around the edges.

Grandmother was always in the kitchen when Granddaddy got home from the office. For one reason, that's where he liked to find her and for another, that's where she was busy getting dinner. So Granddaddy would plunk the Judge down in the Morris chair in the library and hand him Ovid's *Ars Amatoria; Epistulae Heroidum* which he knew full well the Judge couldn't read but would be too proud to refuse. Then he appeared beaming at the door that led from the pantry down a little ramp into the summer kitchen.

And Grandmother would turn toward him, squinting her blue-grey eyes and tilting her fat little body on her tiny feet, like a wren about to surprise a big fuzzy caterpillar. "Papa!" she'd say in what amounted to a muted shout, for Granddaddy was very hard-of-hearing, "Who is in the library?"

"Martindale!" he'd announce, as though he had just netted a rare species of Brazilian butterfly, "and the old fool's making out like he's reading Ovid!"

"Papa! I haven't got a thing for dinner but some boiled beans!"

"Oh, that's all right," he'd say, as he picked up the water bucket and started for the well. "Just put on all the cut glass and open up some of your strawberry preserves and watermelon pickle and he'll never know the difference."

That's how I came to be interested in cut glass.

I must say that my interest was a latent one until one summer twenty years ago when a chance incident fanned the spark into flames. My husband and I were spending a glorious golden month touring the Atlantic beaches. We arrived in Savannah on our wedding anniversary and walked around to an antique store to buy us an anniversary present. We thought we'd like some cut glass finger bowls to use for ice-cream dishes.

The antique store had some all right, as well as other very nice pieces of cut glass, all of which might as well have been solid gold. When we hinted that the price was a bit high, we were informed that on the contrary it was cheap for "English glass." It seems that every piece of glass in the shop was English or Irish.

I picked up a vinegar cruet and asked, "This, too?"

"Every piece I have," the proprietor insisted.

Her vinegar cruet was the twin of the one that Grandmother had used to confound Judge Martindale on Limabean Day, and Grandmother's cruet had most certainly come from Pittsburgh.

The innocence of the Savannah lady was in no way singular to antique dealers. And she had thus, unwittingly, given me the premise for this book.

Collectors and some glass manufacturers have long shared the idea that there was little "old" American cut glass extant in this country, even though statistics clearly show that a great deal of fine lead glass was cut here in the early years. When I declared my intention to dig out all the available information about our American cut glass and consolidate it in a book of reference for collectors and students, several authorities gloomily shook their heads, "Where angels fear to tread!" they warned. Others declared flatly that all cut glass found in this country obviously not of the late nineteenth century was English or Irish.

It seemed to me that our cut glass deserved more consideration. Mr. M. S. Dudley Westropp, formerly curator of the National Museum, in Dublin, Ireland had written a fine book about Irish glass. Mr. W. A. Thorpe of the Victoria and Albert Museum in London had done the same for English cut glass. Surely our own cut glass, which is in many ways finer than either the Irish or the English, should have some record.

The research that followed was tedious and often disappointing. Many early pieces have been labeled Waterford for so long that it was difficult to establish their true source as American. There are available only a half dozen catalogues of glasshouses showing cut glass patterns, and only two of these were published before 1880.

That this first book on American cut glass is far from faultless, I know only too well. There are lapses of time, missing places and patterns, simply because at this point too little is known about either the factories or the glass they produced in localities not mentioned.

England and Ireland have been collecting, documenting, and cataloguing their cut glass for over a hundred years. A century from now the knowledge of our own cut glass will probably be correspondingly accurate and complete, but until such time as other material, catalogues, memoranda, and authenticated pieces come to light, we shall have to do with what we have and try to make a beginning, thus belatedly, on the documentation of American cut glass.

In the preparation of this manuscript, I have been fortunate in having the assistance, guidance, criticism, and encouragement of many wonderful people. I am particularly grateful to Mr. Westropp, now retired from the National Museum of Dublin, who still retains his keen interest in cut glass. Mr. Westropp has been kind enough to check many doubtful examples of early cut glass from our own National Museum, the White House collection, Mount Vernon, and other repositories of heirloom glass.

Dr. Alexander Silverman, Head of the Chemistry Department of the University of Pittsburgh, an internationally famous authority on ceramics, graciously made available to me his numerous papers and articles on American glass, and in addition answered hundreds of questions regarding methods, techniques, and the science of glassmaking.

Mr. Samuel Hawkes, of Corning, New York, gave me suggestions, help, and guidance during all the years this book has been growing. Mr. Hawkes is directly responsible for the identification of many of the more important patterns.

Mr. Frank L. Bryant of Tiffin, Ohio, came to my rescue in the early days with catalogues, suggestions, and answers to problems that seemed to me then almost unsolvable.

Mr. C. U. Fauster of Toledo, Ohio, has been unfailingly generous with material from his meticulously indexed scrapbooks and reference files.

Miss Rose Demorest of the Pennsylvania Room at the Carnegie Library in Pittsburgh has given much time and thought in helping with the outline and research on the text. Miss Catherine Hay and Miss Martha Barnes of the Carnegie Library staff have hunted down obscure references and traced old documentary material. The brunt of searching patent office records and other labyrinths of public information fell upon the slim shoulders of my sister, Mrs. Howard Dobson of Alexandria, Virginia. Without her tireless, willing, and able help, the manuscript could never have been completed.

Mr. Herbert Sanborn, Director of Exhibits at the Library of Congress, first called my attention to the Schoolcraft manuscript on "Vitreology," and Mr. Willard Webb, Director of Stacks there, made my research immeasurably easier by his interested assistance.

Many museums, and libraries, and historical societies have contributed to this book; and I am particularly grateful to Miss Carmen Wilson, Assistant Reference Librarian of the John Crerar Library in Chicago, for her diligent search of the files of the *Crockery and Glass Journal* for the last half of the nineteenth century.

Special mention must be included here also of many individuals who have given time for interviews, and shared with me letters, family records, and special notes. Mr. Ralph Heller, of Monticello College, Alton, Illinois, graciously permitted the use of his thesis, "Edward Drummond Libbey." Colonel Harry C. Fry of Pittsburgh gave me my first lessons in the manufacture of glass and startled the wits out of me by making me my first Prince Rupert drop. Mr. William Anderson of Pittsburgh, Mr. C. W. Meredith and Mr. Leman W. Dolby of Rochester, Pennsylvania, Mr. Henry Fisher of Tiffin, Ohio, Mr. Edward F. Gebhard of Uniontown, Pennsylvania all contributed anecdotes and personal reminiscences. Mr. J. Fletcher Gillinder furnished much of my material on Gillinder glass. Mr. Thomas A. Tripp gave me information on the Pairpoint Manufacturing Corporation and its antecedents. Mr.

Charles Messer Stow of the *New York Sun,* has repeatedly made clippings and photographs available. To Mr. Frank Semple of Sewickley, Pennsylvania and Mr. Milton V. Burgess, of Pittsburgh, I am indebted for the loan of valuable and irreplaceable old reference books. Mr. John M. Graham, 2nd, Curator of Decorative Arts at the Brooklyn Museum; Mr. Louis C. Madeira, IV, of the Philadelphia Museum of Art; Miss Nell L. Jaffe of the Toledo Museum of Art; Mr. Hayward S. Ablewhite, Director of the Edison Institute Museum; Mr. Charles J. Milton, Museum Director of the Oglebay Institute, Wheeling, West Virginia; Mr. H. W. Krieger of the Smithsonian Institution and Mr. John J. O'Connor, Jr., and Dr. E. R. Eller of the Carnegie Museum of Pittsburgh have been ever helpful and willing to supply photographs, acquisition records, and other essential data for tracing the history of glass.

A kindly fate also introduced me to Mrs. Bella C. Landauer of the New York Historical Society, whose collection of mercantile catalogues, cards, and advertising memorabilia was put at my disposal and proved invaluable in tracing factories and dates.

Mrs. Henry C. Lewis of Philadelphia, Mrs. Henry R. Rea of Sewickley, Dr. Florence Kline and Mr. Lowell Innes of Pittsburgh, Miss Elizabeth Wightman, Miss Mary Wightman, and Mrs. Laurence Gouverneur Hoes of Washington, D.C., Mr. Jerome Strauss, Mr. J. A. Lloyd Hyde, of New York, Mrs. Adolph Schmidt, Mrs. W. S. Stimmel, Jr., Mrs. S. N. Benham, Mrs. Lida Snowdon Henesey, and Mrs. John M. Feeney graciously permitted the photographing of prized pieces from their private collections.

To these and to all the other good people who have given so freely of their time, their interest, their encouragement—and have listened so endlessly to the story of American cut and engraved glass—I am deeply and humbly grateful.

DOROTHY DANIEL

◇ ◇

CHAPTER I

CUT GLASS: AN AMERICAN HERITAGE

TODAY we think of cut class as the popular tableware of fifty
years ago. At first marvelously beautiful, it declined at last to
such grotesque forms that even popular taste was outraged and its
early beauty has since been almost forgotten. Actually those hideous
specimens of the 1900s were but the tag ends of an art practiced in
America for nearly two centuries. The time has now come to appreciate our heritage and at long last to safeguard the many exquisite
pieces of cut glass that remain.

American glass was first decorated by cutting at the American
Flint Glass Manufactory of Henry William Stiegel at Manheim,
Pennsylvania, in 1771. Since that date there has never been a year
when glassmakers somewhere in America were not cutting and engraving glass, some of it simple in form, handblown from metal of
indifferent quality, and ornamented with panels and flutes, other
pieces of luxury quality designed for the sideboards of the wealthy
and the tables of important people of the day.

Cut glass is decorated by a moving wheel. Engraved glass is
cut by smaller wheels and left unpolished. Metal (glass in a state
of fusion) that is to be cut deeply or engraved must be of high
quality, composed of heavy lead flint or of a fine grade of potash,
and should be either handblown or blown-molded. The cutting is
always done by hand. Pieces vary in value and importance according
to the purity of materials used, the skill of the manufacturer, and
the artistry and talent of the cutter or engraver. All cut glass is
good glass but some pieces are better than others.

American cut glass has a distinguished inheritance, both ancient

PLATE I

Jar for ointments, 6¼ inches high. Rare piece of ancient glass, probably made in Egypt 668–626 B.C. Concave circle motifs in cut decoration identical to modern bull's-eye. Panel cutting on neck similar to modern flute cutting.
(Toledo Mus. of Art)

and modern. Ancient or antique glass, as it is sometimes called, dates from an undetermined time some two thousand years before the birth of Christ. The earliest known cut glass may have been made five or six hundred years before the Christian era. Pieces have been found of Assyrian, Egyptian, and Roman origin for that period (Plate 1).

Modern glass begins with the sixteenth century when the art of cutting and engraving was revived in southern Europe, and developed four styles, the Oriental, Continental, Anglo-Irish, and American. The American is directly descended from the Anglo-Irish fashion of metal founding and wheel decoration. While such early manufacturers as Stiegel and Amelung were so influenced by their native traditions that the glass produced at their houses resembled the Continental of the same period, the general character of American glass remained closer to the English and Irish.

American glass is either "white," or "green." White glass (the technical term for clear—not to be confused with milk-white) resembles rock crystal. It is clear, transparent, and is produced without a coloring agent. Grades are determined by how closely they approach the ideal of clear crystal. White glass is usually intended for tableware or windowpanes.

Green glass is cheaper, being composed of common sand and other inexpensive ingredients. Little effort is made to obtain clarity or transparency. Green glass is used chiefly for beer and pop bottles or for preserving jars; in the early days it served for milk dishes and window glass.

There are four types of American glass—blown, cut, pressed, and painted. All technical terms unavoidably used in this and later chapters will be found defined in the Glossary.

Blown glass is decorated offhand while the metal is still hot and in a viscous condition. Either it is manipulated into various forms or small pieces of hot glass are added to the original vessel. Trailing, pinchering, applied decoration, teardrops, some overlay, and twirling are possibilities for blown glass.

Cut glass comes second in point of time. Glass is cut after it has been fashioned, annealed, and thoroughly cooled. A finished piece

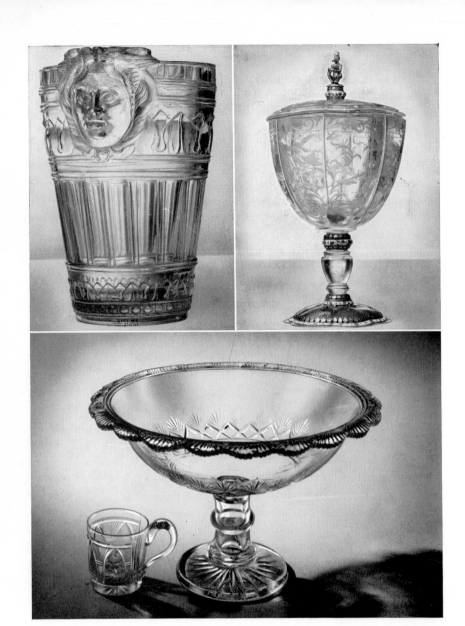

PLATE 2

UPPER, LEFT: *Crystal cup, sixteenth century, German. Pillar motif copied by Anglo-Irish and American cutters.* RIGHT: *Rock crystal chalice, sixteenth century, Italian. Wheel engraving. (Metropolitan Mus. of Art)* LOWER: *Punch cup with arched motif; compote with turned lip. Rare cut glass of Early American Period. (Dr. E. R. Eller)*

which has not yet been applied to the cutter's wheel is called a cut glass blank.

Pressed glass was the latest of the four decorative processes used on American glass. The design is actually pressed on by a plunger and a glass press while the metal is in a viscous state.

Painted glass never attained the popularity here that it enjoyed in Italy, Germany, and Bohemia, but some fine pieces have been produced in America. Stiegel's enamels belong in this category and the glass decorated at Sandwich. Gilding, such as that practiced by the Brooklyn glasshouses, and modern stained glass are all applications of this technique in which luster stains or enamels are applied to cold glass later fired in a kiln to set the decoration.

PERIODS OF AMERICAN CUT GLASS

Modern collectors are most familiar with the glass cut during the Brilliant Period. This was of heavy lead with fine luster and clarity. It was miter-cut in deep splits to form squares, diamonds, and stars in patterns. While such ware was cut extensively from 1880 on, it represents but one of three classifications in American cut glass.

The Early American Period begins about 1771, when according to the well-known authority, Frederick William Hunter, Stiegel's glasshouse at Manheim, Pennsylvania, was entering its most successful period. It ends in 1830, the year the Baldwin bill for the collection of port duties became effective and a high tariff excluded importations.

The Middle Period started in 1830, when a national style of glass was beginning to evince itself, and continued to about 1880. This period reflects the simplicity of contemporaneous life in the popular flute decanters, dishes, tumblers, and compotes. (See Plate 3.)

Methods of manufacturing colored lead glass were developed and fine-line cuttings became popular. The originality and skill of engravers increased. After 1865 it is doubtful if the cut glass industry could have survived the competition of pressed lime glass if the manufacture of lamp shades and chimneys had not come to the res-

PLATE 3

Heavy lead glass compote, flute-cut through purple flashing. 10½ inches high. Rare Pittsburgh glass of Middle Period. Credited to O'Leary, Mulvaney and Co., 1843. (Mrs. Lida Snowden Henesey)

cue of the leading companies. The bonanza that followed the revolution in illumination tided the industry over until 1880, when the cut glass of the Brilliant Period created the greatest market the industry has ever seen.

A combination of fortuitous circumstances brought about the Brilliant Period: new and better glass sands were discovered, natural gas was harnessed as a fuel for furnaces, and electricity was applied to the wheel lathes. Most important of all, prosperity arrived so that almost every family in America could afford cut glass for the dining table. Cut glass had long been the symbol of elegance and leisure. Now it became the hallmark of social prestige. In 1840 there had been eighty-one glasshouses in operation, according to U.S. Census reports. Thirty-four cutting shops employed over a thousand men to make cut glass. In 1876 only eight glasshouses exhibited at The Centennial Exhibition, but by 1900 there were well over a hundred, and the cutting shops running full tilt employed more than three thousand glass blowers, cutters, and engravers. Cut glass became again the standard wedding present, the gift supreme!

REASONS FOR COLLECTING AMERICAN CUT GLASS

Old American cut glass is irreplaceable. It has historical importance, and decoratively, it belongs with the fine furniture of our early years. American cut glass also has very real intrinsic value. A nine-inch berry bowl which cost thirty-five dollars in 1900 would cost one hundred dollars to reproduce today. Labor and materials have so increased in cost that the large-scale production of fine handmade and hand-cut lead glass is no longer profitable. Indeed, it is unlikely that cut glass will be available to most of us again unless we search out what still remains and collect it.

Much fine old cut glass is still treasured in American homes. Because it is fragile and likely to be broken in moving from place to place, the greatest treasures of the early period are in homes of old established communities where there has been continuity of fine living for generations. New England and the South—Boston, Charleston, Savannah, New Orleans, Natchez—are all paradises

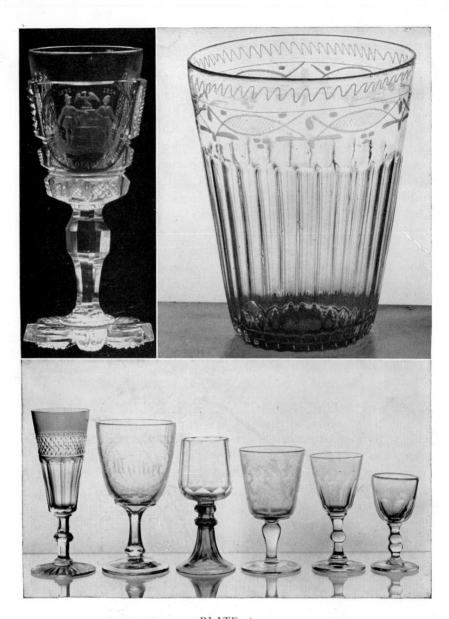

PLATE 4

UPPER, LEFT: *Goblet cut for Dorflinger exhibit, Centennial Exposition, 1876. Arms of Maryland engraved in medallion,* Crescite et Multiplicamini. *(Philadelphia Mus. of Art)* RIGHT: *Stiegel flip, Type 1. (N.-Y. Hist. Soc.)* LOWER: *Wine glasses with flashing, cutting, engraving, and etching. Champagne glass, extreme left, excellent example of gold-ruby flashing. (Author's Collection)*

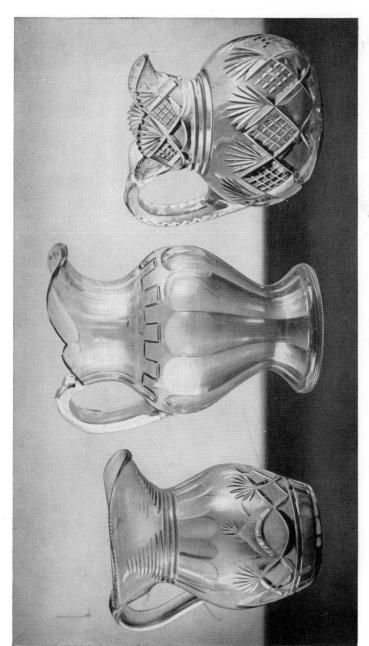

PLATE 5

Pitchers showing progression of form and design. LEFT TO RIGHT: Early American, cut by Bakewell; vesica and English strawberry-diamond motifs, about 1825. Middle Period, fluted, engraving on shoulder; Brilliant Period, globe, English strawberry-diamond motif with American Strawberry-Diamond and Fan pattern. (Author's Collection)

PLATE 6

UPPER, LEFT TO RIGHT: *Decanters showing progression of form. Early American, fluted; Middle Period, partitioned cutting, bull's-eye motif; Brilliant Period, champagne type, hob-star motif.* LOWER, LEFT: *Compote, Brilliant Period, with tear drop.* RIGHT: *Two-way compote, Stourbridge works, 1830.* (*Author's Collection*)

for the collector of cut glass. Fine glass can still be found also in the neighborhoods of the old factories in Pittsburgh, Wheeling, Philadelphia, Baltimore, and certain cities in Massachusetts and Connecticut.

Glass from the Middle Period is not so plentiful as that of the later Brilliant Period, but there is still fine colored and engraved glass to be discovered in shops and private homes throughout the country. When such pieces turn up they should be treasured for cabinet collections. This is particularly true of engraved glass of the Middle Period.

Cut glass of the Brilliant Period is easily identified and there is a quantity of it unappreciated, and perhaps forgotten, tucked away on the top shelves of cupboards in old houses. Once the value of these pieces is realized they will doubtless be brought to view and cherished again. Although the motifs are familiar to most collectors, it is remarkable that in the eighty years since brilliant cuttings first were made, so little information regarding patterns and motif combinations has been recorded.

In this book I have identified and classified fifty patterns of the Brilliant Period with their variations. Some of these patterns are fairly common. Others are rare. Examples of this glass are to be found in all parts of the United States, Central America, Mexico, Cuba, and South America. You, yourself, may have glass of the Brilliant Period stored away in attic or basement. As is the case with cut glass of other periods not all the pieces will be of equal excellence, but some of it will probably be very fine and worth preserving for posterity as examples of an art in which American craftsmen once excelled all others in the world.

This book, the first on the subject, must due to limitations of space confine itself to the obvious guides to classification and identification of American cut and engraved glass. The beginning collector should first classify his own pieces according to period. Those of the same period should then be studied comparatively with reference to metal, form, cutting, motif, pattern, and general excellence of execution. Crude glass should not necessarily be considered early glass. Some early pieces are far better by every standard than those of later years.

PLATE 7

UPPER: *Twelve-inch berry bowl, cut in variation of Russian pattern. Displayed at Columbian Exposition, Chicago. (Carnegie Mus.)* LOWER: *Goblet and saucer champagne, Russian, with engraved crest; cut for White House, 1886, T. G. Hawkes Glass Co. (White House)*

PLATE 8

UPPER, LEFT TO RIGHT: *Berry bowl, 7-inch, American Strawberry-Diamond and Fan. Celery vase, Bakewell, about 1825. Brandy jug, hob-star motif. Jug cruet, pinwheel motif.* LOWER: *Flat candle holders, American Strawberry-Diamond and Fan. Except for vase, all pieces cut by H. C. Fry Glass Co. during Brilliant Period.* (Harry C. Fry)

A collector may find that a fine specimen in his collection cannot be identified with any of the illustrations or descriptions given in this text. So much the better! The cutting of glass is a handcraft. It thrived on individuality and originality. The piece that does not conform to these broad primary classifications gives the collector an opportunity to identify it through study and comparison—and sometimes by luck—until his piece forms another link in the chain of knowledge being forged on this early craft and its craftsmen.

Actually this book endeavors only to state the case—to lay the groundwork for the development of a field of collection hitherto known to few collectors. These for lack of background information have had to approach the largest classification of American glass with the least adequate yardstick of evaluation. Today's careful but enthusiastic collectors are building, piece by piece, the foundation and assembling the documentation for one of the finest heritages of early industry and craftsmanship—American cut glass.

✧ ✧

HOW TO DETECT IMITATIONS

ALL THAT glitters is not gold, but most glass that sparkles is
fairly certain to have been cut. This prismatic brilliance of cut
glass is its most distinguishing feature and the one most difficult to
imitate. Many manufacturers seeking a less expensive but just-as-
good product have tried. Because cut glass has always been the
aristocrat, sparkling on the tables of kings and presidents, it has
been a natural target for imitation. Glass sold as cut-glass-type has
been the result.

So far as the collector of cut glass is concerned there is no glass
that is just as good; glass is either cut or it is not cut. Yet sometimes difficulties stand in the way of identification.

Four types of glass were originally designed to copy cut glass:
blown-molded, pattern pressed lead, pattern pressed lime, and glass
cut on fire-finished pressed blanks. The first three classifications have
become separately collectible so that for the collector of cut glass
there is little danger of confusion with them. Only the fourth is
likely to give difficulty: glass cut on fire-finished pressed blanks resembles true cut glass in weight and pattern and lacks only its essential brilliance and sharpness of cutting.

Blown-molded glass is glass which has been blown into a mold on
which a pattern has previously been carved or cast. While the pattern on many of the early blown-molded decanters, flips, and bottles
copies early cut glass patterns, it will be apparent that the outline of
the design is too smooth and rounded to have been produced by
cutting. Furthermore, these early blown-molded pieces are now so

rare and so prized by collectors of the type that there is little danger of their turning up to confuse the uninitiated.

Pressed lead glass was made before 1827, the date usually given for the invention of the pressing machine; but pressed lead glass did not become a serious competitor of cut glass until after this date. The early patterns copied cut glass designs faithfully, but lead glass was so "lazy" in the press that the edges of the patterns came out soft and rounded, not at all sharp as when cut. Pressed lead glass has the ring of cut glass but it lacks the sharpness of decoration and the prismatic luster. It is usually of low color, grey or smoky. Sandwich lacy is a pressed lead glass.

Pressed lime glass was made after 1865 in great quantity and in a profusion of patterns. Many of the earlier patterns were designed specifically for the press and could not have been cut into lead glass by means of the wheel because of the complicated nature of the design. After 1880, however, when the great vogue developed for brilliant cut glass, some manufacturers did press lime glass into patterns that were exact copies of those used on cut glass. The most obvious copy was the Daisy and Button which duplicated the Star and Hobnail of early lead glass, producing a pressed-glass imitation of the Russian pattern of fine cut ware.

Glass cut on fire-finished pressed blanks can usually be distinguished from fine cut glass by slight ridges or raised places on the inside of the piece *directly* opposite the deeper incisions on the outside. These bulges in the glass are inherent in the method of manufacture. The finest pieces of cut glass are made of good lead glass blanks which have either been blown offhand or blown into a paste mold with no decoration whatever. The inner or refractory surface of such a blank sets in the air. Nothing touches this surface from the time the blank is first made by a glass blower until it is completely cooled and taken to the cutting room. Here the broader aspects of the design, the deep incisions, are made by a rougher. Then a smoother works over the deep incisions and adds the little extra cuttings with the smaller stone wheel. Roughing and smoothing are expensive operations which contribute to the high cost of a piece of fine cut glass.

When a pressed blank is used much expense is saved. A pressed

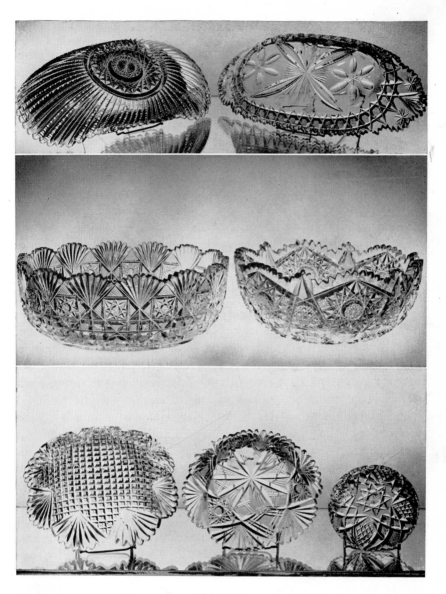

PLATE 9

UPPER: *Celery boat, White House pattern. Bread tray in fine line cutting, Middle Period.* CENTER: *Flat-bottom, 10-inch berry bowl, partitioned design from early Brilliant Period, and standard 9-inch bowl, chair-bottom and hobstar.* LOWER, LEFT TO RIGHT: *Rare, 7-inch, Strawberry-Diamond and Fan plate; 6-inch plate; 4-inch plate. (Author's Collection)*

blank already carries the first deep incisions of the decoration. These have been pressed while the glass was molten. The pressing process was developed to save the manufacturer the cost of hand labor on each and every vessel, the employment of the rougher to cut the first incisions, and the loss of metal resulting from the primary cutting. Some large pieces of cut glass, such as punch bowls, lose as much as a third of their weight in cutting. At least half of this waste was saved by pressing. Pressing, however, left its mark. When the plunger of the press made contact with the hot glass, it destroyed the refractory surface.

Glass that is cut on a pressed blank should probably not be included in a collection of fine cut glass because in a way it is an imitation, the product of a short cut. It is usually of inferior metal, although it does contain lead and will ring. Glass cut on a pressed blank does not have the prismatic luster of true cut glass. The edges of the cuts—especially the deeper ones—are soft, rounded, and smooth. There is lacking that sharp definition of "snap" to the cutting typical of true cut glass. Furthermore, glass cut on pressed blanks gathers dust quickly, fogs more readily, and cannot be polished as brightly as true cut glass. Usually in bowls, nappies, or vessels large enough for such examination those slight ridges or raised places on the inside of the piece are easily felt. They are definite proof that the blank was pressed and fire-finished before its final cutting.

POSITIVE TESTS OF FINE CUT GLASS

When you are in doubt as to whether a piece of cut glass has been completely cut, partly cut, or not cut at all, but decorated by some other means, test it for ring, sparkle, sharpness, and weight. These four tests will also help you to determine the relative quality of the piece of glass you are examining.

1. *Ring.* Strike a piece of cut glass lightly with the side of a pencil or snap it with your fingers and it will ring like a bell. This will always happen unless the piece has a closed top as is the case with carafes, decanters, perfume bottles, and other vessels where

PLATE 10

UPPER: *Berry bowls, 9-inch, Hawkes; 8-inch, Libbey.* CENTER, LEFT TO
RIGHT: *Nappies, hob-star and curved split; broken split; relief cutting in dia-*
mond band, New England Glass Co., 1825. (Author's Collection) LOWER:
Wine service, same company, 1865–1868, sharp-diamond motif, for Maj. Gen.
Judson Kilpatrick. (Smithsonian Inst.)

the nature of the piece smothers the ring. Not all pieces ring alike. In fact, two pieces from the same batch of metal may not ring in the same pitch. Nor is it necessarily true that the finer the glass the longer the ring. Among connoisseurs the ring of cut glass is considered one of its more attractive characteristics and is due to the lead and saltpeter used in its manufacture.

Since American cut glass is usually made of lead, the rule of ring may be almost generally applied, but there are three notable exceptions:

(a) Early pressed glass, designed to copy cut glass, is made of lead, too, and will ring, although it is not cut. It includes the early pressed lead glass pieces of the New England Glass Company, Sandwich lacy pressings, and some early Bakewell. These pieces are few compared to the great amount of standard pressed glass made of soda lime, which has no ring at all. Pressed glass that does ring is easily distinguished from cut glass by the smooth rounded contours of the design and its grey color.

(b) Early Amelung, Philadelphia, and Maryland glass pieces show cuttings and engravings but the ring is short, sharp, and brittle, evidence that lead is lacking as a basic ingredient.

(c) Luster-stained potash glass, sometimes called Bohemian, is frequently decorated with shallow surface cutting. This is cut glass, although it gives when struck the short tinkle of potash glass rather than the bell-like ring of lead glass.

2. *Sparkle.* Hold a piece of fine cut glass to the light and notice the refraction made by the cutting. Only fine cut glass of high lead content has such brilliance. It is this quality which is destroyed by pressing and which manufacturers endeavored, without success, to restore by fire-finishing. Nothing can replace the refractory surface that lead glass establishes in air.

The degree of refraction depends on the ingredients of the metal and the kind and amount of cutting in the design. Glass made and cut in America after 1880 readily refracts light because of the crystalline purity of ingredients used in manufacture and the quick fusion made possible by the adaptation of natural gas as fuel. The refraction is less in Early American pieces due to impurities in the metal and less perfect fusion.

The deep miter cuttings of the Brilliant Period tend to make glass sparkle more than the flatter panel cuttings of the Early or Middle Periods. The copper-wheel engravings of the Middle Period being unpolished have a white surface which does not refract light at all. However most pieces of engraved glass also have cut stems, lips, or bases which are polished to catch the light.

3. *Sharpness.* Run your fingers over the cutting. If the edges are sharp, the glass is cut; if they are smooth, the chances are the design has been pressed, or cut over a pressed blank. The roundness of a cut edge is not to be confused with the deliberate and exquisitely cut and polished smoothness of certain fine cut pieces made in the Early American Period. The Robinson decanter (Plate 45) is an example of the polished cutting of pillar and ring motifs. These are always cut on heavy glass of unmistakable lead content and are so combined with sharp diamond or block cuttings that there can be little question of type.

The feel of this sharpness is a more reliable guide than its visual appearance. Run your fingers over the tops of nailhead diamonds or along the edges of deep miter cuttings. The points *feel* sharp; the sides of the cuttings feel smooth and polished, the edges also have a sharp definition not easily confused with the minutely uneven surface and edge left by the pressing mold.

4. *Weight.* Because of high lead content, cut glass is usually heavy. Approximately sixty pounds of lead were used for every hundred pounds of sand in the manufacture of the blanks for cut glass during the middle and late years of the nineteenth century. It is understandable then that a decanter, compote, bowl, or goblet made of such blanks will be noticeably heavier than the same-sized piece made of glass of no lead content.

However, Amelung and some other pieces of Maryland and Philadelphia glass are exceptions to the rule of weight. These are unusually light due to the calcined seaweed or barilla which was used as the potash ingredient.

Cut glass is, in the final analysis, *good glass.* Whether a wine glass made by James O'Hara in 1804 as bar-ware, a butter dish made by one of the Fisher brothers in New York City in 1825, a goblet engraved by one of the Leighton family in 1850, a decanter cut for Mrs. Abraham Lincoln by Dorflinger in 1861, a punch cup cut for the Russian Ambassador by Hawkes in 1886, or a bowl engraved for Princess Elizabeth by Steuben in 1947, American cut glass is first, last, and always fine glass—the best glass of its time.

Much glass was cut or engraved in individual pieces, particularly goblets and finger tumblers. Decanters were often cut in pairs, (Plate 11) but glass has also been cut in sets since the beginning of the craft in America. Presidents Monroe and Jackson had complete sets cut for the White House (Plates 19, 48) and there is record of other early sets. During the Brilliant Period sets of Russian, Kimberly, Corinthian, and Strawberry-Diamond and Star were relatively common, yet each piece in such sets was an individual achievement. It may have been cut to match other pieces, to give unity to a table setting, but because it represents a handcraft and an artistic skill, it has an individual meaning. It is this that makes the collecting of cut glass such a joy and, in itself, an art.

PLATE II

Fine matched pair of decanters showing sharp-diamond band. Credited to Boston and Sandwich Glass Co. Stoppers are blown and cut. Necks are flute-cut. Almost identical to decanters of same period by New England Glass Co. (Photographs, courtesy Charles Messer Stow, New York Sun)

❖ ❖

CHAPTER III

THE MAKING OF GLASS

I T IS easy to make glass. Volcanoes do it almost every day, but to make fine glass requires skill, experience, and talent. In the early days of glassmaking luck also played a part. Today with modern methods of manufacture nothing is left to chance.

Glass is a fairly stable composition, the result of melting sand with an alkali. There is nothing mysterious about the process, yet man has been trying for four thousand years to perfect it. A collector of cut glass should be able to follow the struggle toward perfection in the pieces he selects. He should know enough about the essential nature of glass to judge for himself whether a piece is wheel-scratched lime glass, fine potash engraved on a wheel, or heavy lead of high or low degree.

Two kinds of metal are used for cut or engraved glass: Bohemian or German flint and lead or English flint. Both have been made in America at various times. Either can be excellent or inferior, depending upon workmanship.

Bohemian or German flint is a soda potash glass which contains no lead. It is usually thin, although it need not be. The thinner pieces give a tinkling sound when struck. Potash or Bohemian flint is mostly of good color but as in some of our early American pieces, it may be slightly low in color and often is noticeably grey. The decoration on such pieces is usually wheel engraving and is rarely polished.

Lead glass or English flint has lead as an essential ingredient. It is soft and can be made in sufficient thickness to absorb the vibration and pressure of the miter wheel. Lead glass has been manufactured

PLATE 12

LEFT: *Rodney decanter with fine engraving. Perhaps from Amelung's works, 1784–1796. (Metropolitan Mus. of Art)* RIGHT: *Pickle dish used at Mount Vernon. Probably by Isaac Gray, Kensington works, 1772–1775. English strawberry-diamond, block, and star motifs. (Mount Vernon Ladies' Assn.)*

in America since the eighteenth century. In this discussion all pieces are assumed to be of lead glass unless otherwise designated because lead glass was the standard American metal for fine cut ware after 1808. We inherited our formulas from the English and Irish and then improved upon their techniques until by the close of the nineteenth century, American manufacturers were making as high quality metal as the world had ever known.

COMPOSITION OF LEAD GLASS

If it were possible to obtain absolutely pure materials to melt under ideal conditions and anneal to perfection, there would be small pleasure in the pursuit of fine old cut glass. Henry Rowe Schoolcraft, writing on the subject of glassmaking in 1812, knew how to make perfect lead glass. Here is his recipe for double flint glass recorded in his own handwriting in his manuscript, "Vitreology or the Art of Smelting":

> "Sand .... 120 pounds (nett)
> Potash .... 30 pounds
> Red lead ...... 90 pounds
> Nitre .... 4 pounds
> Arsenic .... 2 pounds
> Manganese .... 3 ounces"

He adds, "If the materials be such as I have represented they should be, and they be carefully and well prepared, this mixture will produce, so far as depends on the composition, a glass, possessing strength, the weight, the lustre, the purity, density and whiteness of the richest European cut glass." Such perfection was rarely possible during the first hundred years of our glassmaking and for that reason collections present fascinating comparative studies. Early Bakewell glass shows striae, indicating that Bakewell used too much lead and that his fires were slow. Pieces made by George Dummer have air bubbles showing that the fires were too hot. Perhaps this was due to the acceleration of the heat with resin knots, a trick that

PLANT OF THE NEW ENGLAND GLASS COMPANY, EAST CAMBRIDGE, MASS.

PLATE 13

The New England Glass Company as it appeared in 1851. The drawing is a reproduction of one that appeared in Gleason's Pictorial Drawing Room Companion, November 8, 1851. (Libbey Glass Co.)

was patented in 1828 by Dr. Thomas W. Dyott, although the process had been in general use in New Jersey glasshouses many years before that date. Glass made in New England colored down to grey before the use of the Berkshire sands around 1826. All these points are of concern to the collector.

MONKEY POTS AND OPEN TANKS

Glass may be melted in a monkey pot or in an open tank. A monkey pot is a closed cylindrical vessel usually about five and a half feet high with a hole in one side about a foot down from the top. Six or eight or more of these pots are arranged in a circle (the openings facing out) on the floor of a cone-shaped furnace which is usually fired from a pit below the floor. The fire surrounds the pots and the glass is charged and drawn out through the side openings in the pots. Lead glass is made in this manner in order to keep the molten metal free of carbon fumes and other gases of oxidation created in the fire chamber. Lead glass can be made in open tanks and frequently was, but the result is a poor quality of grey or muddy color.

Open pots look like thick-walled wash tubs. They also rest on the floor of a furnace, the fire surrounding them, with the difference that the intense heat passes over the top of the melting glass, thus speeding fusion but also contributing impurities which discolor the metal. Modern tank furnaces are built on the same open-pot principle, except that a tank is larger than a pot, and natural gas is used as fuel.

THE BLOWING OF GLASS

When the ingredients of glass have reached a certain temperature, approximately 2400 degrees Fahrenheit, the molten metal is ready to be worked. At each pot or furnace opening is a "chair," a term that may be applied both literally and figuratively. The chair is a heavy square, wooden seat, with a back and arms extending for-ward beyond the chair itself. This is the blower's seat. He is the

[48]

head man of a group of workmen, usually four, who constitute a shop or a chair, the unit of labor necessary to work each glass pot.

The first man to begin the operation collects a small ball of molten glass called the "gather" on the end of the blowpipe, which is a hollow tube about four feet long. The gatherer puffs a little breath of air into the ball of glass, twirling it the while, and when it has cooled several hundred degrees he rolls the hot glass on a "marver," the metal slab designed to consolidate the metal. The gatherer then delivers the blowpipe to the blower. By blowing and whirling his blowpipe back and forth on the arm of his chair, and by working with tools as ancient as Rome, this man fashions the glass into the desired shape. When the metal becomes too cool to work, he hands it to the servitor, who reheats it in the glory hole, an opening in the furnace made for this purpose.

If the glass is to be flashed, or decorated with an overlay, the servitor brings the blower little globs of colored metal which he drops onto the outside of the hot glass from which the vessel is fashioned.

If the blower is to finish the rim, the servitor attaches a long flat-topped iron rod called a pontil to the end of the vessel by means of a small wad of molten glass, the blowpipe is cracked off, and the workman continues to fashion the vessel holding it now by the pontil. The glass may be reheated many times in the process of hand-fashioning but when it is finally completed the pontil is cracked off leaving the familiar pontil-mark or scar. An apprentice, called a carry-in boy, lifts the vessel on forked sticks or asbestos-covered pinchers and carries the glass to the annealing oven. If a footmaker is to make handles or feet, he works on the glass before it is delivered to the carry-in boy.

MOLD BLOWING AND ANNEALING

Much glass intended for cutting is blown-molded. This it not to be confused with pressed glass, since the mold used is not comparable to a glass press. The early molds were made of cherry or apple wood; later iron molds were used, coated with a paste of resin and beeswax. These were called paste molds. Molds were carved to the general proportions desired for bowl or tumbler. Instead of blowing the glass offhand, the blower first blew the glob of glass slightly, then lowered the glass which adhered to the pipe into a mold suspended in a bucket of water. By blowing and rotating the pipe between his palms he quickly achieved a vessel of perfect symmetry. Because no force other than that of his breath touched the molten inner surface of the vessel, the refractory surface was maintained, thus giving prismatic luster to the finished piece.

Even when perfect materials are melted under controlled conditions, glass will "fly" unless it is annealed, that is, cooled gradually. If glass is cooled quickly, inner tensions are set up which may later be released on contact with a sharp point or even at a slight change in temperature. Then glass explodes or flies to pieces. Glass is annealed in long ovens through which a continuously moving belt carries the pieces slowly from one end where the working temperature is about 1400 degrees Fahrenheit to the other where finished pieces are removed to be packed at room temperature. Even modern annealing lehrs (ovens heated by natural gas) require several hours to complete a satisfactory cooling process.

The undecorated vessel as it is taken from the annealing oven is known as a blank and is stored until needed by the cutter.

◇ ◇

CUTTING, ENGRAVING, ETCHING

IT IS true that all cut glass has been decorated by application to a moving wheel, but there are wheels and wheels, and operators vary greatly in skill. Engraving differs from cutting in the size of the wheel used and consequently in the type of decoration possible. When a piece of glass is engraved, it is held under the wheel and pressed upward toward the engraver and against the wheel. In cutting, the glass is held between the cutter and the wheel and pressed down against it. In both cases the wheels are revolving at high speed. In etching, the decoration is made by the application of a corrosive acid, not by cutting.

The speed of the wheel controls, to some extent, the type of cutting. The earliest power used in England for cutting lead glass was a treadle. The cutter sat or stood at a bench and turned the cutting wheel by pumping a treadle under his right foot in much the same way that grindstones are operated for sharpening axes. Treadle-cutting was confined to more or less simple motifs, such as panels and relief diamonds. A little later apprentices were used to turn the lathes by means of a flywheel, but the boys were not too steady at their work and sometimes lagged behind or got tired and the speed of the wheel was erratic. Even so, the motifs developed a sharper line and some crosshatching was possible; but the lunar slice, favored in England, or the vesica and festoons of Irish decoration did not come until water power was used to speed up the cutting wheels. It is possible that water power was used in Syria and Egypt for cutting glass two hundred years before Christ, since panel scoops and miter squares appear on very early glass (Plate 1).

[51]

GLASS-CUTTING ROOM.

CUTTING SHOP, No. 1,000.

SHOW ROOM OF THE GLASS WORKS.

PLATE 14

UPPER: *Cutting rooms of the New England and of the Libbey glass companies.* LOWER: *Show room of New England Glass Co. (Ballou's* Pictorial Drawing Room Companion, *January 1855.) Epergnes, hanging lamps, compotes, cruets, and apothecary jars were in stock. (Libbey Glass Co.)*

All the methods for turning lathes were used in America (Plate 14). It is particularly likely that water power was used at the Kensington glasshouse in Philadelphia in 1790. Our glassmen were also quick to use steam power for the lathes and Bakewell's glasshouse probably used it as early as 1817. With the help of steam American motifs became deeper, better polished, and sharper than English and Irish cuttings, because foreign glasshouses were slower to adopt new methods. The deep miter cuttings of the Brilliant Period were not made extensively until lathes were equipped with electric motors.

THE CUTTING AND POLISHING OF GLASS

When the vessel to be cut is brought from the storeroom it is first marked by the designer with outlines of the decoration (Plate 15). A rougher next holds the blank against a large, rapidly moving iron wheel, but the wheel does not actually do the cutting. The glass is cut rather by a stream of fine wet sand that drips from an overhanging funnel onto the edge of the wheel and thence to the surface of the glass. The rougher, following the designer's marks, makes the first heavy incisions (Plate 15) and in pushing the glass down against the wheel, he is blind to the contact of wheel and glass. If he sees the work at all, it is through the glass, from inside to outside. There is always danger in miter cutting that the wheel will penetrate the vessel and ruin the blank. In panel cutting, such as that of concave flutes, plain flutes, relief diamonds, or bull's-eye motifs, there is less danger of penetration.

After the rougher has finished with the deep incisions, the glass goes to the smoother. He uses a stone wheel (usually called a craigleith, the name of the natural stone used) to refine the rough first incisions. The smoother also cuts the small lines or motifs indicated by the design (Plate 16).

Deep fine cutting is done with a very narrow wheel or splitter. A slightly flattened splitter may be used for cutting panels, hollows, and circles, but a craigleith miter wheel is more generally employed. The strawberry-diamond motif is produced with the miter wheel as

PLATE 15

UPPER: *"Blank" of a 12-inch plate, with penciled design to guide "rougher."*
LOWER: *Second process. Plate has been "roughed," or cut with first deep incisions. The cut surface of the design is still grey-white from contact with either an iron or a steel wheel and abrasive. Photographs made at T. G. Hawkes Glass Co.*

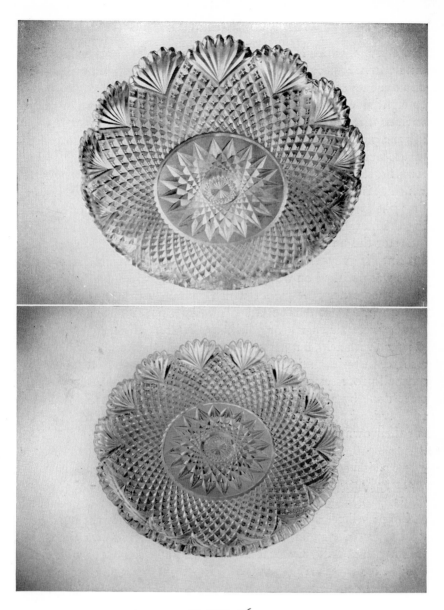

PLATE 16

UPPER: *Third process. Plate has been "smoothed," that is, the stone wheel has been applied to deeper incisions, producing a finer finish. Details of design have been cut in.* LOWER: *Plate has been polished by application to a wooden wheel with rottenstone abrasive. Acid polishing was not in general use before 1900.*

is the prism, which is made by applying the glass to the sides of the miter. Prisms become the edges of facets in a diamond pattern by another movement. Square-cut stars as well as diamonds with three to eight sides are completed merely by moving the piece of glass in various directions against the miter. Buds are made by gently rocking the glass as it is held against the wheel. Outlines of flowers and leaves are perfected by a peculiar rolling motion acquired only by long practice. Serrated or scalloped edges are cut by a panel wheel which acts like a saw in producing right angles. Apprentice boys are first put to work cutting edges since there is no danger of penetrating the metal. Their next job is to cut flute panels.

After the smoother finishes with the design, the surface of all the cut lines is grey-white as in an unpolished engraving. Before 1900 glass was polished on wooden wheels which were made from willow, cherry, or other soft woods which gave a lustrous appearance and left no imperfections on the gleaming surfaces. Rottenstone and pumice were also used for polishing. After 1900 cut glass was often polished with acid, but many collectors feel that hand polishing gives a softer luster than the quicker acid process (Plate 16). In the early days all processes of designing, roughing, smoothing, and polishing were done by a single operator. This slower process is sometimes followed even today by cutters working on special pieces intended for their own use or as gifts.

THE ENGRAVING OF GLASS

Copper-wheel decoration is unquestionably one of the most beautiful types of glyptic ornamentation. It requires more time, skill, training, and natural talent than cutting and compares with cameo sculpturing in its esthetic appeal. Fifty or more small copper wheels are used in engraving. The work is so minute that fine engravings are often studied under a magnifying glass to catch all the exquisite detail. Instead of using a water-and-sand abrasive as in cutting, engravers use a mixture of linseed oil and pumice. Most engravings are left unpolished. The grey-white surface of the engraving ap-

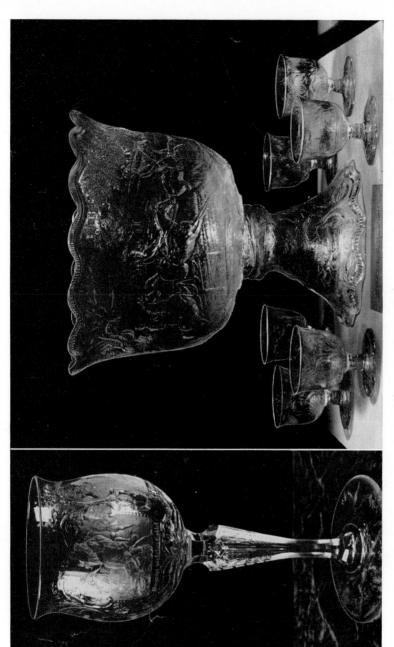

PLATE 17

LEFT: *Edenhall goblet, Hawkes, 1915. Scenes from Longfellow's,* The Luck of Edenhall. *Engraving by William H. Morse. Insured for $5,000. (Samuel Hawkes)* RIGHT: *Punch bowl and cups with unique polished engraving, hunting scenes. Libbey. Gold medal, Columbian Exposition, 1893. (Toledo Mus. of Art)*

PLATE 18

LEFT: *New Bremen covered chalice. Made by John Frederick Amelung in Frederick-town, Maryland, between 1784–1791. (Metropolitan Mus. of Art)*
RIGHT: *Goblet engraved with a view of Mount Vernon about 1876 by the Dithridge Flint Glass Co. (Smithsonian Inst.)*

pears to be in relief against the clear crystal of the vessel. The hunting bowl (Plate 17) is a notable exception.

Engraved glass has always been expensive and many presentation pieces like the Amelung chalice (Plate 18) have been cut with a medallion, inscription, initials, or date. Not all engraving is of equal quality. The early scratchings were fairly simple decorations on Bohemian or potash-flint glass, which would not take the heavier incisions of the cutting wheel; but the later copper-wheel engravings, such as the Edenhall goblet (Plate 17), or modern Steuben pieces (Plate 130) show a perfection never surpassed in the history of glass decoration.

The collector who is not familiar with the technical differences in the pieces of his collection loses much of the story discernible in glass. Knowledge of metal and workmanship helps greatly in placing a piece of glass in its proper locality and period. Some pieces defy classification, it is true, but others have a history to tell to those who can read it. Even if the dates of the three pitchers on Plate 5 had not been established by family record, an astute collector could be fairly certain that the first pitcher was made during the early American period, probably at the Bakewell factory, because of the light metal of high lead content showing striae, the offhand modeling, and the steel-blue shading of the glass in the thick portions. On the other hand he would place the center pitcher considerably later—in the Middle Period—since the metal is heavy, clear, and free of any defect. Although of good color and fine modeling, it lacks the characteristic brilliance of the third pitcher which, by the luster of its metal, as much as by its form and cutting, is easily identified as a product of the Brilliant Period.

It is fun to be a glass detective. Start with your own collection. It will pay you dividends!

CUTTERS AND ENGRAVERS

Cutters and engravers had a pronounced influence on the form and designs of our early glass. Lazarus Isaacs signed a contract with Stiegel in 1773 to cut glass at the American Flint Glass Manufactory, the Manheim glassworks in Lancaster County, Pennsylvania. He was employed as a cutter and flowerer and his work reflects the influence of an engraving style then popular in Germany and Bohemia. Isaacs was to have the sum of £5 10s monthly as pay, a house to live in, a piece of land for a garden, and firewood supplied at five shillings per cord. The contract shows that Isaacs was better paid than most workmen of his day and that he was a man of standing in his community. The finer Stiegel pieces of the later years are credited to him.

Peter William Eichbaum was another colorful German glass cutter who left his mark on early American glass history. He was the descendant of a family in Allemand, Westphalia, which had been glass cutters for generations. When Louis XVI started his ill-timed industrial revival in France, he asked Eichbaum to come to Paris to revive the lost craft, and Eichbaum is said to have been one of the founders of the glass village later known as Saint Louis, a community named for the patron king. It was from the glasshouse there that glass was furnished for the chandeliers and mirrors of the Palace of Versailles.

After the fall of the Bastille, Eichbaum escaped to America through Amsterdam and, because of his friendship with the late Benjamin Franklin, got employment with Robert Morris at the Schuylkill Glass Works in Philadelphia. In 1797 James O'Hara and Isaac Craig seem to have induced Eichbaum to go to Pittsburgh to take charge of their newly erected glasshouse. Eichbaum was not successful as a superintendent. He was a cutter by profession and he was too lenient with the workmen, who criticized him for not being well-informed on glass founding. After a time he leased the works with Frederick Wendt (sometimes written Wentz) but this partnership was short-lived.

Although Eichbaum was interested in the glass business in Pittsburgh for many years, he decided in 1800 to conclude his arrangements with Craig and O'Hara. He opened a hotel and tavern "At the Sign of the Indian Queen" on Front Street near Market Street where in addition to his duties as host, he carried on a business of cutting tumblers and decanters to order. Eichbaum also made chandeliers at his shop, usually from pieces of O'Hara pot glass (Plate

PLATE 19

UPPER, LEFT: *Napkin ring, early Pittsburgh glass, cut in large diamond. Probably by one of Eichbaums for Mary, daughter of James O'Hara. (Alexander Silverman)* UPPER, RIGHT: *Decanter and champagne, Bakewell, engraved by Jardel for James Monroe, 1819. (White House)* LOWER, LEFT TO RIGHT: *Amelung wine; early Pennsylvania goblet, enscribed* Out of Love; *early Pittsburgh wine glass. (Jerome Strauss)*

137). After George Robinson and Edward Ensell began making lead glass, Eichbaum bought his blanks from them, preferring the softer lead metal. The napkin ring (Plate 19) was probably made from Robinson glass by Eichbaum as a present for Mary O'Hara, daughter of his good friend and associate, James O'Hara. It was Eichbaum who introduced the German kugeln, or bull's-eye motif into cut glass decoration in America and also the hexagonal diamond-panel cutting on bottles which he named the "Saint Louis neck."

A. Jardel was another of the famous early engravers. He was a French glassworker who came to Pittsburgh in 1818 and opened a store. He advertised "to engrave and execute everything that may be wished in his line at a moderate price." His advertisement adds: "He has on hand, and will constantly keep an assortment of elegant glassware of every description." When business wasn't too good at first, a postscript appeared: "A few gentlemen can be accommodated with genteel boarding."

Later Jardel pieces became recognized as superb examples of the craft and it became a fad to own anything engraved by him. He no longer took in boarders. The vases presented by Bakewell to Lafayette on his visit to Pittsburgh in 1825 are signed by Jardel and the wine glasses and claret jugs made at the Bakewell glasshouse for the White House at the order of James Monroe were cut and engraved by him (Plate 19).

Louis Vaupel, who came to the New England Glass Company in 1856, is one of the spectacular engravers of the Middle Period. His work is similar to that of old Bohemian engraving and depicts hunting scenes, trees and flowers, animal groups, and naturalistic landscapes.

Henry S. Fillebrown was one of the skillful engravers employed at the New England Glass Company from 1860 to 1880. There is a more characteristic American motif in the Fillebrown engravings than in those by Vaupel. Fillebrown used the grape, ivy, strawberry, and wild rose motifs in addition to birds and fishes.

Several of the Leighton family were talented engravers. Lura Woodside Watkins, in her book on *Cambridge Glass,* mentions a set of heavy tumblers engraved by Henry Leighton. One of these carries the Leighton coat of arms. The William Leightons, Senior

PLATE 20

LEFT: *Drinking glass engraved with chapel of Our Lady the Blessed Virgin Mary, at Coldspring, N. Y. Solid vaseline-colored glass.* RIGHT: *Crystal drinking glass flashed with red. New Orleans scene. Copper-wheel engraving in style of Boston, Brooklyn, and Philadelphia cutters, 1830–1850. Rare pieces. (Jerome Strauss)*

and Junior, were engraving glass at the Hobbs, Brockunier glass house in Wheeling, West Virginia, during the late years of the Middle Period.

While there were many other fine engravers about this time and during the early years of the Brilliant Period, the work of only two has been definitely identified. Joseph Locke's engravings and cameo work for the New England Glass Company are museum pieces. William O. Bowen, a student of John Northwood, also engraved glass of exquisite beauty.

William H. Morse, whose work is more recent (1915 to 1925) than the Brilliant Period, was one of the most skillful engravers in American history. Contemporary engravers at the Corning Glass Center cutting pieces for Steuben carry on the fine tradition. Many modern pieces are so skillfully engraved they seem to be in three dimensions.

ETCHED GLASS

Etched glass is not a type of cut glass, but it is of interest to the collector who needs to understand the etching process in order to distinguish it from engraving. Etching and engraving are by no means the same thing. Etched glass is not cut. Unlike engraved glass which is decorated by a moving wheel, etched glass is made by the application of a corroding acid. We might say that etching is a matter of surface deterioration, but that hardly seems a fair description of the method in the hands of such skilled craftsmen as Joseph Locke, some of whose exquisite pieces are shown on Plate 21; nor does it do justice to the work of the English master, John Northwood, whose replica of the Portland vase was done in part by etching. The trouble with the etching of glass in America seems to have been that except for Locke's work, it was not developed here as an independent art, but used as an imitation of cutting.

Etching was described as early as 1812 by Schoolcraft, who called it "engraving" in his manuscript on Vitreology: "When a vine or flower is required upon the surface of a glass this [is] done by simply using a copper wheel of the size of a cent, with water. These ornaments are, however, most accurately engraved by the fluoric acid which is used in the same manner upon glass that aqua fortis is upon copper; the surface is first covered with a coat of wax and rosin, and the figures drawn, by sharp instruments, that cut through and remove the coating. The liquid acid is poured on, and immediately corrodes the glass. When deep enough its effects are stopped by pouring on water." The early American compote from the collection of Lowell Innes (Plate 22) is a rare example of the early technique of etching. Bleeding of acid under the edge of wax resist is clearly shown. The etched surface has been cut through with wheel engraving.

All etching is done by exposing glass to a corrosive agent, usually, but not always, some form of hydrofluoric acid. The process of etching varies according to the type of "resist" or wax used to cover areas not to be exposed for decoration, the method of applying the pattern, and the kind of acid used to fix it. The various qualities of etching depend entirely on the use and composition of these three factors.

NEEDLE ETCHING

The simplest technique of etching employed a sharp instrument to mark the design and an acid vapor to fix it. This method known as needle etching was followed by many American glasshouses including those at Sandwich, Cambridge, Pittsburgh, and Wheeling. In *Reminiscences of Glass-Making* Deming Jarves gives this description: "The glass to be operated upon is first coated with a ground of wax and the design to be etched is then traced through the wax with a sharp instrument. In a shallow lead basin some powdered fluor spar is then placed and a sufficient quantity of sulphuric acid poured upon it to convert it into a thin paste. The glass to be etched is now placed in the basin to which a gentle heat is applied when the vapor of the acid is disengaged and attacks the traced lines from which the wax has been removed. The operation is completed in a few minutes, the glass is removed and the wax cleaned off with warm oil of turpentine. All those parts which have remained covered

PLATE 21

Pitchers etched and signed by Joseph Locke. LEFT TO RIGHT: Flight of Mary and Joseph; Otus and Ephialtes with Mars in Chains (amberina glass); Grape design; Uncle Remus illustration for which Locke was noted. (Hist. Soc. of W. Penna.)

with wax are now clear as before while the other parts drawn by lines have a frosted appearance."

These early etchings can be distinguished from engravings by the needlelike tracery of the pattern. This is never deep, and the lines are often disconnected because little pieces of wax have escaped the needle and held the acid from the glass. Wine glasses, finger bowls, tumblers, and other lightweight bar and tableware were often decorated with needle etching in conventional designs of loops and scrolls with a multiplicity of fine lines. Early freehand pieces of original design are worth while, but the later pieces with machine-traced patterns are of little value.

PLATE ETCHING

Plate etching in its simplest form was patented in 1859 by James Napier, who had learned the method in Glasgow, Scotland. Napier's idea was to fix a print or lithograph with printer's ink to the surface of the glass by an ordinary starch paste. After the appliqué was dry, he subjected the entire piece to acid three times, and washed it with water. The Napier method was not reliable and was soon improved upon in the American development of plate etching, but pieces with early Napier etchings are priceless. They were frequently made of flashed glass (glass coated with a film of another color). The picture appears as a colored outline against a white frosted background.

Plate etching has been done continuously in America since the development of Napier's patent. It is used to etch crests, shields, and elaborate designs on goblets, tableware, and bar-ware. In this type of etching the master pattern is first made on a metal plate. This is covered with wax and the excess scraped off. A tissue is then laid over the plate and pressed down so that when it is removed, the wax adheres, covering it except where the etched lines have appeared on the master plate. The tissue is then placed on the piece of glass to be etched, and the uncovered section of the glass is coated with wax inside and out. It is then exposed to acid according to the Napier method (Plate 22).

PLATE 22

UPPER: *Ritchie and Wheat pitcher, Wheeling, W. Va., 1830, and Pittsburgh pitcher with applied handle and acid-etched landscape, about 1900. (Author's Collection)* LOWER: *Early American compote, 6¾ inches high, hand-molded stem, folded rim on foot. Decorated by early etching process and wheel cutting. (Lowell Innes)*

PLATE 23

UPPER, LEFT: *Punch cups, oriental scenes, etched by Joseph Locke. (Harry C. Fry)* LOWER, LEFT: *Crystal chalice cased with blue. Overlay of silver filigree. Cut stem and foot. Made in Pittsburgh by Locke in early 1900s. (Hist. Soc. of W. Penn.)* RIGHT: *Champagne pitcher etched by Locke. (Smithsonian Inst.)*

FREEHAND ETCHING

The finest etching results when a skilled artist cuts the pattern through the wax resist without stencil or pattern to guide him. Toward the end of the nineteenth century there were a number of talented freehand etchers at work in America, among them Joseph Locke, friend and associate of Edward Drummond Libbey. Locke developed his own technique and his own resists for etching. Several of his pitchers are illustrated on Plate 21. One is of Amberina glass, a heat-treated metal which Locke invented and patented along with Pomona and Peachblow glass, while he was with the New England Glass Company. Many of his pieces show both engraving and etching, but their distinguishing characteristic is the evidence of two and three layers of etching which makes parts of the design appear in relief. The edge of a leaf or the outline of a pattern will be more pronounced than the rest of the design. Locke used only hydrofluoric acid to get the bright, deep, triple-edged outlines, but for the mat and satin etchings he used hydrofluoric acid with alkali or ammonium fluorides. The chalice (Plate 23) is a most unusual Locke piece. It is a crystal glass cased in blue and then decorated with a partial silver overlay. The foot was cut on a lathe, but the silver was applied in a filigree etching. Locke made a number of these chalices, only two of which are known to exist. They represent a degree of craftsmanship rarely attained by any glassworker in any country.

Fine examples of etched glass such as the best Locke pieces are rare and should be treasured as samples of a specialized art craft (Plate 24), but the average acid-decorated ware was of little value when it first came on the market and is of no greater value to the collector. Today a potash glass finger bowl with a needle-etched border may be bought for ten or fifteen cents, but a lead glass finger bowl *engraved* with the same pattern is worth ten or fifteen dollars.

PLATE 24

UPPER: *Brandy jug, engraved by one of Leightons, and claret pitcher, George and P. C. Dummer, 1825–1830. (Author's Collection)* LOWER, LEFT TO RIGHT: *Etched Uncle Remus glass and pitcher with marine scene, wine glass with typical wheel cutting. All three by Locke. (Alexander Silverman)*

❖ ❖

CHAPTER V

CAMEO AND INTAGLIO GLASS

A FEW very beautiful glass ornaments made in America were sculptured from glass of two or more layers with engraver's tools. These pieces are known as cameo glass when the outside coating—usually white opaque glass—is carved or etched away from the colored undercoat to leave the desired figure in cameo relief. Cameo glass is the direct opposite of intaglio cutting in which the decoration is incised or sunk into the background. Since the sculpturing of glass requires quality metal and considerable artistic skill, both expensive necessities, no great number of pieces were cut and those that remain are highly valued.

The technique of cameo cutting was not used extensively in England until the late years of the nineteenth century and has never been commonly practiced in America, but the method was developed centuries ago. The famous Portland vase was very likely cut in the early years of the Christian era, since it is believed to have been the burial urn for the ashes of Roman Emperor Severus who died 235 A.D. Then the secret of the technique seems to have been lost. Nothing similar appeared in modern times until Josiah Wedgwood's reproduction in 1790. Today the collector of cameo glass does not seek utilitarian tableware but brooches, pendants, plaques, scent bottles, jewellike snuff boxes, jars, vases, and rose water bottles decorated with cameo medallions.

It requires the combined skills of designer, glassmaker, and sculptor to produce a piece of cameo work. The process is intricate. For example, when a vase is to be made the design must first be outlined on paper. This is given the glassmaker who then prepares a cup of white opaque glass of the required size. In this cup he places a mass of dark blue or green or whatever color is desired for the background of the vase. He must take care to drop the colored glass into the very bottom of the cup and to push the mass down carefully until the cup is filled. If this operation is not managed skillfully, air blisters will form between the background and the opaque casing. Next the entire mass is marvered or rolled on a metal slab after which it is blown into the desired size and shape and most carefully annealed, for if there should be the slightest internal strain the piece will fly under the sculpturing pressure. After annealing, the opaque shell is carved away from the background leaving the design in white relief. It is supposed that Chinese cameo glass (Plate 25) was carved in this manner, and authorities believe that the Portland vase was made the same way.

ARTISTS IN CAMEO GLASS

Cameo artists of the late nineteenth century developed a method combining etching and carving techniques. John Northwood, Joseph Locke, and Frederick Carder all produced pieces with this revised process. John Northwood's work was outstanding. He applied the etching principle to cased glass (made with layers of different colors) which he covered with a bituminous resist. On this he drew the outline of the design. Then he cut away the coating from the background and put the glass into a bath of hydrofluoric acid. In the bath the white top layer of glass was etched away until only the blue background remained. At that point the design looked like a silhouette. Using copper wheels and a combination of emery and oil as an abrasive, Northwood ground down the design to give it a rough modeling. He finished off the cameo cutting with engraver's tools. For his reproduction of the Portland vase he had made special mushet steel tools varying from one-eighth to one-sixteenth inch in thickness and ground to give three cutting edges.

The original Portland vase, probably the most famous piece of cameo glass in the world, is only ten inches high and seven wide. On it appears the story of Bacchus and Ariadne in white carved

PLATE 25

UPPER: *Bottom of Portland Vase with figure of Paris.* LOWER: *3½-inch, Chinese, cameo-glass snuff bottles with stoppers. Opaque white glass. Blue overlay on left; rose amber on right. (Alexander Silverman)*

PLATE 26

Reproduction by Wedgwood of Portland Vase in jasper ware. Original, in British Museum, is the most famous piece of decorated glass in the world. A cameo frieze of white glass is carved against a dark blue background and represents the marriage of Peleus and Thetis. (Alexander Silverman)

glass against a dark blue background. The vase was found in 1630 in a marble sarcophagus under Monte del Grano near Rome by a member of the Barberini family and was sold to Sir William Hamilton, who in turn sold it to the Duchess of Portland for whom it is named. In 1786 the third Duke of Portland bought the vase at an auction of his mother's art treasures for £1029. It was lent to the British Museum in 1810, and because cameo sculpturing in glass was not known to craftsmen of that day, the vase was supposed to have been carved from stone. One day a madman struck it with a cane. When it shattered there was no doubt that it was made of glass. After restoration it was placed in the Gold Room of the British Museum, where it remained for one hundred and nineteen years. In 1929 it was offered at auction in London by Messrs. Christie, Manson & Woods. The high bid of $143,000 was refused and the Portland vase was returned to the British Museum, where it is today.

In 1790 Josiah Wedgwood made the first reproductions of the Portland vase (Plate 26) in blue and white jasper ware (a type of porcelain perfected by him in 1775), which is translucent when thin and yet hard enough to grind and polish. He is believed to have made fifty copies. Not more than twenty are now known to exist, of which some may have been made after his death. The original pieces sold for fifty guineas each, a sum insufficient to pay for the manufacture. One of the original reproductions sold in 1892 for £215 5s. It was John Northwood who made the first reproduction in glass and Philip Pargeter, a fellow workman, who cased the blue glass for him in an opaque white enamel glass shell.

The Pegasus vase (Plate 27) was also carved by Northwood. It was exhibited with decoration obviously unfinished at the Exposition Universelle in Paris in 1878. It is now part of the Gellatly Collection of the Smithsonian Institution. The Northwood vase (Plate 27) is distinguished by a green background, and traces of basic color have been left in the cameo. This piece is from the Alexander Silverman Collection.

Three contemporaries of John Northwood came to America and were associated closely with the glass industry here. Joseph Locke, whom we have already mentioned, made many fine cameo pieces.

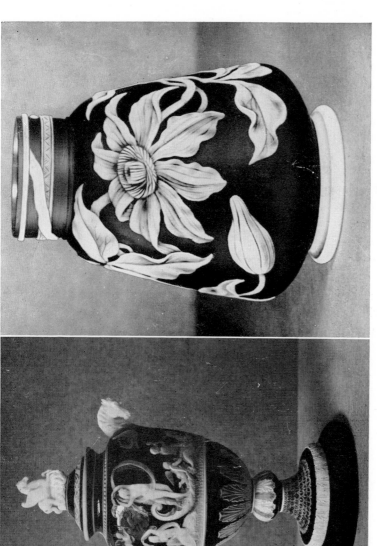

PLATE 27

LEFT: *Pegasus Vase*, 21½ *inches high, famous piece of cameo glass carved by Northwood, 1876–1878. Dark blue body, opal overlay, depicting the* Triumph of Galatea and Aurora. *(Smithsonian Inst.)* RIGHT: *5-inch cameo vase, also by Northwood. Green background, white opaque overlay, cut in cameo. (Alexander Silverman)*

Notable are his brooches, plaques, and scent bottles. Frederick Carder was a master craftsman in the art of cameo, applying the technique to scent bottles (Plate 28). William O. Bowen, a pupil of John Northwood, set up shop in South Brooklyn in 1883. Unfortunately some of Bowen's work was sold as imported "Northwood" cameo glass, although it was made from American metal and in this country. Bowen employed several sculptors and was himself prolific. They cut small vases, scent bottles, cologne bottles, brooches, and plaques. The small bottle in the Alexander Silverman Collection is believed to be a Bowen bottle.

IMITATIONS OF CAMEO GLASS

Because it was costly, rare, and beautiful, cameo glass was copied. In the real article the cameo is carved from glass and is an integral part of the vase or box. In the imitation, the cameo is cast of white china and pasted to a piece of colored glass to achieve the cameo effect. Careful examination of the place where the cameo joins the background will reveal the fraud, since the carved cameo blends—almost bevels—into the background. A piece of white glass or china which has been pasted on will show a definite line of demarcation when scrutinized under a magnifying glass.

The familiar encased silhouettes were also not produced by the cameo technique. Collectors will see these mounted in old door knobs, ash trays, paperweights, inkwells, drawer pulls, and tiebacks. Popular during the middle years of the nineteenth century, they were made in profusion by the Bakewell company. The material was china clay and supersilicate of potash, a mixture which could withstand the 1400 degrees Fahrenheit or the working temperature of the lead metal in which they were encased. The Clinton silhouette (Plate 43) is an example.

Sometimes colored pink and blue bottles and decanters are found with clay silhouettes encased in the glass. These pieces have frequently been credited to glassmakers in Bristol, England, but since many are labeled Shrub and shrub was primarily an American drink, and since our glassmakers were adept in the use of the clay sil-

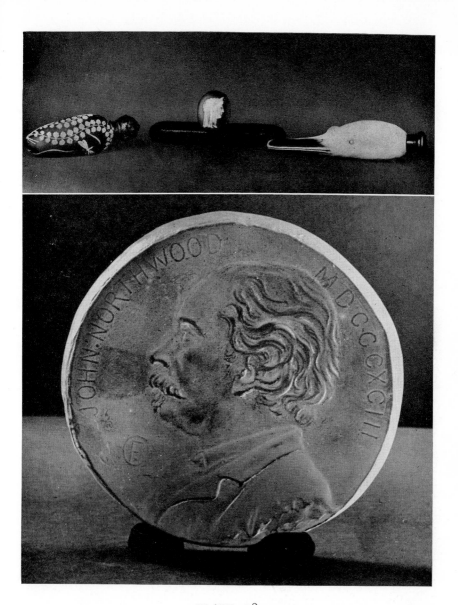

PLATE 28

UPPER, LEFT TO RIGHT: *Rare pieces of cameo glass. Yellow-green scent bottle
with fern and butterfly in white cameo, probably by William O. Bowen, 1885;
beige glass, cameo cut, by Locke; blue scent bottle, white overlay, swan's-head
form, by Frederick Carder.* LOWER: *Head of John Northwood cast by Carder.
(Alexander Silverman)*

houette, it is possible that many so-called Bristol shrub bottles are American products. Of course, these clay silhouettes should not be considered as cameo glass since they are not in themselves made of glass nor are they sculptured.

INTAGLIO CUTTING

Many collectors consider intaglio cutting the finest of all decoration for glass. This Italian process, which produces the opposite effect from cameo carving, is also done with engraving tools and small copper wheels. Designs are usually left with a dull silvery grey finish, but intaglio cuttings may also be polished. The finer the shading in the sculpturing and the greater the precision with which the parts are cut into one another, the better the piece. The artistic composition, as well as the execution of the design, is important. The majority of American intaglio cuttings are worthy of cabinet collections, but some pieces should command higher prices than others.

Intaglio pieces are not common. Usually they are decorative objects such as mantel ornaments, candlesticks, sweetmeat jars, cologne bottles, cigarette, powder, and candy boxes. As with cameo glass the cost of intaglio was so great that tableware was rarely cut. The few berry or center bowls, decanters, finger bowls, and sandwich plates which have appeared are highly valued.

Intaglio work was popular about 1900, particularly the fruit designs cut on crystal blanks. These had to be of first quality and heavy to take the deep incisions. The slender square vase made by the Fry company (Plate 29) is a fine example of an intaglio cutting in which the design is well adapted to glass. The workmanship is exceptional. The intaglio plate (Plate 29) is a Hawkes piece. Intaglio cutting was also done by the J. Hoare Company in Corning and by the L. Straus Company of New York City, but little of it appeared in America until near the end of the Brilliant Period. Then cutters adopted the intaglio method in an effort to save their failing fortunes. Although intaglio was well received, its popularity was not sufficient to save the cut glass industry.

PLATE 29

UPPER: *Intaglio-cut dish, gold and red paint fired over the design. Dugan Glass Company, 1905. (Philadelphia Mus. of Art)* LOWER, LEFT: *Hawkes plate cut with intaglio Iris pattern, miter-cut leaves and star. (Smithsonian Inst.)* RIGHT: *Intaglio cut vase by H. C. Fry Glass Co. with fine adaptation of design to form. (Harry C. Fry)*

As with cameo cutting there were no definite patterns for intaglio work. Each piece was the individual creation of the cutter-designer, and designs were adapted to the articles on which they were cut. Usually the decoration was realistic rather than geometric. Some intaglio cuttings are classed together as fruit, flower, or figure patterns, but there are no identifying pattern names.

◇ ◇

CHAPTER VI

COLORED CUT GLASS

R ED, blue, violet, green, yellow, and amber pieces of glass made
and cut in America are valued by collectors and are not so
rare as has commonly been believed. But collecting colored cut glass
requires even more knowledge than collecting clear glass and is an
expensive business, if you limit yourself to *genuine* pieces. In fact,
Czechoslovakia has reproduced the old glass so extensively that
even a pair of rare Pompadour luster candlesticks with sparkling
prisms from the Sandwich Glass Company rather loses distinction
from having been copied so much. There is, however, undeniable
beauty in a collection of colored cut glass. The majority of the
pieces were designed to be ornamental rather than useful, although
a number of bases for whale-oil lamps have been found.

Many pieces were made for the mantel, the sideboard, or the
side table. Vases, mantel and apothecary jars (both with covers)
are prized pieces. Choice decanters can be found in amber, green,
or red, with or without matching wine glasses of one color or of
red with white overlay. A collection of wines and cordials makes a
brilliant cabinet, but the glasses are rare, particularly the early ones.
Some finger bowls in the Lincoln set with green bands and similar
sets with red bands and casings may be found, and a few plates.

Colored and cut perfume bottles, however, were made in profusion, particularly at the time of The Centennial Exhibition in 1876.
The earlier ones are, of course, hard to find. They were made of
yellow, amber, and ruby glass at the Boston and Sandwich Glass
Company as early as 1827. During the Middle Period, salve and
powder jars and smelling-salts bottles were also cut.

[83]

There are four types of colored glass: one color all through, two or more colors cased together, one color flashed or overlaid with another, and glass of one color to which a luster stain has been applied. Of these, cased glass is the finest; cut glass of one color, the rarest; flashed or overlaid glass the most common; and stained glass of least value. All four kinds were cut and engraved.

Colored glass was essentially a product of the Middle Period, although some pieces appeared earlier and later than that time. Before 1830 the New England Glass Company made red wine glasses which are interesting because they show the use of etching during the Early American Period, but it was not until between 1827 and 1830 that Deming Jarves started making a variety of pot metals for cut glass blanks at the Boston and Sandwich Glass Company. His colored glass remained preeminent until 1880. However all the colored glass did not come from Sandwich. Much of it was made also at Cambridge, Pittsburgh, and Wheeling.

CUT GLASS OF ONE COLOR

Both single Bohemian flint and double lead flint were used for pieces of one color. Sometimes red glass goblets were mounted on white glass stems and feet, or yellow pitchers were given either crystal or opaque white handles. If the body of the vessel is all one color, the piece is said to be of one color regardless of foot, handle, stem, cover, or other additions. The amber goblet (Plate 30) is an example of cut glass of one color. The cutting on such glass is usually a repetitious use of a simple motif such as bull's-eye, flute, fringe, flat or nailhead diamonds.

CASED GLASS

Glass with layers of different colors is called cased glass, since one color actually encases another. Theoretically any number of casings can be made. Usually but two colors are used, three are sometimes found, four or five are rare. Only fine metal is used for

PLATE 30

UPPER, LEFT TO RIGHT: *Middle Period goblets (1) panel cut (2) amber with flat diamond (3) blaze with step-cut foot (4) American application of vesica motif (5) modified rummer. (Author's Collection)* LOWER: *Wine glass, New England Glass Co. Red-gold encased in crystal with crystal stem and foot. Flute cutting. (Toledo Mus. of Art)*

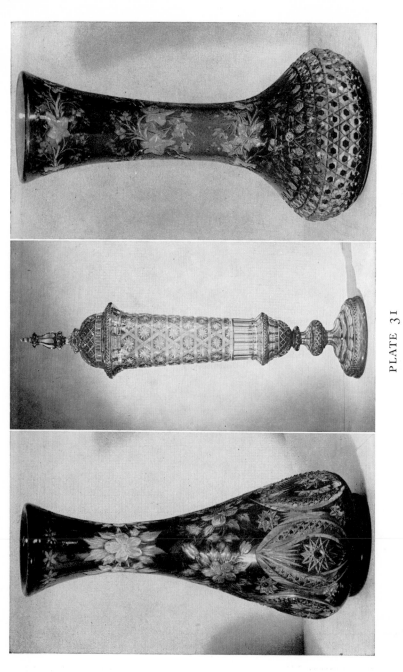

PLATE 31

LEFT: *Cased vase, green over crystal; hob-star and chair-bottom motifs with engraving. C. Dorflinger.* CENTER: *Apothecary jar, New England Glass Co., 1845. Crystal with gold-ruby overlay. Bohemian influence in top and foot. (Toledo Mus. of Art)* RIGHT: *Vase, crystal cased with red. Hobnail motif with engraving. C. Dorflinger. (Vases, Philadelphia Mus. of Art)*

casing and the best pieces are offhand. The color for the outside case is blown first to the size and shape of the finished vessel. This piece is transferred to the pontil and cracked off from the blowpipe. Then a second gather of another color is made, which in glass of two casings, becomes the inside color. The second color is blown into the outer shell until the two blowings are exactly fitted to one another, or encased. If a third or fourth color is used, the process continues with each additional color being encased in the one previously blown. The same process is followed when glass is cased in a paste mold. The outside layer is blown first into the mold and the inner one blown into it.

Before 1890 it was considered essential for the layers of cased glass to be of the same nature: lead glass was cased only with lead, potash only with potash. After 1890 copper ruby was sometimes cased on a lime glass body. Since lead glass requires less coloring and has a natural luster lacking in lime glass, the difference in metals can usually be detected in the varying brilliance of the layers.

The casing of glass requires considerable skill. It is essential that the different gathers be worked at the same temperature and that annealing be done with utmost care to avoid splitting. After a cased piece has been annealed it may be either cut or engraved (Plate 31). A red-over-crystal or green-over-crystal casing offers an effective background for the delicate designs of wheel engraving (Plate 32). Costly pieces involving so much skill in making and decorating were usually destined for presentation or exhibition purposes.

FLASHED AND OVERLAY GLASS

In flashing a gather of glass of one color is covered, while hot, with a thin layer of another color. This double gather is achieved by dipping the first quickly into the hot metal of the second. The metal is then worked out on a marver or metal slab and blown and worked as though it were originally of one piece. In flashed glass the thin layer is on the outside, whereas in cased glass the two layers are of almost equal thickness. (When overlay glass is cut,

PLATE 32

UPPER: *Service, with U. S. coat of arms, ordered by Mrs. Lincoln from Dor-flinger.* LOWER, LEFT: *Blown, gold-ruby wine glass, 4¾ inches, engraved by Louis Vaupel, New England Glass Co. (Brooklyn Mus.)* RIGHT: *Wine glass, replacement to Monroe service. Engraved green bowl on crystal stem and foot. (Both services, White House)*

this difference in thickness is easily detected.) In flashed glass the two layers are actually blown together as a unit, in cased glass one is blown into the other. Flashing implies the use of glass of different colors. Casing may be of different colors, but the term is also used to designate two or more casings of the same color but of different composition.

Overlay, with which American collectors are familiar, is an application of the technique of flashing. True overlay originated with early Bohemian and German workmen and was introduced to America at the Boston and Sandwich works. First a gather of glass, either crystal or colored is made. Then small pieces of a contrasting color are applied and spread over the surface. Finally the glass is reheated and the vessel shaped as one piece. This was the method used for much of the Sandwich overlay in opaque colors (Plate 33).

While flashing and overlay are not technically the same, the methods are so similar that the terms are often used interchangeably. In flashing the entire outer surface of a piece is originally covered with a thin coating of a contrasting color. This is then cut away, leaving the design; in overlay the outside color is applied in streaks or patches and worked out from there, the decoration usually being made by cutting on a wheel.

LUSTER-STAINED GLASS

Any of several metallic stains may be applied to cold glass after it is fashioned and annealed. A luster stain is applied as a varnish to the inside or outside of the glass which is usually clear and of indifferent quality. After it is painted the glass is heated in a kiln to fix the color. Usually a copper luster is used, which stains the outside red; but purple, green, yellow, or blue may also be obtained. The decoration on such pieces usually consists of superficial cutting of poor design and careless workmanship. Luster-stained ware was a cheap imitation of fine cased glass.

METHODS OF COLORING

Glass is colored by the introduction of small amounts of certain metallic oxides into the clear batch. Manganese in varying quantities produces pink, blue, or purple. Antimony and oxides of cobalt and copper also produce blue. Iron and carbon turn glass yellow or amber. Uranium and copper make it green. The intensity and clarity of color varies with the proportions of the oxides and the purity of the materials. It was discovered that the character of the metal also has a bearing on the color. Lime glass, for instance, requires a stronger agent than lead. Rate of fusion and purity of ingredients also affect color. Batches that result in fine clear flint also produce fine colored glass. Each manufacturer had his own recipes which he guarded carefully, keeping them secret sometimes even from his superintendent. A simplified color chart is given below, but it is only suggestive:

Blue glass . . . oxides of cobalt, copper, antimony, and manganese

Yellow glass . . . silver, carbon (coke or anthracite), sulphur, iron, chromium, and uranium

Green glass . . . chromium, protoxide of copper, protoxide of iron, uranium, or combination of blue and yellow glass

Violet glass . . . binoxide of manganese, oxide of gold, or a combination of red and blue glass

Red glass . . . oxide of gold or suboxide of copper

Black glass . . . excess of manganese, or iron, or other oxides

Opaque or Opal glass . . . cryolite, fluor spar, feldspar, borax

In the early days it was the practice to melt first a batch of pure flint. A small quantity of clear glass was dipped out, cooled, and pulverized. The coloring oxides were added to this powdered glass and after thorough mixing, the oxides and clear crystal glass were remelted in the original batch. This laborious method was followed at the Bakewell and Page plant and at the New England Glass Company before the formulas of the Leightons came into common use. The earlier method was tedious and expensive and in reheat-

PLATE 33

LEFT: *Barber-shop bottle, emerald-green with white opaque overlay. Probably Sandwich. (N.-Y. Hist. Soc.)* TOP, RIGHT: *Sandwich candleholder, opaque white over crystal, over sapphire-blue. (Mrs. Lucy E. Marshall)* LOWER, RIGHT: *Rare whisky tumbler. Grape design applied in pulverized white glass. New England Glass Co., Early American Period. (Toledo Mus. of Art.)*

ing, colors often lost considerable intensity. It is interesting to note that while the glass recipe book kept by Thomas Leighton and his son John is still intact, its contents are the secret of the Leighton descendants.

The formulas used at Sandwich, for amber, gold, blue, opal, crystal, white, and Pompadour or pink enamel had been devised by George L. Fessenden and William E. Kern. In a series of articles in the *Glass Industry Magazine* for 1936, these formulas are discussed by the eminent authority, Dr. Alexander Silverman. He had known Kern, who was a gaffer at Boston and Sandwich Co. from 1852 until 1867. According to Dr. Silverman, the Fessenden amber used nutgall as an agent: "Nutgall is the gall from young twigs of certain plants which grow in Syria and Turkey. The accumulation on the twigs is caused by eggs which are deposited by insects. The excretion contains two to four percent of gallic acid and fifty to sixty percent of tannic acid." Such an analysis indicates to what lengths the glassmen of the Middle Period went to secure the right coloring agent for their batches.

The Kern formula for the familiar olive-green employed uranium and green chrome. Lamps were frequently made of this green glass combined with an opaque casing or overlay. Such pieces may be later than 1867 but usually they date from 1850 to 1866. The canary-yellow and yellow enamel overlay pieces were Fessenden colors used at Sandwich between 1866 and 1885.

RUBY GLASS

Red or ruby glass has long been a favorite with collectors, and many recipes were used to produce the various types—the blood-ruby for casing lead glass; copper-ruby, pot and gold-ruby for casing French flint without lead; and gold-ruby for casing the best English lead flint. Gold-ruby is brighter than copper-ruby, which absorbs light. The copper has a purplish cast while the gold is more scarlet than crimson (Plate 33).

There is a story told of the Leighton boy who on his way to the glasshouse stopped each morning at the bank to pick up twenty-dollar gold pieces to throw into the batch. Of course, the process of obtaining ruby-glass was not so spectacular. The first Leighton recipe appears in the books of the New England Glass Company for 1848, but red glass was made at Cambridge long before that time, the earlier pieces being copper-ruby, the later ones gold-ruby. The opaque Pompadour pink enamel so popular at Sandwich for use on luster candlesticks was made with gold and oxide of tin. The champagne glass from the author's collection (Plate 4) is an excellent example of gold-ruby flashing.

QUALITY OF COLORED CUT GLASS

Pieces of colored cut glass are first judged in the same way as pieces of clear cut glass. Are they heavy, brilliant in the light, and are the patterns sharp to the touch? Do the open pieces ring when struck? If the glass passes these primary tests of fine lead quality, it should then be scrutinized for clarity of color.

Lead glass takes a more brilliant hue than glass of any other composition. When different colors of lead glass are cased, the result is a piece of first quality. Value increases with the number of casings, and is also affected by the craftsmanship revealed in the cutting or engraving. Cased glass is, of course, worth more than stained glass. If you are in doubt as to whether a piece has been cased or stained, examine the bevel edges left by the cutter's wheel. Notice the bleeding of one color into another. Bleeding is proof of casing or heavy flashing and reveals thickness of layers. Glass stained with a luster has a flat tone. Any cutting shows a definite edge, a straight line, since the luster is of minute thickness and does not bevel out under the wheel. Luster staining on old pieces will show signs of wear not to be confused with indications of poor workmanship. Actually very little stained glass was cut in America. Almost all stained cut glass was made in Bohemia, but pressed stained glass was made in America.

Evidence of surface gilding on a fine piece of cut glass does not detract from value. Gilding was fashionable during the middle years of the nineteenth century. When the heat in the kiln was not sufficient to fix the gilt paint, it wore off with the years. Traces of gilding are usually indications of age and authenticity.

MAKERS OF FINE COLORED CUT GLASS

Colored cut glass from the Brilliant Period is rare, although some was made in Pennsylvania by the Phoenix Glass Company at Monaca (largest producer 1880 to 1890), by C. Dorflinger & Sons at White Mills, and by Gillinder & Sons of Philadelphia.

During the Middle Period many houses produced fine colored cut ware, but the following companies manufactured it in quantity:

Bakewell, Page and Bakewell Company, Pittsburgh, Pennsylvania

Boston and Sandwich Glass Company, Sandwich, Massachusetts

Brooklyn Flint Glass Works, Brooklyn, New York

Cape Cod Glass Company, Sandwich, Massachusetts

C. Dorflinger & Sons, White Mills, Pennsylvania

Fort Pitt Glass Works, Pittsburgh, Pennsylvania

Hobbs, Barnes & Company, Wheeling, West Virginia

Jersey City Flint Glassworks, Jersey City, New Jersey

Joseph Stouvenel & Company, New York City, New York

Mulvaney and Ledlie Glass Company, Pittsburgh, Pennsylvania

New England Glass Company, Cambridge, Massachusetts

◇ ◇

CHAPTER VII

ENGLISH, IRISH, OR AMERICAN?

IN THE years that I have been collecting Early American cut glass, I have found but two pieces of English and three of Irish, although I have examined thousands of items not previously identified in catalogued collections. It is true that many of the pieces were represented as English or Irish, but further investigation proved them to be unmistakably American. Mr. Westropp, formerly of the National Museum of Dublin, reports similar experience. In an examination of a hundred or more photographs of glass identified in American collections as English or Irish, he found only two pieces that might possibly have been made in his country. All others he declared were *not* Anglo-Irish.

Even before 1830 our production of cut glass was far greater than that of either England or Ireland. And our wares stayed at home because of the ready market here and also because of the prohibitive foreign duties. In view of the established facts of domestic production and of the foreign records of exportations, it appears conclusive that any piece of cut glass known to have been in this country before 1830 can be accepted as American until proved to be English or Irish.

The possibility of English origin is particularly remote. Single pieces, either family heirlooms or gifts, were doubtless brought to this country from England by individuals. Today these pieces are usually documented by family records and are thus catalogued in private collections or in museums. In the last twenty-five years some antique English cut glass has been imported duty free under the customs exemption for commodities made before 1830. Such glass is generally expensive and so expertly catalogued that it is unlikely to confuse the collector of Early American cut glass.

According to Mr. W. A. Thorpe, curator in the Victoria and Albert Museum in London and a foremost authority on English glass, almost no English cut glass was exported to the Americas. It went instead to the Continent. This left the glass export trade to the West solely to the Irish, who were politically more compatible with their American customers.

IRISH EXPORTS AND AMERICAN PRODUCTION

American records of imports before 1827 are unreliable, but the Irish export figures were carefully kept. These figures, compared with our records of production, indicate that before 1830 three times as much cut glass was made in America as was imported from Ireland. The Irish export figures which establish this ratio are those recorded by Mr. Westropp in his book, *Irish Glass*. Figures on American manufacture have been taken from contemporaneous statistics. There are, of course, no completely accurate figures for the Early American Period. At the time, many manufacturers did not report their production. Some reported but did not classify their products as tableware, cut, or plain. Furthermore, industry was scattered and communication difficult so that many houses doubtless did a thriving business of which we have at present no knowledge. If information comes to light on more manufacturers who were cutting glass before 1830, the ratio of three to one in favor of American origin may conceivably be doubled or even tripled.

In any case we do know that from 1809 to 1812 no glass entered our ports legally, that after 1830 very little was imported because of the increased tariffs, and that twenty years later Irish glasshouses ceased to operate.

The first Irish customhouse record of Irish glass export to America is dated 1784 when 1,200 tumblers were shipped to Philadelphia and 5,136 to the Carolinas. In 1785 more glassware (not tumblers or bottles) was exported to the value of £204/10s. In 1786 the factories of Waterford shipped £215 and other Irish houses £28 worth. In 1787 some 1,200 tumblers were sent to New York City and 8,240 more in 1788. The following year New England, presumably Boston, imported 4,416 Irish tumblers. Apparently very little glassware other than tumblers was shipped before 1790. At the end of the ten-year period, 1784 to 1793, before any effective tariff measure had been adopted here, Ireland had sent 88,684 tumblers to Pennsylvania; almost as many to New York; 66,871 to New England; approximately 5,000 to the Carolinas— 247,231 in all. The total value of other glassware for this ten-year period was £6,877, or approximately $30,908.26 at the then current rate of exchange.

In the next ten years from 1794 to 1803, New York imported almost twice as many tumblers as all other states during the previous ten years. The value of glassware (other than tumblers and bottles) imported from Ireland from 1794 to 1803 was within a hundred pounds of the figure for the previous ten years, or £6,978. But the total number of tumblers imported soared to over a million and a half. Not an inconsiderable number of tumblers! However, when we consider their mortality and compare this figure with that of the Rochester Tumbler Company, whose output less than fifty years ago was two million tumblers every two weeks (of which only a very few survive), we can be sure that the chance of any considerable number of Irish tumblers from this ten-year period lasting through the intervening one hundred and forty years is, to say the least, remote.

By 1810 our manufacturers were in active competition with the Irish importers. No drinking glasses were shipped that year to Pennsylvania or to New England although New York imported 205,200, the Carolinas, 144,414, and Maryland, 20,160. The total value of other glassware imported from Ireland in 1810 was £4,932. The same year the Pittsburgh glassworks produced lead glass to the value of $30,000, and American dominance of the industry had begun.

After the War of 1812 fewer tumblers and more glassware of other types were imported. For American manufacturers the three "bad" years of which contemporary critics complained editorially were 1815, 1816, and 1817, when Irish and English manufacturers were sending shiploads of merchandise into America from stocks built up during the war. Irish export figures show that cut glass was a large item in Ireland's bid for American trade. In 1815 we imported 577 tumblers and £7,774 worth of other glassware; in 1816, 4,320 tumblers and £27,962 worth of glassware; in 1817 only 1,600 tumblers and £22,991 worth of other pieces. In 1818 no drinking glasses were imported and the value of other glassware was only £20,651. (See Appendix VI for the complete Irish Export Chart.)

Upon such slender figures as these has grown the legend that all old cut glass found in America is Waterford. As Mr. Westropp says in *Irish Glass,* "It seems curious that out of the vast quantities of old Irish glass that has been broken, such a very large amount of the Waterford glass should have escaped destruction!" And in a recent letter to the author he comments, "The important thing to remember regarding genuine Irish glass is that it is rare anywhere, even in Ireland."

Over a longer span (1812 to 1822) the total imports as shown on the Irish Export Chart were approximately £132,000, not including drinking glasses and bottles. Although this is not such a tremendous amount it sufficed to frighten American glassmakers into taking measures to check Irish competition. In 1827 our tariff laws became effective, manufacturers breathed easily once more, built new chimneys, and imported additional workmen from England and Ireland.

However, even during the earlier lean days our records indicate that American manufacturers of fine cut ware produced more than the three-to-one ratio shown by exporters' invoices. Using the base total (in round numbers) of £132,000 from the Irish Export Chart and allowing the rate of exchange then current of $4.45 per £, we find that the value of the imports over the ten-year period, 1812–1822, would be approximately $587,400.

Meanwhile in America, Pittsburgh makers alone produced $110,000 worth in 1817. The New England Glass Company's output was $65,000 in 1818. The Hamilton works at Albany, New York, were also in production until 1815. Isaac Duval made fine decanters in Wellsburg, Virginia, after 1813. Henry Rowe Schoolcraft was making cut glass whisky tumblers at Lake Dunmore, Vermont, at approximately the same time. The Fisher brothers and John Gilliland produced fine glass in New York City for the last two years of the period, and the South Boston Crown Glass Company was still in operation. For these several glasshouses an estimated annual production of $25,000 is most conservative. If we add this low estimate to the larger known figures, we find that America's average annual production of cut glass from 1812 to 1822 may easily be reckoned in excess of $200,000.

The Irish figures include exports to the Indies, Nova Scotia, and Newfoundland. Even so, the average annual export value in dollars would be roughly $58,740, or considerably less than one-third the value of cut glass that we know was produced in this country. We can conservatively conclude, therefore, that pieces of early cut glass found here are three times as likely to be American in origin as Irish.

DIFFERENCES IN COLOR

In the color or tinct lies the main difference between Irish and American glass. Tinct in clear lead glass results either from impurities in the sand or other ingredients, faulty fusion of materials, or lack of balance in the ingredients. English or Irish glass is assumed to be clear glass unless otherwise specified. Colored glass pieces— red, blue, yellow, cased, flashed, or stained—were Continental innovations. Colored glass was never made in any appreciable quantity in either England or Ireland until after 1830.

Early American cut glass is clearer than either Irish or English. Our sands contained fewer impurities than those available to Irish manufacturers and so required less manganese in the batch as decolorizing agent. When glass of high manganese content is exposed to sunlight for a period of years it takes on the blue tinct known as high color.

On the other hand, glass fired by a slow uneven fire becomes a victim of slow fusion and ages down to grey or is said to take dark color. Because American glasshouses adapted coal to the furnaces

PLATE 34

UPPER: *Oval, cut glass compote, 8 inches high, late eighteenth century. Irish, probably Waterford, slightly blue-white. (Mrs. Henry R. Rea)* LOWER: *Typical American compote. Round, 9-inch diameter, crystal-clear, leaf border, no cutting on stem. About same period, Bakewell, 1810. (Carnegie Mus.)*

early in the nineteenth century fusion was rapid enough, along with our clean sand, to produce crystal-clear glass of good color. It is true that some of our early lead glass does age up to blue or down to grey, and some even shows characteristic lead striae; but it is generally and predominantly clearer than Irish glass of the same period. As Mr. Westropp remarks in *Irish Glass,* "Most of the Irish glass has a rather dark color . . . genuine Waterford glass is decidedly the whitest [i.e. clearest—ed.] of the later Irish glass. The idea has long existed that Waterford glass is always to be known by its dark or bluish tint, but every piece of genuine Waterford glass that I have seen has no trace of dark tint. Waterford glass will not have the same whiteness and brilliancy as modern cut glass, but compared with other contemporary Irish glass, it appears white."

DIFFERENCES IN WEIGHT AND FORM

Early American pieces are generally of lighter weight metal and consequently of more graceful form than Irish pieces, and they rarely have the turned lip so often seen on Irish compotes and bowls. Two compotes of similar period illustrate these differences (Plate 34). The round Bakewell piece is deeply cut in the English Strawberry-Diamond pattern. It has a hand-made foot. The color has greyed only slightly with age and striae are visible. The Irish piece has a curved flat-prism cutting, sometimes called an inverted arch, combined with perpendicular blazes. The shape is oval, which is typical of Irish footed bowls or compotes, and the foot has been molded and then cut over, also characteristic of Irish pieces. It is blue-white and looks solid and heavy; beside it the American piece appears light and graceful. Although both pieces are made of metal of high lead content and both ring well, it is difficult to see how their national identities could be confused.

DIFFERENCES IN QUALITY

There are, of course, many fine family pieces of English and Irish glass in private collections and museums in America, but on the whole those of which Mr. Westropp speaks in the text supporting the Irish Export Chart were not of first quality glass. In fact, the finer pieces of early cut glass found in this country are more likely to be American; the pieces of cheaper quality lead metal with scratched decoration can usually be identified as part of the Irish export shipments. Deming Jarves makes this point clear in his *Reminiscences of Glass Making* when he refers to these same exports from Ireland.

"At that time [before 1812] the articles of flint glass imported by the earthenware trade were confined to a very few articles, such as German straw tumblers, cruets, salts, and plain decanters of cheap fabric; of the finer articles, to cut finger tumblers, sham diamond-cut dishes, and Rodney decanters; a quality of glass and cutting that would not at the present day command one-fifth of their then cost." What Jarves refers to as a German straw tumbler is a goblet with a stem; a finger tumbler is a short, wide-bottomed, six-ounce whisky tumbler; sham diamond cutting refers to the concave diamond known in England as the flat-relief diamond; Rodney decanters are those sturdy everyday decanters with mushroom tops, no neck rings, and broad flat bottoms, which were in common use in taverns, inns, and on shipboard. These articles of glassware did not compare favorably with the deeply cut, fine glass tableware being made contemporaneously in America.

DIFFERENCES IN MOTIF

Early American glass, with the exception of that produced by manufacturers of German apprenticeship, copied the lead glass of England and Ireland. This was natural since manufacturers, craftsmen, and customers were predominantly British. The cutting followed the English and Irish system of motifs, hence the erroneous assumption that all glass cut with the English strawberry-diamond, fringe, or flute motif was of English or Irish origin. The most important single motif used in Irish glass of the early nineteenth century was the large double-cut diamond, known as the English Strawberry-Diamond (Plate 35). In English glass it appears in narrow zones or horizontal chains of diamonds. In Irish glass, particularly from Cork, it was combined with chains of vesica-shaped curves.

English and Irish patterns often partition the design, and by 1830 it appears overcrowded with a tendency toward miniature cutting of the old motifs. In America this trend did not appear. Cutters took the English strawberry-diamond, the blaze (which we call fringe), and the nailhead-diamond motifs and worked them into patterns to please themselves. Although the English continued with the miniature treatment until 1851, generally using the same motifs and the same application of pattern, America had changed styles completely by 1830.

The vesica motif was used extensively in Irish glass, almost never in American cutting. The large lozenge-shaped panel typical of Cork glass was copied extensively by American cutters but in combination with other motifs like the pillar and flute. The arched cutting, the pendent semicircles of fine diamonds, the inverted arch, sometimes called swag (Plate 36), with star and splits were favorite designs in Irish factories, but rare in American.

Where American cutters used the flat-panel cuttings they applied them to band designs such as combinations of the Saint Louis (concave diamond) cutting with fish-scale motifs and with large squares. The claret-pitcher (Plate 24) illustrates panel cutting as used in America. This piece is believed to be from the glassworks established by George Dummer in Jersey City, New Jersey, in 1824. It is of good color and a heavier metal than was used by Pittsburgh or Boston glasshouses of the same period. The small dish (Plate 10) shows the American use of the diamond band. It was made at the New England Glass Company in Cambridge, Massachusetts, about 1818.

The decanter (Plate 35) shows the kugel, a polished circle about half an inch in diameter. The kugel is perhaps the most character-

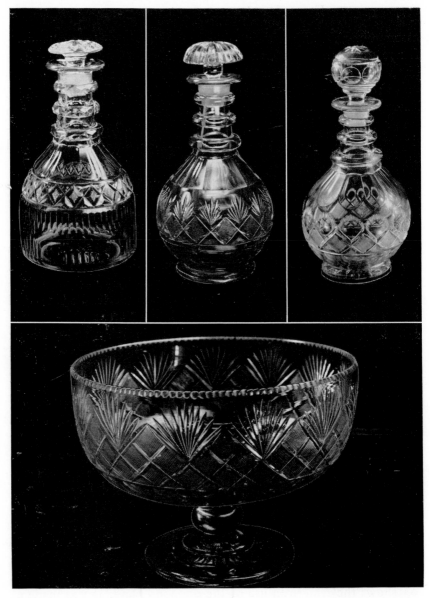

PLATE 35

UPPER, LEFT: *Madeira decanter, probably Waterford.* CENTER: *American decanter, Kensington works.* RIGHT: *American, Bakewell.* LOWER: *American compote, English strawberry-diamond motif. Presented to Washington by George Mason. Probably Kensington, about 1790. (Bakewell decanter, Harry C. Fry; other pieces, Mount Vernon Ladies' Assn.)*

PLATE 36

istic motif of early Bohemian and German cutting; it rarely appears on early English pieces. Later the figure was used on English and Irish glass and was known as the roundelet, puntie, or printie. German cutters used this round figure extensively on American pieces, combining it with the partitions and strawberry-diamond bands pleasing to their English employers. This decanter is the work of one of the Eichbaums, either Peter William or Arnold, who, as his father's student, used the kugel extensively. The motif became very popular in America and was later known as the Bull's-Eye.

To sum up, it is well to remember that there is almost no early English glass in America which has not already been catalogued, or imported in recent years, and that Irish glass, while more plentiful than English, is rare. (See Plate 36.) Anglo-Irish and American glass made before 1830 are alike in essential ingredients of metals and types of wheel cutting, but pieces differ individually in quality, color and use of pattern motifs. If collectors of American cut glass will become familiar with the authenticated pieces of Anglo-Irish glass in art galleries and museums, they will be less likely to confuse our own fine cut glass with that of another country.

◇ ◇

CHAPTER VIII

THE EARLY AMERICAN PERIOD, 1771–1830

THE Early American Period is the most interesting to many collectors since it presents challenging problems of identification. The pieces have particular appeal because of the indomitable personalities of their makers who worked at a time of fierce competition with English and Irish rivals. Collectors treasure them as examples of a craft in which our country excelled very early.

Although there is considerable evidence that glass was made and cut in America before 1771, there are no records before that year and no specimens of cut glass known to have been made earlier. We must therefore start the chronology of American cut glass with the output of the Stiegel glassworks at Manheim, Pennsylvania, in 1771. Later perhaps cut glass of both potash and lead formulas will be found dating back to the middle of the eighteenth century. Such glass may come from the first Philadelphia glasshouse, commonly called The North Liberties Glass House.

Meanwhile, the Early American Period begins in 1771 and closes in 1830 with the Federal tariff restrictions against imported glass and the subsequent boom in domestic glass manufacture. This coincides with the beginning of a national reaction against foreign styles in decoration and the resulting development of American design.

TYPES OF EARLY AMERICAN CUT GLASS

There are two kinds of early American cut glass. This is not true in the later periods. The early glass may be thin, Bohemian or

German flint, or it may be the so-called double-flint or heavy English lead glass.

The Bohemian flint has some resonance, but it is not at all like the heavier English lead glass. Bohemian flint is usually not as good color as lead glass. It will not take deep cutting but it has been used successfully for wheel scratching and engraving. Stiegel glass was made from a formula combining the techniques of both German and English glassmakers. It was definitely a potash glass, but it contained some lead although not enough to make it a true English lead glass. Amelung glass was Bohemian flint of the soda barilla type, a trait that accounts for its lighter weight.

Other Philadelphia and Baltimore companies making glass of potash formula adhered more strictly to Bohemian-German traditions. One collector told me that he had a rule of thumb for identifying Early American glass: "If it isn't as light as Amelung and isn't as heavy as Stiegel, then it must be either Philadelphia or Baltimore." This is neither infallible nor scientific, but it is a practical guide for a beginner.

English flint or lead glass was the standard American metal used for the cut glass with which we are familiar. It was used in Philadelphia before 1800, and after 1830 almost all American cut ware was of lead glass. Not all early lead glass was blown in double-flint thickness, however. Bakewell's, George Robinson's, and other early glasshouses such as those of Trevor and Ensell of Pittsburgh, the Johnson works in Maryland, and Vermont and New York glasshouses with which Henry Rowe Schoolcraft was associated, blew thinner pieces which they nevertheless cut on miter and panel wheels. These pieces have the characteristic ring of true lead glass.

COLOR AND PATTERNS

Early American cut glass may be considered to be clear crystal unless otherwise specified. Although some colored glass was manufactured toward the end of the period—such as that credited to Isaac Duval of Wellsburg, Virginia (later West Virginia), or Jarves of Sandwich, Massachusetts—these colored pieces were not commonly cut but were blown and decorated offhand. Colored cut glass is principally a product of the Middle Period.

Generally the metal of the early glass is of good quality, although some of it will show bubbles, also striae due to high lead content. While the American metal is clearer than that of foreign glass, it still has a mellowness that shades to silver or grey in the shadows. It is not of the same luster as glass of later periods. This greying down is due to age, impurities in the ingredients, and poor conditions of fusing prevailing before 1830.

The patterns resemble the English and Irish, but they are applied in a way that is distinctly American. The frequent use of the roundelet or kugel on Pittsburgh pieces of this period, the single star made with parallel miter splits on the bottoms of articles made by the Dummer brothers, and the panel curves and crosshatched fields of the New England Glass Company, are indications of American originality in adapting foreign patterns. The shapes of vessels for this period also indicate a creative attitude. The pieces are hand polished on wooden wheels so that they have a soft luster quite different from the later brilliance obtained by wheel polishing at high speeds or by acid baths.

While the value of glass from the Brilliant Period can be fairly well reckoned by multiplying the price in 1880 or 1900 by three, no such evaluation is possible for cut glass of the Early American Period. Pieces are rare, which adds considerably to value, and they are irreplaceable—defying duplication.

We have at this point records (see Appendix V) of over thirty glasshouses that were in production during the Early American Period. Undoubtedly others may be discovered as time goes on and research continues. Only a listing can be made of many glasshouses of this period since no example of their cut glass has been identified. In the case of Stiegel, Amelung, Bakewell, and the New England Glass Company, however, there are a number of well-documented pieces. The important houses from which we have either tangible evidence of work or important clues to output are discussed below.

STIEGEL'S MANHEIM GLASS WORKS, 1771–1774

According to current records, the first American cut glass was made at the American Flint Glass Manufactory where, between 1771 and 1774, workmen were scratching leaves, birds, and flowers on the quite unique Stiegel metal. Many collectors are familiar with the texture, color, and patterns of this glass. During the three years that the works were in operation they turned out a quantity of exceptionally interesting pieces which do not fit usual classifications of American glass.

Stiegel himself knew little of the technicalities of manufacture. He hired workers from England, Ireland, Italy, Germany, and Bohemia, and the glass produced by these men combines their various traditions. Stiegel glass is a Bohemian flint, relatively thin. Cut and engraved pieces are usually clear, of low color tending to grey. The metal does, however, contain some lead which Bohemian flint customarily does not. The decoration of tulips and birds is German rather than English, and the flips and case bottles often follow English forms. Other Manheim pieces are of the Italian school of handblown decoration. The finest Stiegel cuttings were made by Lazarus Isaacs of Philadelphia, who worked at Manheim from June, 1773, until the closing of the factory in 1774.

Stiegel workmen used engraving and diamond-point scratching in their decorations. Many pieces have a diamond-engraved mark, a letter, or a series of two or three letters cut into the glass, an indication of true Stiegel, although not all Stiegel pieces have such marks.

The primary authority on Stiegel glass is Frederick William Hunter, whose book, *Stiegel Glass,* was privately printed in 1914. This book is rare but is available in the art rooms of most libraries. Hunter lists fourteen basic motifs for Stiegel glass. (See Appendix III.) Several of the more common Stiegel patterns are illustrated (Plates 37 and 38).

PLATE 37

Stiegel engravings. UPPER, LEFT: *Bottle with tulip pattern (Hunter, Type III).* CENTER: *Flip (Hunter, Type III).* RIGHT: *Covered flip, engraved with flower spray (Hunter XI).* LOWER, LEFT: *Bottle, engraved with two-handled basket containing plant (Hunter, Type VIII).* RIGHT: *Wine glass (Hunter, Type XIII). (Metropolitan Mus. of Art)*

PLATE 38

UPPER: *Stiegel pieces.* LEFT: *Flip with flower.* RIGHT: *Mug with handle, engraved with love birds and heart enclosed in sunburst (Hunter, Type X). (Metropolitan Mus. of Art)* LOWER: *Pickle dish with crude G.W. on base, used at Mount Vernon in Washington's time. (Side view, Plate 12.) Probably cut 1772 to 1775 at Kensington works. (Mount Vernon Ladies' Assn.)*

PHILADELPHIA GLASSHOUSES

There were at least three manufacturers of tableware in the Philadelphia district during the early period. The Northern Liberties Glass Facture (later sometimes called the Kensington works, though not to be confused with Elliotts' Kensington Glass Works) advertised in 1772 for broken flint glass or cullet and for workmen. Some authorities believe that this house dates back to 1691. It was purchased in 1820 by a group of workmen from the New England Glass Company, who about that time established the Union Glass Company for the manufacture of fine flint ware.

The Kensington Glass Works was owned by John Elliott and Company of Philadelphia. The Elliott brothers and their associate, Isaac Gray, probably produced glass of double flint similar to that being made in England. The pickle dish and custard cups from the Mount Vernon Collection (Plates 38, 39) may possibly have been made by the Elliotts. The metal is clear and of good color. The cutting follows Irish motifs but the shapes are distinctly American.

The third Philadelphia glasshouse was believed to have been founded about 1780 by Robert Morris and John Nicholson who erected kilns and other buildings on the west bank of the Schuylkill River below the bridge near the falls of the Schuylkill. This is where Eichbaum was first employed on escaping to this country. It is believed that the works were situated at the falls to obtain water power for turning lathes. Since Eichbaum was primarily a cutter and not well versed in manufacture, it is likely that the Schuylkill Glass Works used a simple potash formula similar to that of Stiegel's, except that it contained no lead. Many decanters accredited to Amelung and similar to those on Plate 40 may be from either the Northern Liberties or the Schuylkill Glass Works.

AMELUNG'S NEW BREMEN GLASS WORKS AT FREDERICK-TOWN

Amelung, like Stiegel, was German. His conception of flint glass was Bohemian glass, but he was a skilled artisan who followed his

PLATE 39

UPPER: *Syllabub glasses from Mount Vernon. Stemmed cups with diamond band, probably 1825–1830, Pittsburgh. Cup on right probably by Isaac Gray at Elliott works in Kensington, late eighteenth century.* LOWER: *Sweetmeat glasses, probably Philadelphia, late eighteenth century. (Mount Vernon Ladies' Assn.)*

PLATE 40

Amelung decanters. Non-lead metal, low color in thicker parts. Flute cutting around bottom. Swag and rose design. Shape similar to that of more common Rodney decanters of the same period, late eighteenth century. Original stoppers. (Mrs. Adolph W. Schmidt)

own formulas. Amelung glass is noticeably light in weight and is generally of better color than Stiegel. Only the decoration is similar, the same light-wheel engravings suited to Bohemian flint.

There are two kinds of Amelung glass, both rare. One is exemplified by the fine chalice, the other in the more common commercial Rodney decanter on Plate 41.

Amelung came to Maryland from Germany about 1784 and established the New Bremen Glass Works at Frederick-town in Maryland. There he set up a fine village with schools for the children. His glassworks are an important link in the history of American cut glass. Some of his workmen came from Stiegel's glasshouse, and later, after Amelung's failure, went West, thus continuing the early tradition in glassware manufacture.

Amelung was one of the first to plead for protective tariff, and he was tireless in his efforts to promote home industry. He earned the respect of George Washington, Thomas Jefferson, Pennsylvania's Governor Thomas Mifflin, and Charles Carroll, an early Maryland statesman, who spoke in defense of Amelung and his Frederick-town glasshouse in the first Congressional debates on taxation.

Amelung failed and in 1796 the fires at the New Bremen Glass Works were drawn. But the plant was not a complete loss until 1804, when it was sold at receiver's sale. Young Frederick Amelung, who had worked with his father, then became an employee of James O'Hara in Pittsburgh.

GLASSWORKS AT PITTSBURGH

Col. James O'Hara established the first glassworks west of the Alleghany Mountains in 1795, for the manufacture of porter bottles. The project was not successful and the works were soon torn down. The following year, however, O'Hara entered into partnership with Isaac Craig for the manufacture of green glass and built a new glasshouse across the river from Pittsburgh at Coal Hill, producing the first bottle at the new works in 1797. In 1800 he employed William Price, an English workman, to manufacture

PLATE 41

UPPER, LEFT TO RIGHT: *Rodney decanter with Saint Louis neck, celery vase, stemmed champagne glass, all cut in Early American Period. (Dr. Florence Kline)* LOWER, LEFT: *Chalice, engraved with arms of Pennsylvania. Amelung, 1784–1796.* RIGHT: *Rodney decanter, concave diamond or Saint Louis neck, attributed to Philadelphia, late eighteenth century. (Metropolitan Mus. of Art.)*

PLATE 42

UPPER: *Whisky tumblers and brandy glasses. Probably early Philadelphia glass, similar to Amelung. (Dr. Florence Kline)* LOWER, LEFT: *Only authentic pieces of clear tableware by James O'Hara, "Pittsburg" works, 1800. Flute cut. (Hist. Soc. of W. Penna.)* RIGHT: *Wine glass cut in Philadelphia for Washington. (Smithsonian Inst.)*

PLATE 43

UPPER: *Rare tumbler with clay silhouette of De Witt Clinton. Made by Bakewell while his hero was governor of New York and had hopes of presidency in 1829. (N.-Y. Hist. Soc.)* LOWER: *Typical Bakewell glassware of the same period with English strawberry-diamond motif. (Dr. Florence Kline)*

cut glass at the Pittsburgh Glass Works. Only three pieces of O'Hara tableware are authenticated (Plate 42). Other pieces, according to the O'Hara letters, were sold to taverns and inns along the National and Philadelphia pikes. After Benjamin Bakewell entered the lead glass field in Pittsburgh, O'Hara discontinued the manufacture of tableware.

In 1807 George Robinson and Edward Ensell built the first closed-pot furnace for the making of flint glass in Pittsburgh. They were in partial production when Benjamin Bakewell, an Englishman whose importing business had failed in New York following the Jefferson embargo, came to Pittsburgh and bought out Robinson's interest. A year later he also bought Ensell's share and the firm name was changed to B. Bakewell and Company. It was controlled by the Bakewell, Page, and Pears families until 1882.

Until around 1850 Bakewell's was one of the leading manufacturers of lead cut glass in the country. The metal was clear and bright, although thinner than that made by the New England Glass Company, the Elliotts, or the Dummer brothers. Cuttings usually followed English and Irish patterns with emphasis on the English strawberry-diamond and similar crosshatching. Due to the great influence of the Eichbaum family (by now proprietors of their own cutting shop) on the apprentice cutters at Bakewell's, German motifs such as the kugel cutting were also much used (Plate 43).

After he had been bought out by Bakewell, Edward Ensell joined forces with Frederick Wendt, who had worked with Eichbaum at O'Hara's glassworks in Pittsburgh, to form the Pennsylvania Flint Glass Works. This company, which was in operation at Pittsburgh under a succession of different partners from 1810 to 1895, made lead glass handblown into interesting shapes. The metal was thin and the decoration followed the German style of wheel engraving. Designs were left unpolished. Probable examples of Pennsylvania Flint Glass Works tableware are shown on Plate 44.

John Robinson, a gentleman glassmaker of Stourbridge, England, came to America at the suggestion of the Bakewell family who had offered him an interest in their booming glass business. However, on his arrival the arrangements were not agreeable to

PLATE 44

Blown wheel-engraved glass. Thin metal of good lead content, somewhat greyed. Engraving follows German patterns. Early American. From Pittsburgh area, sometimes called Birmingham glass as it was made at Birmingham, across the Monongahela River from Pittsburgh. (Dr. Florence Kline)

PLATE 45

LEFT: *Authenticated decanter from Stourbridge works, 1823. Unusual short pillar cutting and horizontal pillars around neck. (Misses M. and E. Wightman)* UPPER, RIGHT: *Whisky tumbler with polished flute cutting.* LOWER, RIGHT: *Decanter of heavy metal and fine pillar cutting, probably Stourbridge. (Philadelphia Mus. of Art)*

Robinson who organized his own company and went into production in 1823 under the firm name of the Stourbridge Flint Glass Works. The company was never large and was not rebuilt after the great Pittsburgh fire of 1845, but the heavy glass produced here is of interest to collectors because of its exquisite quality and precision of cutting. The decanter on Plate 45 is an authenticated piece of Robinson glass; note the use of pillars and half pillars, a distinctive Stourbridge motif in American glass of this period.

NEW ENGLAND GLASS COMPANIES

Deming Jarves credits Thomas Caines with introducing the manufacture of lead glass into New England. In 1812 Caines induced the proprietors of the South Boston Crown Glass Company, of which he was superintendent, to erect a six-pot furnace in part of their large unoccupied manufactory in South Boston. Their output was probably much the same as that known to have been made later by the New England Glass Company at Cambridge and the Boston and Sandwich Glass Company at Sandwich.

About this time Samuel Swift, Epaphras Jones, and Milo Cook obtained the exclusive right to manufacture clear flint glass in Vermont and hired Henry Rowe Schoolcraft as technical advisor. Schoolcraft built a glasshouse at Salisbury, Vermont, where he was superintendent until the winter of 1814, when he went to Keene, New Hampshire. He made all kinds of decanters, tumblers, and wine glasses at the Vermont Glass Factory. His pieces were flute or fringe cut with deeply ground-out bottoms.

The New England Glass Company, organized by Deming Jarves and his associates at Cambridge, Massachusetts, in 1817 had the longest continuous history of any glass company in America. It was in production under the same name until 1888 and its successor, the Libbey Glass Company, is still in business. Generally pieces from the New England Glass Company are heavier than Bakewell glass and are cut in solid panel and miter patterns, wheel-polished. The small salt dish (Plate 46) is a fine piece. The relief cutting is similar to that used later by the Boston and Sandwich Company, but a

PLATE 46

UPPER: *Three Boston and Sandwich pieces.* LEFT: *Honey jar with plate, sharp-diamond motif, 1825–1830. (D.A.R. Mus.)* CENTER: *Bonbon dish to fit silver basket. Sharp-diamond band with arched pillars. (Mrs. L. G. Hoes)* RIGHT: *Salt dish, 2¼ inches high. Polished diamond band, scalloped top. (Smithsonian Inst.)* LOWER: *Early New England decanters. (Smithsonian Inst.)*

PLATE 47

LEFT: *Decanter with cut rings on neck and repeated pattern of triple-miter crosshatching, about 1827. Probably not original stopper. (Toledo Mus.)*
RIGHT: *Celery vase, 1830, said to have belonged to the Bradford family of Massachusetts. Both cut by New England Glass Co. (Smithsonian Inst.)*

family record establishes this piece as having come from the Cambridge glasshouse.

In 1825 Deming Jarves left the New England Glass Company to establish his own works, the Boston and Sandwich Glass Company at Sandwich, Massachusetts. His cut Sandwich closely resembles glass from the company in Cambridge, and in many cases cannot be distinguished from New England Glass Company products. The metal is heavy and of fine color and the cutting is characteristic of the period (Plate 49).

GLASS COMPANIES IN THE VIRGINIAS, NEW YORK, AND NEW JERSEY

In 1815 in Wellsburg, now in West Virginia, but then part of Virginia, Isaac Duval operated one of the first works to specialize in fine lead glass and especially in the making of cut decanters in color. The half-pint decanter (Plate 143) is believed to be a Duval piece.

Fourteen years later, in 1829, John Ritchie opened a glasshouse in Wheeling, West Virginia. Their metal was clear and solid. Fortunately we have enough authentic specimens to be able to identify Ritchie patterns with some accuracy. Note the use of the panel and flute with roundelet (Plate 49).

Before the end of the Early American Period several glasshouses had been established in New York and New Jersey. In 1820 the Bloomingdale Flint Glass Works was founded in New York City by Richard Fisher, a skilled English glasscutter who had come to America in 1810. Because it was against the law for glassworkmen to leave England, Fisher was smuggled into America in a barrel. He first became a member of the firm of Emmet, Fisher and Flowers (1815–1817), which failed and sold out to Jarves and his friends who founded the New England Glass Company. Richard Fisher with his brother John established the Bloomingdale works on land along the east bank of the Hudson River between what are now Forty-eighth and Fiftieth Streets. Here the Fisher brothers made cut glass of superb quality. The metal is not so heavy as that

PLATE 48

LEFT TO RIGHT: Decanter, part of service ordered by President Andrew Jackson from Bakewell and Company, Pittsburgh. Complete set cost $1,451.75, January 27, 1830. Syllabub cups and champagne glasses by same company for the Biddle family, about 1825. (Philadelphia Mus. of Art)

PLATE 49

UPPER, LEFT: *Pickle dish, Boston and Sandwich, 1830.* RIGHT: *Pickle dish, New England Glass Co., 1825. (D. A. R. Mus.)* CENTER: *Syllabub cups and whisky tumbler, Ritchie glasshouse, Wheeling, W. Va., 1830.* LOWER: *Wine glasses, John and Craig Ritchie. Heavy metal, polished flute cutting (Oglebay Inst.)*

PLATE 50

UPPER, LEFT: *Small cruet, cut in hexagonal diamonds. (Carnegie Magazine)*
RIGHT: *Whisky tumbler, star-cut, used by Washington at Mount Vernon.*
Late eighteenth century, probably from Philadelphia. (Smithsonian Inst.)
LOWER: *Salt cellar, decanters, and oil bottle, probably from Stourbridge, by*
John Robinson, 1825–1830. (Dr. E. R. Eller)

PLATE 51

Flute-cut decanters with trailed neck rings, unusual in American decanters of this period. Made by R. B. Curling and Sons, Pittsburgh, 1828. Mushroom stoppers with knob are interesting. (Carnegie Magazine)

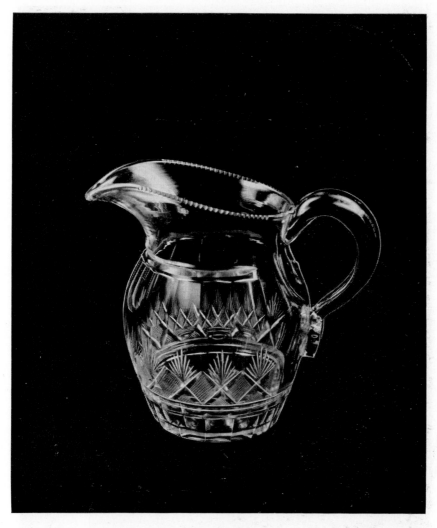

PLATE 52

Pitcher authenticated by family record as having belonged to Thaddeus Chadwick, Washington, D. C. Believed to have been made in Philadelphia at the Elliott glasshouse. English strawberry-diamond motif with fan, typical of glass cut in America before 1827. (D. A. R. Mus.)

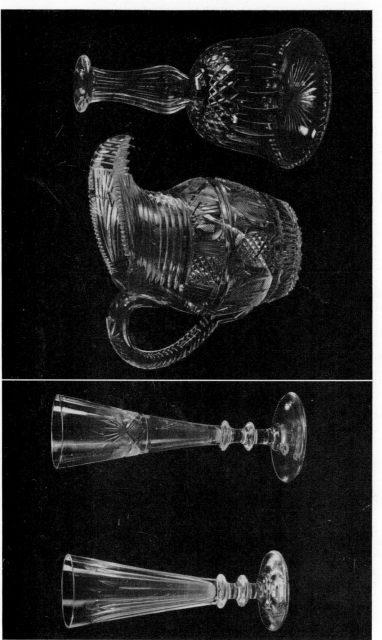

PLATE 53

LEFT: *Champagne glasses used by Washington at Mount Vernon, credited to Philadelphia glasshouses. (Mount Vernon Ladies' Assn.)* RIGHT: *Pitcher with partitioned cutting, arches, and crosshatching. Carafe with flute and block motifs. Both New England Glass Co., Early American Period. (Smithsonian Inst.)*

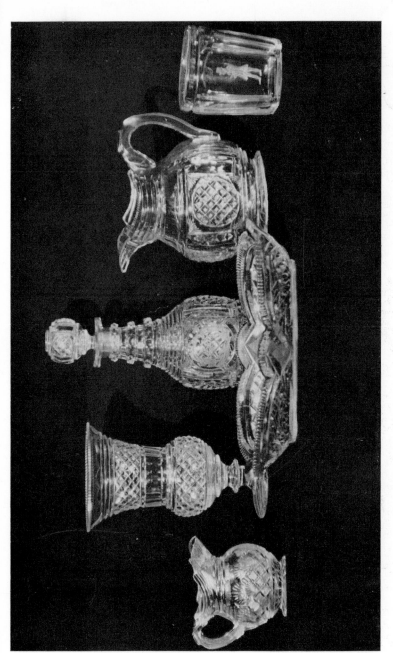

PLATE 54

Bloomingdale glass, from the New York glasshouse of Richard and John Fisher. Early American Period. Motifs of English strawberry-diamond, horizontal prisms, and diamond bands, popular in early nineteenth century. Tumbler on right is engraved. (Photographs, courtesy Charles Messer Stow, New York Sun)

PLATE 55

Cut glass sugar bowl and cover attributed to Brooklyn Glass Works, 1823, established by John L. Gilliland. Glass is of high lead content, fine workmanship, and good design in English rather than Irish tradition. (N.-Y. Hist. Soc.)

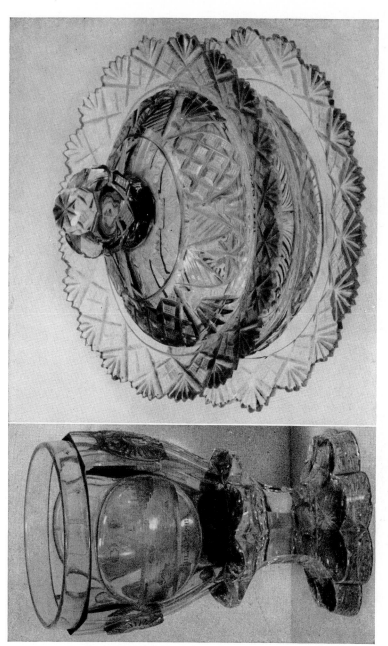

PLATE 56

LEFT: *Goblet or firing glass, probably part of set made by George Dummer at Jersey City for members of his lodge. Harbor of Philadelphia engraved on medallion. Heavy metal and scalloped foot. (Philadelphia Mus. of Art)*
RIGHT: *Covered butter dish, Gilliland, Brooklyn Glass Works. (N.-Y. Hist. Soc.)*

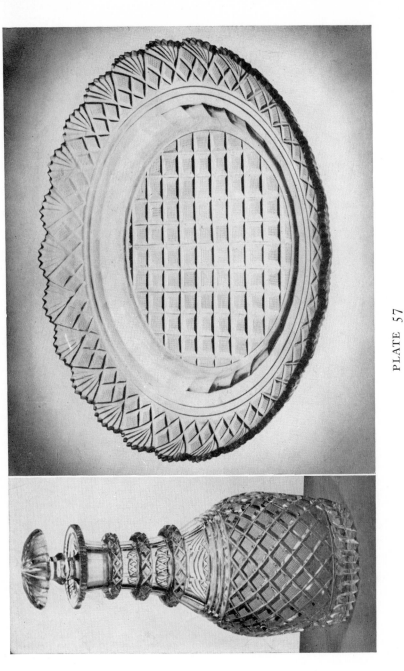

PLATE 57

Decanter and plate, 9¼ inches in diameter. Both credited to Gilliland of Brooklyn works. Gilliland glass, notable for fine detail and elaborate use of old motifs, is rare, although a comparatively large amount was produced from 1823 to 1868. (N.-Y. Hist. Soc.)

from the Elliott, New England, or Dummer glasshouses, but it is of good weight, follows rather elaborate Irish forms, and is well cut (Plate 54). One of the partners in the Fisher brothers glass enterprise in Bloomingdale was John L. Gilliland. He withdrew from the company in 1823 to establish the Brooklyn Glass Works in Brooklyn, New York. This manufactory was in production for many years and the glass was heavy, clear, and cut in designs similar to those used by the Fishers or by Bakewell, except that Gilliland employed the heavy fan scallop long before it was in general use. It is doubtful if this motif was ever used so successfully by any other company (Plates 55, 56).

Another early glassmaker, George Dummer, started in business in New York at Albany. Apparently he learned the glass business at the Hamilton works there. Then in 1824 he set up shop as a glass broker and importer at 110 Broadway in New York City and opened his own glassworks across the Hudson in Jersey City, with his brother, P. C. Dummer, as partner. There were forty-four wheels run by steam in the cutting shop. The metal was heavy, handblown, of good color, free of bubbles. The Dummers cut the single star on the bottom of pitchers and decanters as shown on the claret pitcher on Plate 24. They also used curved splits, which was unusual for such early ware.

PROBLEMS OF IDENTIFICATION

Most of us hope to identify our pieces with one locality, or glasshouse, or in the case of engraved or beautifully cut ware, with an individual cutter. But such knowledge is not requisite for the enjoyment of early American cut glass. Almost any early piece is worth cabinet space whether it came from Cambridge, Pittsburgh, or Wheeling. Possibly, in days to come, additional information will come to light to make positive identification possible. It was not until 1927 that we knew very much about John Frederick Amelung and his ware. The Robinson pieces (Plate 45) were not identified until 1948. The fact that a piece fails to fit into a classification in this book or look like one of the illustrations does not make it less valuable as an example of early American cut glass. I have chosen such pieces as could be credited with some authority to specific localities and in some cases to specific glasshouses. These illustrations are intended only to serve as guides to the cataloguing of other pieces of the same general period, metal, design, and pattern.

◇ ◇

CHAPTER IX

THE MIDDLE PERIOD, 1830–1880

FOUR kinds of cut and engraved glass are identified with the Middle Period. First in point of time are the pieces with flute cuttings. First in intrinsic and artistic value is the engraved glass. Probably first of all in interest to the beginning collector is the colored, flashed, and cased ware, and first in rarity are the pieces with so-called fine-line cuttings.

The Middle Period is identified with a new feeling of nationalism. During the Early American Period we were an infant country with newborn industries to foster. We followed the fashions of our forefathers and imitated styles popular in the mother countries. As a result, there was great similarity in metal, designs, and patterns between American glass and that produced contemporaneously in England, Ireland, and on the Continent. By 1830 there was a reaction in the thinking of our manufacturers, statesmen, and people against foreign ideas. Tariffs became effective. By sponsoring domestic crafts and shutting out foreign competition, manufacturers developed and protected new industries in young America. The glass industry in particular prospered under tariff protection. New glasshouses were built and established works prospered as never before. (See Glasshouse Chart, Appendix V.) With industrial independence came a preference for domestic styles and designs. The simplicity of the flute-cut decanters, compotes, and pitchers suited American customers and heavy cut glass articles appeared on every well-appointed table. Because of this popularity it is still possible to find intact many fine pieces of fluted glass from the Middle Period. Indeed, decanters with diamond-cut rings and steeple stoppers are relatively common (Plate 58).

PLATE 58

Typical decanters of Middle Period, Pittsburgh area. LEFT TO RIGHT: *Two fluted decanters with neck rings; footed type, grape engraving and diamond-band cutting. (Ditheridge and Co. and William Phillips made similar tableware.) Panel cutting; Saint Louis diamond. (Hist. Soc. of W. Penna.)*

THE MIDDLE PERIOD, 1830–1880

The evolution of American industry did not stop with the impetus of tariff protection. American enterprise and originality discovered short cuts and produced less expensive wares both for export and domestic sale. Pressed glass, a typically American product, flooded the market, first in lead glass, later in pieces of lime glass. While the difference between a fine cut piece of lead glass and a pressed imitation was obvious, the imitation spoiled the market for the higher priced cut pieces. To avert disaster, manufacturers of fine glass either converted to pressed ware or made cut pieces which the pressing machine could not duplicate. Some houses, notably in Pittsburgh, went the commercial way and produced the less expensive pressed ware in quantity. Others, particularly the New England and Brooklyn houses, refused to yield and developed the engraved technique for quality glass.

Colored glass was the child of the engraving art for it was soon obvious that if engraving on crystal was beautiful, it was infinitely more so when cut through a color. Such was the status of the glass industry at the time of The Centennial Exhibition in Philadelphia in 1876. Fine pieces exhibited there illustrate the best in glass decoration of the Middle Period (Plate 59).

The period closed on a definite note of industrialism. Between 1876 and 1880 new fuels were used to produce a brighter glass fused under controlled conditions. Lathes were speeded up. Materials were more accurately weighed, purified, and founded, and the end of the Middle Period came simply because the Brilliant Period had begun.

FLUTE CUTTINGS OF THE MIDDLE PERIOD

Flute cutting, sometimes called Colonial Flute, is identified with the Middle Period because of the quantity of glass cut in this pattern between 1830 and 1880. Actually the flute was cut before 1830 and can even be traced back to the panel cuttings of the eighteenth century, but for every one example of Early American flute-cut glass there are hundreds from the Middle Period. After 1830 the style becomes more ornate on heavier, brighter crystal like the half-pint

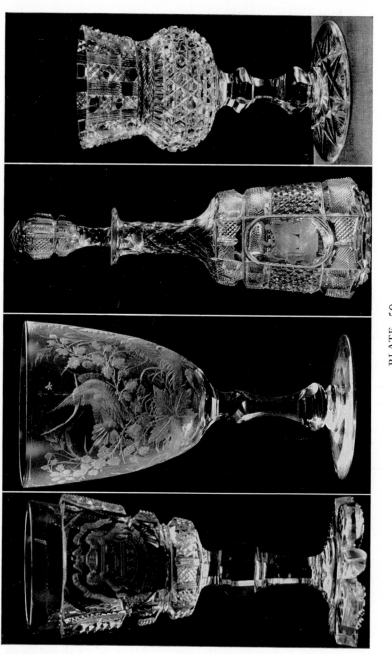

PLATE 59

LEFT TO RIGHT: *Exhibition pieces cut for Centennial Exposition, 1876. Goblet engraved—Virtue, Liberty and Independence, J. F. Hartranft (Governor of Pennsylvania); Goblet engraved by Gillinder; Dorflinger decanter honoring Philadelphia. (Philadelphia Mus. of Art) Wine glass, Centennial pattern, New England Glass Co. (Brooklyn Mus.)*

decanter (Plate 60) accredited to the Sweeney glasshouse in Wheeling. Notice that the decanter was apparently blown for flute cutting
and that it has the typical tapering neck. The steeple stoppers were
a development of the flute style.

Flute cuttings were made by practically every glasshouse in business between 1830 and 1845, and pieces have been found from all of
them. The West Virginia houses were particularly adept in designing fluted tableware as is shown in the Sweeney and Ritchie pieces
(Plates 61, 62, 63). In time flutes were combined with engraving
and other decoration as shown in the pitcher on Plate 5. This piece
is later, probably about 1850, and while it retains the flute style, it
also has a wheel cutting which has been left unpolished. The bottom
is engraved in a pattern to match that on the shoulders. This pitcher
is accredited to the O'Hara works of the James B. Lyon Glass Company of Pittsburgh, a descendant of the old Union Flint Glass
Works established by Hay and McCully in 1829.

An old invoice gives the price in 1858 of one dozen, hollow,
flute-cut goblets at twelve dollars a dozen. One dozen flute-cut
champagne glasses sold for eight dollars. A cut scalloped-top spoon
glass cost three dollars, and a cut square-top celery dish sold for
three dollars. A seven-inch bowl with a bull's-eye cutting and a flute-
cut stem cost five dollars.

ENGRAVED DECORATION

Glass was engraved in America in the later years of the eighteenth century. It is still being engraved in the twentieth, but the peak
of production and popularity was reached during the Middle Period.
The earliest pieces of this era are of clear glass and the engraving
is unpolished. Later, engraving was used on glass of two colors
(usually blue on white or red on white) or on glass of three colors
—blue, yellow, and white.

American metal of the Middle Period was predominantly lead
glass. The glass used for engraving in the Early American Period
was thin and usually soda-potash. Foreign glass engraved in the
middle nineteenth century was customarily high-grade potash. De-

[143]

PLATE 60

*Flute-cut decanters. Straight sides of first decanter indicate earliness. (N.-Y. Hist. Soc.)
Half-pint decanter with blown stopper is unusual, of W. Va. glass. Ringless decanter, far
right, Pittsburgh. Variety of steeple stoppers. (Author's Collection)*

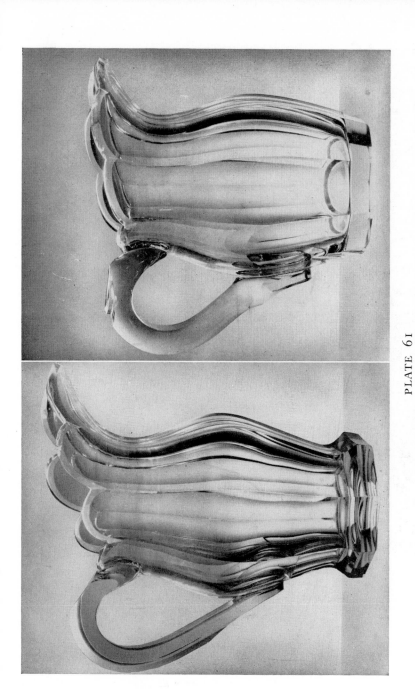

PLATE 61

LEFT: *Authenticated pitcher from glasshouse of John and Craig Ritchie, Wheeling, W. Va., about 1830.* RIGHT:
Pitcher by M. and R. H. Sweeney of same locality, about 1835–1840. (Oglebay Inst.)

PLATE 62

UPPER: *Pair of celery vases, Sweeney Glass Co., Wheeling, W. Va., about 1840. Typical cutting on foot.* LOWER: *Sweeney decanters with flute cutting adapted to heavy lead glass. Sweeney glass rivals quality of modern crystal. Does not color down like other early, heavy lead glass. (Oglebay Inst.)*

PLATE 63

termining the type of metal helps in the identification of pieces of engraved glass.

Middle Period engravings are on the whole delicately fine and precise. The themes are usually historical or mythological. The earlier engravings are of conventional patterns with broader wheel marks and a sketchier delineation than that of the minute, exquisite work found in the copper-wheel engravings of the Middle Period. These, seen a little way off, actually seem to be sculptured in relief. The pieces most commonly engraved were decanters, bottles, wine glasses, cologne bottles, cruets and pitchers (Plate 64).

COLORED, FLASHED, AND CASED GLASS

Colored glass of the Middle Period was elegant and costly. Fine examples may still be found but they are more rare than pieces of crystal glass. Red was favored and the New England Glass Company made much crystal flashed with gold-ruby which was then cut through in diamonds, stars, and prisms, or engraved in pictorial designs. Blue and green were also popular. Dorflinger glass was world famous for its clear green flashing.

FINE-LINE CUTTINGS

Fine-line cuttings of the Middle Period are very rare. Notice on Plate 65 the double cutting, the pattern cut through the crosshatched bands. This is a typical fine-line cutting for the period. It is sometimes called a triple cutting because the field has been cut all the way round in fine lines on a triple miter. It was then cut in the opposite direction on the same wheel to make a field of miniature diamonds. Finally the flower or vine or other design was cut into the crosshatched field on a panel wheel. Glassmen used fine-line cuttings in an effort to compete with the pressed glass imitations of miter-split patterns. It was difficult, almost impossible, to get a fine-line reproduction with a press. Only the triple miter wheel could cross-hatch flowers, leaves, and bands. Decanters, tumblers, goblets, wine

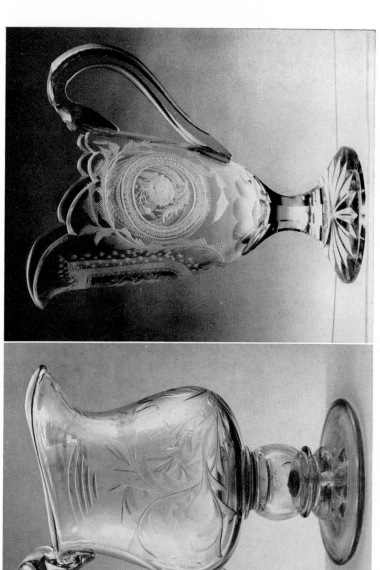

PLATE 64

LEFT: *Presentation piece, 10⅞ inches high, New England Glass Co., 1845, to M. E. Jacops, whose name is engraved on front. Bulbous stem encloses coin dated 1845. (Brooklyn Mus.)* RIGHT: *Promotion sample, Hobbs, Barnes Company, Wheeling, W. Va. Initials, H. B., engraved in shield on front. (Oglebay Inst.)*

PLATE 65

UPPER, LEFT: *Unusual berry bowl with fine-line crosshatching cut through in floral pattern, Middle Period.* RIGHT: *Bowl with partitioned design, early use of hob-star. (Author's Collection)* LOWER: *Ritchie punch bowl, unusual piece for this house, resembles Gilliland technique. (Philadelphia Mus. of Art)*

glasses, bread plates, and bowls (Plate 65) were cut in fine-line patterns.

Considerable difference will be noticed in the metal used by various manufacturers through the Middle Period. Much of the glass was a clear lead crystal glass such as that of the pieces accredited to the Dummers, the Sweeneys, and the New England and Brooklyn companies. Glass with color was made by the New England Glass Company, Hobbs, Barnes and Company in Wheeling, West Virginia, as well as by the Mulvaney and Ledlie Company at Pittsburgh. At Dorflinger's in Brooklyn, a thin glass of fine quality was made and this was often colored and decorated with fine-line cuttings.

The metal of the earlier pieces was usually slightly grey, with the exception of those from Wheeling which were always of good color. Later pieces have a clearer metal. Contrary to the usual rule, fluted pieces of high color, that is with a light blue or more especially pink tinct, are later than those showing grey.

GLASSHOUSES OF THE MIDDLE PERIOD

Ten years after tariff laws made the manufacture of fine tableware profitable in America there were eighty-one glasshouses in operation. According to the census of 1840 there were thirty-four cutting shops with ten to a hundred frames in each. The figures do not indicate how many of the shops were run by the eighty-one manufacturers, but it is likely that each cutting shop represented at least one manufacturer. In some cases two manufacturers supplied glass to the same shop as was the case in Brooklyn when Joseph Stouvenel manufactured his own glass but amplified production with blanks from the Gilliland and Dorflinger works.

There were more than a thousand men cutting and engraving glass from 1840 to 1855 and the annual product was worth over $1,500,000. In New Jersey there were four cutting shops. Two were out-cutting (i.e. independent) shops and two were associated with glasshouses, the Jersey City Glass Company and the Camden County works. In Pennsylvania there were fifteen cutting shops.

PLATE 66

PLATE 67

Many glasshouses of the Middle Period were descended from those founded during the Early American Period. Some like Bakewell's, the New England, and the Boston and Sandwich companies continued under the same names. Others changed hands a dozen times in their forty or fifty years of existence, but the character of the glass produced in the same place usually remained the same because of the equipment in the glasshouse. Forty new companies began the manufacture of cut ware about 1840.

By 1865, according to some authorities, there were only eight houses engaged in the production of fine cut glass. These were the New England Glass Company, the Mount Washington Glass Company, the Bay State Glass Company, the Union Glass Company, and the Boston and Sandwich Glass Company (all in New England), Gilliland's South Ferry Works, Christian Dorflinger's glasshouses at Brooklyn, and the Dummers' glasshouse in Jersey City. It is possible that this figure is low for, in addition to these eight, there were a few houses that were still producing cut glass in small amounts after they had converted to lime glass.

There is a tendency to blame the invention of the lime glass formula for the decline of the cut glass business in America. The popularity of pattern glass undoubtedly did have an effect on the manufacture of luxury ware, but the War Between the States and the resulting hard times that made the necessities of life more important than elegant tableware were also factors. By 1860 there were only two hundred and twenty-five cutters and engravers employed in the eastern glasshouses, chiefly in New York, New Jersey, Boston, and Philadelphia. In Brooklyn, E. V. Houghwout and Company, Joseph Stouvenel, and Hoare, Burns and Daily were running cutting shops. In Pittsburgh and Wheeling the glasshouses had for the most part converted to the manufacture of pressed lime glass.

From 1865 to 1870 the larger manufacturers found it necessary to reduce output because of the popularity of etched and sandblast decorations for lamps, shades, and globes. Then the panic of 1873 all but ruined the remaining houses. Only J. Hoare survived as an independent cutting shop, thanks to his close association with Amory Houghton, Senior, of the Corning Glass Works.

In 1876 when The Centennial Exhibition opened in Philadelphia there were few exhibitors. The New England Glass Company, the Mount Washington and Boston and Sandwich companies, Christian Dorflinger, and J. B. Dobelmann of Brooklyn, were represented. There were also a few pieces of cut glass and colored engraved glass among the Hobbs-Brockunier pressed pieces. William Gillinder, whose Franklin Glass Works set up a complete production exhibit, also showed cutting methods and sold souvenir cut pieces along with his cheaper sandblast and stained wares. But out of the slender showing of the once thriving industry blew the spark that was to ignite again the mighty furnaces of America's cut glass industry and start a boom in luxury tableware never before equaled in this country—or in any other.

◇ ◇

CHAPTER X

THE BRILLIANT PERIOD, GLASSHOUSES, 1880–1905

C UT GLASS reached the height of its popularity in America following The Centennial Exhibition in Philadelphia in 1876. Before this time and for a few years afterward American glass cutters used the technique of fine-line cutting and copper-wheel engraving, which distinguished the Middle Period. After 1880 and until 1905 glass craftsmen designed the deep miter cuttings. These decorations on heavy crystal became known as brilliant cuttings and were produced in a profusion of patterns as late as 1915. But the popularity and quality of craftsmanship were already on the decline and reached an all-time low just prior to World War I.

Glass cut during the twenty-five-year span of the Brilliant Period is characterized by crystal-clear quality of metal, deep and sometimes curved miter cuttings called splits, and such motifs as the hobstar, fan, notched prism, and single star. It is this glass which the average American thinks of as cut glass. It is heavy, usually beautiful, and undeniably fine. It was always costly. This was our grandmothers' glass which we washed and polished on Saturday mornings —the glass sold unlisted in barrels at auction when it became mother's unhappy task to close up the home place.

Today it is possible to assemble fine collections of American cut glass at a fraction of the original cost because value and growing rarity are not yet realized. Only fifty-odd years ago cut glass still had such a tremendous vogue that it was the preferred wedding and anniversary gift, and the valued possession of millions of American housewives. Before the turn of the century, women who had never heard of Waterford, Bakewell, or Cambridge, acquired sets in patterns of Middlesex, Devonshire, Parisian, Russian, Polar Star, and Kimberly. A standard table setting consisted of goblets, wines—champagne, claret, and sherry—ice-cream dishes and plates with ice-cream platter, finger bowls with plates, salts and peppers, candlesticks, butter patties, compotes, bonbon or nut dishes, celery boats, one or two nappies of various sizes, berry bowls, punch cups, and pickle dishes. In fact, during the Gay Nineties everything appeared in cut glass that could be served either at room temperature or chilled. Heat was then, as it is now, the mortal enemy of cut glass.

A complete setting in any one of the ornate patterns was so expensive that most women acquired cut glass as they did silver: six or eight pieces at Christmas, and six or eight more on the next anniversary. Sometimes they had only a few dearly prized pieces such as a celery boat, ice-cream platter, or punch bowl. Since quantities of glass were cut, it is remarkable and perplexing that so little of it appears today.

Consider a single pattern, the Russian, for instance. There is scarcely a magazine article, newspaper story, or reference to cut glass in the press of the late nineteenth century that does not mention the "popular Russian." Probably no other design was so well-known or so generally used. In 1886 the White House ordered a complete service of Russian from the T. G. Hawkes Glass Company for the use of President Grover Cleveland, and additions were made during the Benjamin Harrison and second Grover Cleveland administrations. When Theodore Roosevelt moved into the White House he found the supply inadequate and reordered, adding highball glasses to the goblets, tumblers, wine and cordial glasses of the original service. These were the first highball glasses to be ordered for the White House. The same pattern continued in use for state dinners until 1938 when, in the administration of Franklin D. Roosevelt, replacements became too expensive and a complete service of a more modern but less costly pattern was ordered (Plate 68).

Indeed it would be difficult to estimate the quantity of glass cut in the Russian pattern that was made and sold in this country during the last twenty years of the nineteenth century. Yet today collections of matched sets are few. They will continue to be difficult to assem-

PLATE 68

UPPER: *Ice-cream tray. Libbey Glass Co. (Mrs. John M. Feeney)* CENTER: *Finger bowl and sherry glass, Russian pattern engraved with coat of arms of White House, 1886. (White House)* LOWER: *Twelve-inch plate. Venetian Pattern, T. G. Hawkes Co. (See also Plate 97.) (Smithsonian Inst.)*

ble until women become aware of the possible value of the cut glassware packed away in the attic or forgotten on some dark shelf.

REASONS FOR POPULARITY

There were several reasons for the tremendous vogue of cut glass
during the Brilliant Period. Business conditions made it possible for
women to indulge in expensive tableware. The society of the eighties
and nineties was gay and given to dining in style. Cut glass was a
luxury suited to elegant and elaborate entertaining. Had it been
developed in the days of depression around the middle of the nineteenth century, there would have been no market, and a house which
specialized in heavy cut ware would have failed.

After 1880 refinements in the industry itself made it possible to
cut glass more deeply and more accurately so that great brilliance
was achieved. Soon after the War Between the States, James Lyon
in Pittsburgh saw the advantage of converting his coal furnaces to
gas, and the industry was quick to follow his lead. Gas heat was con-
trollable. Glass so manufactured could be fused more quickly and
completely. It came out clear, bright, and flawless. Lehrs or annealing ovens heated with natural gas, the development of feeding-up
brushes for polishing, and other technical improvements during the
last two decades of the century replaced the primitive techniques of
the old glasshouses. Modern methods of preparing and measuring
heat and weighing ingredients created the means of making exceptionally fine cut glass.

Undoubtedly The Centennial Exhibition in Philadelphia in 1876
played a genuine part in popularizing American cut ware. Although
there had been local fairs and regional industrial exhibits before
this time, it was not until railroad travel became relatively common
that great numbers of American women were able to get about and
see things for themselves. Quite unexpectedly the exhibits of cut
glass at the Centennial proved to be the most interesting of all to
women. The Boston and Sandwich Glass Company exhibited their
Fern pattern. The Mount Washington and the New England Glass
companies both cut Centennial patterns. Christian Dorflinger from

White Mills, Pennsylvania, had a large exhibit as did the Hobbs-Brockunier Company of Wheeling, West Virginia.

By far the greatest attraction, however, was the complete glass-works set up and operated right on the exhibition grounds by Gillinder and Sons of Philadelphia. Here could be seen the actual processes of melting, blowing, annealing, cutting, and engraving. Each woman visiting the exhibit was given a small souvenir and most visitors bought additional pieces, many engraved with initials or date. Of these souvenir pieces $96,000 worth were sold and taken back to Iowa, Georgia, Ohio, and California to publicize the new cut ware. Today a collection of such souvenirs would make a most interesting cabinet. Slippers, leaves, hats, match holders, pin trays, and bonbon dishes could all be included.

TRADE-MARKS AND OTHER IDENTIFICATION

Many collectors attempt to identify each piece of glass in their collections with a specific glasshouse. There are three general clues to sources of the Brilliant Period—pattern, metal, and trade-mark. Only the acid-etched trade-mark insignia may be taken as infallible.

Toward the close of the nineteenth century leading glasshouses felt the need of identification for their fine ware not only to avoid confusion with inferior domestic glass but to establish American quality. Between 1895 and 1905 many trade-marks were registered. Some were in use for only a short time. Many were printed on paper and glued to the glass. These soon washed off or wore away. Houses that adopted the acid stamp were not always consistent in its application, and of course much fine glass was cut before the trade-mark came into common use. Many valuable pieces from the Brilliant Period are marked, however, and it is a short cut to identification to be familiar with the most common trade-marks (See Appendix IV).

Pattern and metal are indications—although sometimes inconclusive ones—of source. Patterns such as Wheat (Fry), see Plate 75, Kimberly (Libbey), Croesus (J. Hoare), and Louis XIV (T. G. Hawkes) may be catalogued with certain identification, but more common patterns such as Russian and Bull's-Eye were so widely copied by all glass cutters that pattern does not give an infallible clue to manufacturer.

While individual houses had certain characteristics, these cannot be taken as absolutely reliable but only as general guides to the work of various manufacturers. For instance, Dorflinger glass is usually considered to be of lightweight, that is thinner, metal than Hawkes, Libbey, or Fry; yet some fully credited pieces of Dorflinger glass are a quarter of an inch thick (Plate 69). These pieces are the exception, to be sure; but similar exceptions may be pointed out in the work of other glasshouses.

The bulk of the fine cut glass of the Brilliant Period was produced by the better known and well-established glasshouses. However, it is important to recognize that there were over a thousand cutting shops in operation during the twenty-five years of the Brilliant Period and not all of these turned out creditable work of lasting quality. Some only recut pressed blanks. Others were in business for so short a time that there is little record of their output.

Cutting shops bought their blanks from glass manufacturers, frequently on specification. The similarity of metal found in glass produced by different cutting shops, as for instance the Buffalo Cut Glass Company of Batavia, New York, and J. Hoare of Corning is due to the fact that blanks were supplied to both by the Corning Glass Company which had no cutting shop of its own. It is apparent that two cutting shops such as Hope Glass Works, Providence, Rhode Island, and Meriden Cut Glass Company, Meriden, Connecticut, buying their glass from the same source—in this case, Pairpoint Corporation—on the same specifications, produced confusingly similar ware.

It is then, because of the similarity of metal, the widespread use of identical patterns, and the inconsistent use of trade-marks that only outstanding characteristics of the work of each glasshouse may be considered typical.

PLATE 69

Water pitcher, 7¼ inches high, globe-shaped, partitioned design combining American and English strawberry-diamond and fan motifs. Made by Christian Dorflinger in 1897 at White Mills. (Brooklyn Mus.)

IMPORTANT GLASSHOUSES

The following glasshouses are listed in the order in which they or their parent companies were established:

I. LIBBEY GLASS COMPANY, Toledo, Ohio

New England Glass Company, Cambridge, Massachusetts, 1817–1878

New England Glass Company, W. L. Libbey and Son, Proprietors, Cambridge, 1878–1888

W. L. Libbey and Son Glass Company, Toledo, 1888–1893

Libbey Glass Company, Toledo, 1893–

Libbey glass is heavy, of thick metal, and deeply cut (Plate 70). Even the smaller figures in the designs are well defined. The glass is clear and flawless, does not age, but retains its sparkle and snap. Libbey made much use of the hob-star motif which his cutters called the "rosette" because of the many points and the raised center of the star. After 1895 all of the larger pieces were marked with an acid trade-mark stamp. Pieces made before 1904 are usually of good form with sharp, well-defined cutting. The later vases, bowls, and pitchers are heavy and ornate. After 1905 Libbey patterns made much use of the pinwheel motif. Libbey never used pressed blanks.

The Libbey Glass Company, successor to the New England Glass Company, carried on the fine traditions of craftsmanship and design. The parent company had not been able to survive the lime glass competition of the late Middle Period. After sixty years of operation as one of the nation's leading cut glass manufacturers, it was offered for sale in 1877. William L. Libbey, trained at the Mount Washington glassworks in South Boston, was then the general manager. He obtained a lease on the company in 1878 and changed the name to the New England Glass Company, W. L. Libbey and Son, Proprietors.

After his death in 1883, his son, Edward Drummond Libbey, continued to operate the new company through trying days of deficit and labor strife. The fortunate incident of hiring a young Englishman, Joseph Locke, an accomplished technician and etcher, helped

PLATE 70

UPPER: *Creamer, small, stemmed jelly dish, and sugar bowl, cut in simple hob-star motif. Libbey Glass Co., 1900. Brilliant Period. (Author's Collection)* LOWER: *Twelve-inch plate, Harvard border, flower center. Cruet and decanter in various combinations of notched prism and hob-star motifs, also Libbey. (Libbey Glass Co.)*

the company for a time, but even the popularity of his inventions of colored art glass—Amberina, Pomona, Peachblow, and Agata—did not prevent a deficit of $40,000 in 1888. That year E. D. Libbey moved the company to Toledo, Ohio, where he hoped to meet competition through the use of natural gas as furnace fuel.

He reorganized as the W. L. Libbey and Son Glass Company, Successors to the New England Glass Company, but two years later, in 1890, it became expedient to drop the name of the parent company and the New England Glass Company gave up the ghost and surrendered its charter. In 1893, when fine cut glass tableware and electric light bulbs had brought prosperity, the Toledo company changed its name to the Libbey Glass Company and as such it continued to make fine cut glass through the remainder of the Brilliant Period. The Libbey Glass Company, now a division of Owens-Illinois, continues to produce fine cut tableware. "Windswept" is a modern cutting in their "Premier" line.

2. PAIRPOINT CORPORATION, New Bedford, Massachusetts
　　Mount Washington Glass Company, South Boston, 1837–1869
　　Mount Washington Glass Company, New Bedford, 1869–1896
　　Pairpoint Glass Company, New Bedford, 1865–1896
　　Pairpoint Corporation, New Bedford, 1896--1938
　　Gundersen Glass Works, Incorporated, New Bedford, 1939–
　　The Pairpoint Corporation and its predecessors were all fortunate in having skilled designers. Considerable fine crosshatching appears on their pieces (Plate 71) and frequently small areas of wheel engraving will be found in combination with older motifs. Earlier patterns tend to use older forms in modern combinations with fans and stars. Late patterns used the bull's-eye, fan and prism, and Saint Louis diamond, but even in the closing years of the period when other houses were turning out hectic scrambles of half a dozen motifs, Pairpoint patterns remain in good balance with studied composition.

The Mount Washington Glass Company also supplied blanks to other cutting houses including the Meriden Silver Plate Company and the Wilcox Silver Plate Company of Meriden, Connecticut, and later the J. D. Bergen shop. If you have an old plated silver castor frame with cut glass bottles, it probably came from Meriden and the glass was very likely cut on Mount Washington blanks. Much of this metal, however, was of poor quality with air bubbles and striae. It was not always well fused. Some ruby bowls for insertion in silver frames were made by the Mount Washington company. Generally speaking, pieces showing defects were made about 1865 to 1870 before the Brilliant Period and should be attributed to the parent companies rather than to the Pairpoint Corporation.

The Mount Washington Glass Company was started by Deming Jarves in 1837 for his son, George. It was at that company that William L. Libbey learned the glass business. In 1860 he became part owner and in 1866, after acquiring sole ownership, he moved the company to New Bedford, Massachusetts, where he later sold out his interest. The new owners merged the older company with its neighbor in 1896 to become the Pairpoint Corporation, which produced much fine glass during the remainder of the Brilliant Period.

The Pairpoint Corporation stopped making cut glass in 1938. In 1939 Robert M. Gundersen bought the old glasshouse and resumed the manufacture of handmade cut and engraved glass under the new name. Gundersen Glass Works, Inc., is no longer in operation.

3. C. DORFLINGER AND SONS, White Mills, Pennsylvania
    Long Island Flint Glass Works, Brooklyn, New York, 1852–1863
    Greenpoint Glass Works, Brooklyn, 1860–1863
    Wayne County Glass Works, White Mills, 1865–1881
    C. Dorflinger & Sons, White Mills, 1881–1921

Dorflinger glass is always of fine clear metal and excellent workmanship (Plate 32). Any genuine piece is worthy of a cabinet collection. Much of it was cut in colored and cased glass, the Dorflinger green being a particularly fine bright color. It was frequently blown thinner than contemporaneous pieces and cuttings were sharp. In 1883 John O'Connor, cutting shop superintendent, designed the Parisian, (Pattern 3) the first design with the curved miter split. Repetitious use of this motif distinguishes Dorflinger cuttings of the first ten years of the Brilliant Period.

PLATE 71

UPPER: *Inverted berry bowl and pickle dish, with hob-star. (Author's Collection)* CENTER: *Claret, tumbler, and sherry glass in Dorflinger's adaptation of New England Glass Co.'s Middlesex (Pattern 6.) (Brooklyn Mus.)* LOWER: *Celery vase in notched prism, butter dish in Harvard, compote in Harvard with Rose. Pairpoint Brilliant Period. (Mrs. John M. Feeney)*

Christian Dorflinger, founder of the company, was one of the truly great glassmen of America. An Alsatian by birth, he learned his trade at Saint Louis, Lorraine, where more than fifty years before him one of America's first glass cutters, Peter William Eichbaum, had helped to establish the glass industry. In 1846, Christian came to America at the age of eighteen to enter the glass business. In 1852 he started the Long Island Flint Works in Brooklyn for the manufacture of chimneys and shades for kerosene lamps. Anxious to try his hand at fine flint and colored glass, he built the Greenpoint Glass Works in Brooklyn in 1860 for the production of cut glass tableware. It was at this factory that the Lincoln service was made. In 1863, because of ill health, Christian sold his interests in Brooklyn and retired to White Mills, Pennsylvania; but by 1865 he was back in business again manufacturing fine lead glass. He formed a partnership with his sons, William, Louis, and Charles, in 1881 and with them made and cut fine glass during the entire Brilliant Period. Christian died in 1915 and six years later the company was dissolved.

4. GILLINDER AND SONS, Philadelphia, Pennsylvania
    Franklin Flint Glassworks, Philadelphia, 1861–1868
    Gillinder and Sons, Philadelphia, 1868–1871
    Gillinder and Sons, Greensburg, 1883–1892, affiliate of the
        United States Glass Company, 1892–1949
    Gillinder Brothers, Incorporated, Port Jervis, New York,
        1912–
Much glass of extra fine brilliance and cut in old English solid-field motifs during the early part of the Brilliant Period is Gillinder glass from the old Franklin Flint Glassworks. William Thynne Gillinder, or Old Gillinder as his employees called him, specialized in lamps, lamp shades, and chandeliers from the start of his American venture in 1861. But many other pieces of fine metal and workmanship were also made at the Franklin works (Plate 67), where he prided himself on being an expert glassman. William Gillinder had written a book about glass which was published in England in 1851, and he was considered an authority on metals. He did not approve of the newfangled curved split, hob-star, and rosette motifs so

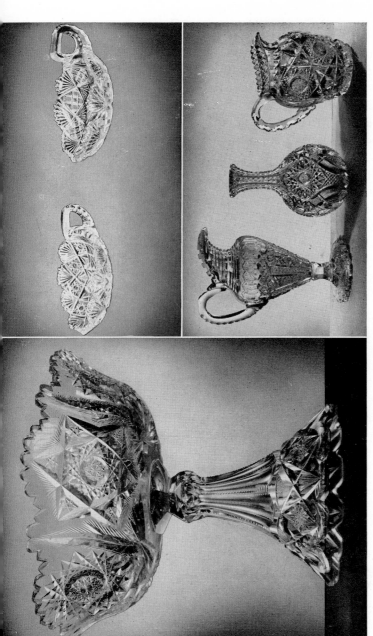

PLATE 72

LEFT: *Compote in Rajah pattern from Libbey. (Smithsonian Inst.)* UPPER, RIGHT: *Bonbon dishes by Hawkes in Gladys pattern; by Dorflinger in fan and block. (White House)* LOWER: *Pieces from late Brilliant Period showing overuse of motifs. Note crenulated top on pitcher. Carafe in Libbey's Columbia. (Mrs. John M. Feeney)*

his Franklin works cut the old-fashioned solid fields of hobnail, strawberry-diamond, and single star and block which he had known in England until competition forced adoption of modern patterns.

In a letter from the late James Gillinder, Jr., grandson of the founder, the work of the company is described: "The first cuttings made were copies of the Irish [English?] Bristol. The factory did . . . . considerable . . . . cutting, particularly . . . . lighting glassware. We did cutting through a frosted surface producing the Colonial designs of grapes, etc. Sandblasting was not invented until 1876 by Telghman of Philadelphia. The method we used [for frosted glass] was to apply the sand by means of a wire brush to a rapidly rotating piece of glass on a spindle of a lathe."

William, the founder of Gillinder and Sons, was born at Gateshead, England, in 1823. At seven he went to work in the glass factory at Mexborough. After becoming one of England's most prominent glassworkers and head of the British Friendly Society, a labor organization, he came to America in 1854, to become superintendent of the New England glassworks. The job did not turn out as promised so with his wife and five children he started for the West by way of Pittsburgh. At Saint Louis, he was employed at the bottle works of George W. Scolley.

Like his contemporary, Christian Dorflinger, Gillinder was quick to see the possibilities of the kerosene lamp and in 1861 he opened a small glasshouse on Maria Street in Philadelphia. When the neighbors complained of the soot from his furnace, he moved to Oxford Street. In 1863 he took into partnership Edwin Bennett, one of the founders of the Bennett Potteries in East Liverpool, Ohio, but five years later Bennett sold out to William's two sons, James and Frederick, and the company became known as Gillinder and Sons.

After William's death in 1871 the company was moved to Greensburg, Pennsylvania, in the early years of the Brilliant Period, and in 1892 it became an affiliate of the United States Glass Company. In 1912 two of William's grandsons established a glasshouse in Port Jervis, New York, under the name of Gillinder Brothers, Incorporated. The company is still in operation although they are making no cut tableware today.

[170]

PLATE 73

UPPER: *Pieces from Col. Harry C. Fry's collection made by his father in Rochester, Penna., early in twentieth century.* LOWER: *Seven-inch nappy, cut at Franklin Works of Gillinder and Sons Co., Philadelphia. Overornament had already appeared in 1903.*

5. T. G. HAWKES GLASS COMPANY, Corning, New York, 1880–
(Steuben Glass Company, 1903, subsidiary of the Hawkes
company until 1918 when Steuben was sold to Corning Glass
Company.)

In 1889 two patterns of the T. G. Hawkes Glass Company, the
Grecian (Pattern 9) and the Chrysanthemum (Pattern 21), took
the grand prize at the Paris Exposition, thus establishing a record
and a reputation for American cut glass. Hawkes glass has been of
fine quality since the founding of the company. Pieces cut since 1895
are trade-marked, the smaller ones with an H, the larger ones with
a shamrock enclosing two hawks. Both marks are still used by the
company. (See Appendix IV.) This was the only company to mark
every piece (after 1895). The glass is heavy, being of high lead
content, and of crystal purity. Goblets made of thinner metal than
the other pieces ring for almost thirty seconds with a clear bell-
like tone.

Thomas G. Hawkes, founder of the company, was one of the
most distinguished glassmen in America. A descendant of the
Hawkes and Penrose families—makers and cutters for five generations in Dudley, England, and in Waterford, Ireland—Thomas
came to Brooklyn, New York, in 1863 to practice the family trade.
In 1880 he set up shop in Corning, New York, cutting fine glass on
blanks made to his own specification by his friend Amory Houghton,
Senior, of the Corning Glass Works.

In 1903 Hawkes manufactured his own blanks for cutting and
with his son, Samuel, and Frederick Carder of Stourbridge, England, he established the Steuben Glass works in Corning, New York.
Hawkes crystal was cut on blanks manufactured at the Steuben
subsidiary until 1918 when the Steuben works were sold to the
Corning Glass Works.

The Hawkes Glass Company was liquidated following the death
of Samuel Hawkes in 1959, and the factory closed in December
1962. Penrose Hawkes, a descendant of the founder operates the
Hawkes Crystal Shop in Corning, New York, where some engraving is still done on Hawkes blanks.

PLATE 74

UPPER: *Plate, unusual piece of Brilliant Period cutting with hob-star motifs on strawberry-diamond field.* LOWER: *Plate, fine example of triple-miter cutting in bands. Medallions engraved with fruit baskets and cornucopias. Both 12-inch plates belong to the T. G. Hawkes permanent display at Smithsonian Inst., Washington, D. C.*

6. THE PHOENIX GLASS COMPANY, Monaca, Pennsylvania, 1880–
So much colored cut glass was made by the Phoenix Glass Company that there is always danger of accrediting all colored cut glass of the Brilliant Period to this Beaver County glasshouse. Organized in 1880 the company specialized in cut glass of all colors as well as in cased and flashed glass. Green over white was a favorite combination; amber, blue, and red glass were also cased and cut in patterns new at that time—chair bottom, hob-star, and notched prism combinations. Colors were usually very clear and brilliant and metal always of lead. The overlay or colored casing was thick enough to show considerable bleeding into the white, especially on the miter splits, although the crystal glass was very much thicker than the colored casing. Solid pieces included goblets in amber, blue, and red with cut stems and Saint Louis diamond cutting on the bowls, and blue blown wine glasses with cut stems and feet.

The Phoenix Glass Company was founded in August, 1880, at Monaca, called Phillipsburg in the early days. Just across the river is the site of the old Rochester Tumbler Company and the H. C. Fry Glass Company. Much fine engraved and colored glass of the Middle Period had come from Phillipsburg. This prompted Andrew Howard and W. I. Miller to organize the Phoenix glassworks for the manufacture of cut ware in 1880 with a capitalization of $30,000. So well did Phoenix colored cut glass sell that in 1887 the capitalization of the company was increased to a quarter of a million dollars. By 1891, the capitalization was $700,000 and the company began to make fancy hand-painted and stained lamp shades which sold on the New York market for as much as five and six hundred dollars for a single shade.

7. THE UNITED STATES GLASS COMPANY, Tiffin, Ohio
   Pittsburgh, Pennsylvania, 1892–1939
   Tiffin, 1939
   The formation of the United States Glass Company in 1892 was an important factor in both the growth and the doom of cut glass tableware. It is impossible to accredit accurately the work of any one of the seventeen affiliating companies, as each participant lost

[174]

its individuality in the merger. Although certain popular patterns, such as the Kaiser (Pattern 49), were cut by the parent company, the identity of the pieces was lost in the volume production of the big holding company. Typical patterns are those which could be cut in volume with very little small-wheel detail. (Plate 116.) This company used pressed blanks and all possible short cuts in production. While the glass is of fairly good quality, cutting bears the telltale stamp of mass production.

On the whole, cut glass from the United States Glass Company is not comparable to that of the Libbey, Pairpoint, Dorflinger, or Hawkes companies and did not command so high a price in the contemporary market. However, collectors who have followed the course of such fine companies as Bryce Glass of Mount Pleasant, or Hobbs-Brockunier of Wheeling, Pennsylvania, may be interested in the list of companies consolidated in September, 1892, to form what at that time was the largest glass company in the world, and the dead end of much fine individual production.

The holding company was formed on July 1, 1891, but did not function as a distributing agent until the next year. The following glasshouses became participating companies: Adams and Company, Pittsburgh; Bryce Brothers, Mount Pleasant, Pennsylvania; Challinoir Taylor & Company, Tarentum, Pennsylvania; George Dungan & Sons, Pittsburgh; Richards and Hartley, Tarentum, Pennsylvania; Ripley & Company, Pittsburgh; Gillinder & Sons, Greensburg, Pennsylvania; Hobbs Glass Company, Wheeling, West Virginia; Columbia Glass Company, Findlay, Ohio; King Glass Company, Pittsburgh; O'Hara Glass Company, Pittsburgh; Bellaire Goblet Company, Findlay, Ohio; Nickle Plate Glass Company, Fostoria, Ohio; Central Glass Company, Wheeling, West Virginia; Doyle & Company, Pittsburgh; A. J. Beatty & Sons, Tiffin, Ohio. (The Hobbs Glass Company was what remained of the once internationally famous Hobbs-Brockunier Company; the O'Hara Glass Company was the successor to the formerly important James B. Lyon Glass Company.)

The Bryce Company is now (1964) again producing cut tableware independently in Mount Pleasant, Pennsylvania.

[175]

The Tiffin Art Glass Co., Tiffin, Ohio, cuts a few "Hawkes" patterns using the old "Hawkes" trademark.

8. H. C. FRY GLASS COMPANY, Rochester, Pennsylvania, 1900–1929

No finer cut glass has ever been made in America than that produced by Henry Clay Fry at his Rochester glasshouse in the first few years of the twentieth century (Plate 75). Any piece of Fry glass is now a collector's item because of the superb quality of the metal, the precision of the cutting, and the originality and composition of the patterns. Fry glass compares favorably with the finest quartz crystal produced today. It has depth, excellent color, brilliance, and luster, but its distinctive characteristic is the unusual shape of the handmade blanks.

There was a theory among old glassmen that the secret of the Fry brilliance was not alone in his formula, which was extravagantly high in lead combined with the finest ground quartz obtainable, but in the coincidence of high fusion. Ordinarily flint or lead glass furnaces with their tall chimneys were built near transportation, at dock or river level, or at a railroad siding. Fry, however, had been the victim of floods from the Ohio River when he was manager of the Rochester Tumbler Company. He therefore selected for his own glassworks a site on a hill high above the Beaver Valley, and he built his own railroad siding up to the glasshouse on top. Thus the tall stacks of the chimneys towered over the countryside and the fires drew with a furious draft. It was this combination of pure ingredients and greatly accelerated fusion which are thought to have produced the remarkably crystal-clear Fry glass.

Henry Clay Fry, founder of the company, was another of the colorful glassmen of the Brilliant Period. Traveling for the William Phillips Glass Company of Pittsburgh, Fry met Abraham Lincoln in Illinois before he became President and interested him in the domestic manufacture of cut glass. Many students believe that the international popularity and market dominance of American cut glass can be traced to President Lincoln's sponsorship of the industry in 1861.

As superintendent at the O'Hara glass works under James B. Lyon's ownership, Fry had been a leader in fine-line cuttings during

PLATE 75

UPPER: *Twelve-inch plate by Hawkes with combination of cutting and engraving. (Smithsonian Inst.)* LOWER: *Mayonnaise bowl in swirled Wheat pattern with step cutting on base; compote with air-twist stem; small jug, about 1905, with buzz or pinwheel motif. All Fry glass. (Harry C. Fry)*

the Middle Period. As president of the Rochester Tumbler Company in 1872, he had manufactured 80,000 dozen tumblers a week and sent them to all parts of the world. Before this time tumblers had been used principally for whisky. Fry invented and perfected heat-proof tumblers for commercial jellies and jams and also glass jars for home canning. As president of the National Glass Company combine, Fry bought Mike Owens' invention for pressed blanks and so started the eventual decline of the cut glass business to which he also contributed so much.

Vaudeville acts, touring the country in the early years of the twentieth century, invariably visited the H. C. Fry Glass Company, because all the glass bell ringers of the entertainment world came to Fry for their ringing tumblers, jugs, tubes, and bells. It was a common sight to see a vaudeville musician tuning up at one end of the Fry cutting shop. The old H. C. Fry chimneys are still standing, and although the furnaces are in ruins, some of the pots are still in place.

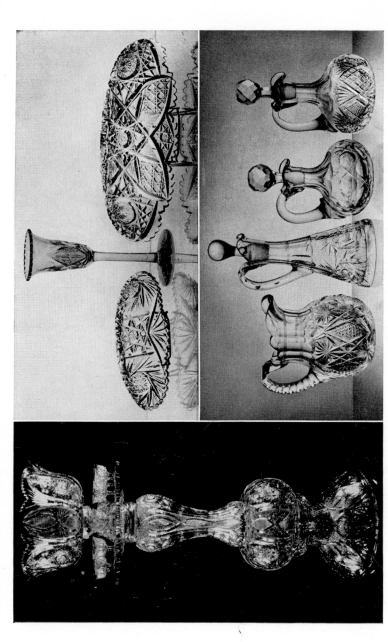

PLATE 76

LEFT: *Cut glass punch bowl, 5-part pedestal, 12 glasses. Rochester pattern, H. C. Fry Co., 1905. Height 4½ feet. Weight 150 pounds. Largest composite piece of cut glass in the world. (Carnegie Mus.)* RIGHT, UPPER: *Pickle dish, parfait glass, celery boat. Brilliant Period.* LOWER: *Late pitcher and cruets. (Author's Collection)*

PLATE 77

Saint Louis bowl, the largest single piece of cut glass in the world, 25 inches in diameter, 24 inches high, capacity of 4 gallons. Cut by John Rufus Denman for the Libbey exhibit at the World's Fair in 1904. Appraised at $24,000 in 1946 when it was presented to the Toledo Mus. of Art.

❖ ❖

CHAPTER XI

PATTERNS OF THE BRILLIANT PERIOD

I T IS easy to recognize patterns of the Brilliant Period. The
designs are more deeply cut and more intricate than those of
the two earlier eras. The familiar motifs of hob-star, curved split,
notched prism, and chair bottom are combined with the older and
simpler motifs of hobnail, fan, strawberry-diamond, and block.

About the year 1880, several almost simultaneous developments
in the glass industry made possible these more intricate cuttings.
First, the use of natural gas made fusion of metal more rapid and
annealing more perfect so that the final product was crystal clear
and could be a very heavy type of glass. Then electricity was
adapted to the cutter's lathe. This so speeded up the stone cutting
wheels that much deeper designs were possible. Finally an automatic
polishing device and the designing of curved miter cuttings led to
greater variety in the necessarily geometric designs. Copper-wheel
engravings of the Middle Period rarely appear in the Brilliant
Period until about 1900 when, to recoup the fading glory of the
industry, a few manufacturers cut flowers and fruits in intaglio.

A complete listing of the thousands of patterns produced by name
or number in hundreds of cutting shops during the Brilliant Period
is not possible. Some patterns of which a few stray pieces sometimes
turn up, were cut in limited quantity, proved impractical, and were
then withdrawn. There are no records of these transients. However,
some fifty fully documented patterns cut by leading glasshouses were
produced in sufficient quantity to be available now to the collector.

In the classification that follows, standard patterns are empha-
sized and the variations listed under them. The name and patent

[181]

design of the original patentee has been considered the standard. Frequently a glass cutter or manufacturer would design, patent, and produce an original design under his own name. The next season other glasshouses, seeing its popularity would copy the same pattern under another name or offer a design under the same name with just enough variation to obtain a new patent listing.

Pattern names applied to designs of the Brilliant Period are more easily followed in the early years. The Russian (Pattern 1), for example, is definite, as easily recognized on a goblet as on a bowl or pitcher. The Middlesex (Pattern 6) is definite, as are Strawberry-Diamond and Fan (Pattern 18), Venetian (Pattern 20), Parisian (Pattern 3), and a number of others that are classified.

Toward the end of the period, however, patterns became ornate and confused. For this reason, pattern names mean less after 1900 than in the first twenty years of the period. The older glassmen who still remember the later years of the Brilliant Period speak of such designs as "Chair Bottom and Star" or "Flower and Diamond Combination," or "Pinwheel and Bull's-Eye." Although most of the hybrids had specific pattern names, there were so many variations that the cutters themselves no longer recall them.

Collectors who have examples of these later cuttings (not listed among the better known and older patterns of the Brilliant Period) should study the Motif Chart (Appendix I) and apply the proper motif designations to individual pieces. Generally there will be two definite motifs used in a pattern. Pick out the two dominant recognizable ones and, if this combination does not fit into any classification already defined either as standard pattern or variation, identify your design by a combination of the names of the two principal motifs. Common combinations include hob-star or single star or pinwheel with any one of the following: curved split, hobnail, notched prism, bull's-eye, chair bottom, block, or strawberry-diamond. Although these cuttings are usually later ones, they are not necessarily so. During the entire Brilliant Period many pieces were cut without a pattern in the smaller shops, and in the large shops single pieces were always being cut without a pattern on the

[182]

inspiration of the moment. Such pieces—often made by the cutters for their own use or as gifts—are frequently of fine craftsmanship and should be included in collections.

The fifty patterns classified here in chronological order indicate to the collector the trend of design from 1880 to 1905, the duration of the Brilliant Period. The motifs dated here should also help him to place with fair accuracy almost any unlisted pattern in his own collection. He is safe in assuming that an unlisted pattern which combines a curved split with any other motif was probably not cut before 1882 or 1883, even though the piece in question is apparently old. A pattern which included the notched prism motif as an integral part of design in combination with bull's-eye, block, or any other single motif probably followed the Nautilus pattern of 1896. The pinwheel motif denotes cutting after 1900 in any case, and probably later than 1905. Any realistic cutting of flowers or fruit in intaglio indicates that the pattern was cut toward the close of the Brilliant Period or even as late as 1910.

The pattern names have been taken from three sources: I have used old catalogues where they were available, I have drawn on the memories of several veteran glassmen, and I have consulted the design patent records from the United States Department of Commerce. In a few cases the name of the pattern is included on the letters patent.

It is to be remembered, too, that all the time Brilliant patterns were being designed and cut, variations on the old stand-bys were also being cut on more modern blanks. Strawberry-Diamond and Fan is given as a standard (Pattern 18) but the strawberry-diamond motif without the fan was cut in solid fields on a number of blanks. The old English hobnail and the American block motifs were also cut on nappies, particularly square-shaped ones, and on saucedishes. Because of their sparkling metal and not because of motif or pattern, these few pieces are classified as of the Brilliant Period. Actually the same motifs were cut during the Early American and the Middle Period, but any piece of hobnail, strawberry-diamond, or block made after 1880 will have the luster and snap characteristic of the Brazilian (Pattern 15), Kimberly (Pattern

[183]

23), or other patterns definitely of the Brilliant Period. In such pieces consider age marks and color rather than pattern as a guide to classification.

Patent records are available for only a relatively small number of cut glass designs. Some houses never did patent their designs; some patented only those challenged by other houses; some patented designs they never actually cut; and many houses stopped patenting when it became apparent their designs were still not protected from copying. Although the classification below is given in the order of patent dates, in so far as these are available, it is not an infallible guide to the first appearance of certain designs. Leighton's Bowknot (Pattern 5), for instance, was patented in 1886, but did not appear until 1887, when it was contemporary with a variation, Miller's Maltese Cross (Pattern 5, variation), and with Middlesex (Pattern 6). Chrysanthemum (Pattern 21) was patented in 1890, but was certainly known before that time as it won a prize at the Paris Exposition in 1889.

1. RUSSIAN

The Russian pattern is a refinement on the old Star and Hobnail cut in Brooklyn and Pittsburgh as early as 1863. It was designed by Philip McDonald, a cutter employed by Thomas G. Hawkes of Corning, New York. The designer secured patent papers for it on June 20th, 1882, and assigned the pattern to his employer. Soon afterward one of the most influential glass dealers and importers of the nineteenth century, Richard Briggs of Boston, came to Hawkes with an order for a complete banquet service to be cut for the Russian Embassy in Washington. McDonald's design was selected, became tremendously popular, and was thenceforth known as the Russian.

In June of 1885 another complete service in this pattern was ordered for use at state dinners in the American Embassy at Saint Petersburg, and in 1886 the White House at Washington adopted the same pattern, with the addition of an engraved eagle crest. The first highball or iced-tea glasses were cut by C. Dorflinger and Sons

PLATE 78

Russian, Pattern 1

Reproduced from catalogue of the T. G. Hawkes Glass Company

for Theodore Roosevelt. Although additions and replacements were later made to this service, many of the original pieces still appeared at state dinners during the administration of Franklin D. Roosevelt and the set was in use until 1938, when a less expensive service was ordered.

It would be impossible to list the pieces cut in the Russian pattern, since everything that could be cut was eventually represented. Not every company, however, cut all kinds of pieces; for instance, T. G. Hawkes cut small bonbon and olive dishes in 5-inch crescents, 7-inch oak leaves, and hearts of varying sizes. The same shapes were cut in smaller sizes for pin trays. Some of the plates have a shell scallop, but early pieces have plain borders.

The plates cut by Dorflinger in the Russian pattern usually have a 24-point star in the center, a very early use of this motif. Earlier plates, bowls, and nappies cut by the Hawkes company usually show a solid cutting. Later this company also adopted the 24-point star in combination with the Russian pattern because of the greatly reduced cost of production, but this was after trade-marks were used and all such Hawkes pieces are marked. (See Appendix III.) The Russian pattern was much copied by manufacturers of pressed glass and was called by them Daisy and Button.

Russian is one of the patterns for which prices are known. With some local variation but with a fairly standard retail mark-up of 33 1/3 per cent, the following prices prevailed in 1890 for pieces of high quality: bonbon dish, 7-inch oak leaf, $12.50; butter tub with plate, $23.00; cologne bottle, 8-ounce, square, $10.00; compotes, 8-inch, $15.00; 9-inch, $20.00; 10-inch, $25.00; 12-inch round nappie without handles, $18.00; punch bowl with pedestal, 15-inch, $125.00. Today, goblets cut in the Russian pattern with an engraved crest similar to those supplied to the White House from 1886 until 1938, are listed at an approximate retail price of $750.00 per dozen; sherry and cordial glasses, $600.00 per dozen.

CLASSIFICATION.

1. Basket, 10-inch
2. Bonbon or olive dishes, 5 and 6-inch round; 5-inch crescents

3. Bowls, 7, 8, 9, 10, and 12-inch; flat-bottomed, square, round, and oval
4. Bread plate, 10-inch oval
5. Butter dishes, individual, 3-inch, flat or stemmed
6. Butter tub with plate
7. Candlesticks and candelabra
8. Celery dishes
   a. boat, 4½ by 11 inches
   b. vases, 10, 12-inch, straight or stemmed
9. Champagne jug, 2-quart, straight with handles, without cover
10. Claret jugs, 1-pint, 1½-pint, 1-quart, with handles; matching or lapidary stoppers
11. Cologne bottles, 4, 6, and 8-ounce, narrow-necked, square, globe, and round
12. Cocktail glasses
13. Compotes, 8, 9, and 10-inch; round, short, or tall-stemmed
14. Cruets, 6 or 8-ounce, tapering or globed
15. Decanters, 1-pint, 1½-pint, 1-quart; narrow, ring-necked, and globe
16. Finger bowls, 2½ by 5 inches
17. Goblets, tall and short-stemmed, globed, tapering, and bell
18. Highballs
19. Ice-cream platter, 7 by 12 inches
20. Mustard jar
21. Nappies
   a. 7, 8, 9-inch square, with or without handles
   b. 7, 8, 9, 10, 12-inch round, without handles
   c. 6 by 9-inch oblong
22. Pin trays, 4-inch oak leaves, hearts, and crescents
23. Plates, 6, 8½, 10, and 12-inch
24. Powder box, with glass or metal tops
25. Punch bowl, 15-inch with pedestal
26. Punch cups, with handles
27. Rose bowl
28. Salts, table and individual; globed, square, and tub
29. Saucedishes, 4 and 4½-inch shallow
30. Sherbets, flat or stemmed, with handles

[187]

31. Smelling-salts bottles
32. Spoonholder, 3½-inch by 7½-inch oval
33. Sugar bowls, globed, standard, and tub; with or without cov ers; with or without handles. Older pieces without handles.
34. Sirup pitcher, globed, with or without silver tops
35. Toothpick holders, square, round, flat, and stemmed
36. Tumblers, water and whisky
37. Vases, tall, straight, or stemmed
38. Water pitchers, straight or globe
39. Wines, champagne, claret, cordials, hock, Madeira, sherry

VARIATIONS.

Ambassador. Crosshatched, as in the old English strawberry-diamond.
Canterbury. The hobnail cut in a simple star.
Cleveland. Combines two circles of straight, undecorated hobnail motifs with Russian.
Persian. Changes the simple star motif to a many-pointed hob-star figure. Expensive and rare, appears chiefly in 8, 9, and 10-inch nappies with straight sides, and 7, 8, 9, and 10-inch berry bowls.
Polar Star. Increases size of larger star motif in proportion to smaller hobnail.
Spider Web. Combines Russian with Strawberry-Diamond and Fan pattern.

COLOR. Clear, green, ruby, amber, amethyst, blue, yellow. All very rare.

ORIGIN. The name, Russian, originated with the T. G. Hawkes Company, but the pattern or one of its variations was later cut by virtually every glasshouse.

TRADE-MARK. None, since trade-marks were not adopted until after this pattern had reached its peak of popularity.

2. COBWEB

Patent design papers for the Cobweb pattern were taken out in 1883 by George Hatch, a glass cutter at the Meriden Flint Glass

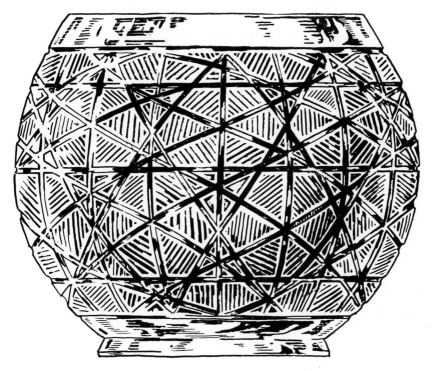

PLATE 79
Cobweb, Pattern 2
Reproduced from the files of the United States Patent Office

Company. Hatch had an idea for a *tout ensemble* never before applied either in the cut glass industry or in interior decoration. He says in his letters patent: "This ornamentation applies to the various articles included in glassware . . . such as sets including shades for lighting-fixtures, as well as articles of table service, whereby the entire glass in the apartment will all correspond."

The Cobweb pattern resembles the triple miter cuttings of the Middle Period rather than the deep miter cuttings of the Brilliant Period. However, because of the date of Hatch's patent and the shapes on which the design was cut it is rightly assigned to the Brilliant Period. It is a very rare pattern but exciting to search for, especially for lamp collectors.

CLASSIFICATION.

1. Bowls, 6, 7, 8, 9-inch
2. Celery vase
3. Compotes, on high standard, without cover; on low foot, covered; both 8-inch
4. Goblets, straight, tapering sides, plain rim
5. Lamp bases
6. Pitchers, straight or globe-shaped
7. Shades for lighting fixtures, globe or flaring; other shapes may have been cut, but none are now known

VARIATIONS. None.

COLOR. Clear; may have been cut in color, red perhaps, but no known pieces exist.

ORIGIN. Meriden Flint Glass Company, Meriden, Conn. It is doubtful if this pattern was ever cut by any other company.

TRADE-MARK. Pattern discontinued before the trade-mark was adopted, so that no piece is marked.

3. PARISIAN

The Parisian pattern was the first to make use of the curved miter split. It was patented in May, 1886, by John S. O'Connor, designer

PLATE 80

Parisian, Pattern 3

Reproduced from the files of the United States Patent Office

and cutting shop superintendent for C. Dorflinger and Sons and was assigned to the company which manufactured cut glass blanks and began cutting the new pattern immediately. It became popular almost at once and started a trend in cut glass decoration which continued through the first two decades of the twentieth century.

The Parisian pattern is comparatively simple. It consists of curved splits with alternate fans and old strawberry-diamond cross-hatchings. Each piece has a star bottom. An exclusive Dorflinger pattern, it is now rare.

CLASSIFICATION.

1. Berry bowls, 7, 8, 9, and 10-inch
2. Berry dishes, 4½ and 5-inch, shallow
3. Bonbon or olive dishes, small, round, 4½ and 5-inch diameter
4. Celery vase
5. Cruets, 6, 8, and 10-ounce
6. Finger bowls, 4, 4½, and 5-inch, shallow and deep
7. Goblets, taper and bowl-shaped, 6½ inches high
8. Plates, 6, 8½, and 10-inch
9. Saucedishes, 4½ and 5-inch, shallow

Parisian was undoubtedly cut in compotes, claret jugs, water pitchers, tumblers, and other tableware as it was one of the most popular Dorflinger patterns of the period; but no such pieces are now known.

VARIATIONS. Several Straus cuttings are variations of Parisian. Other glasshouses developed patterns on the curved-line principle but they are too distinctive in character to be confused with Parisian. All variations used the curved-line split in combination with the star; the original has only the bottom starred.

COLOR. Clear only.

ORIGIN. C. Dorflinger and Sons, White Mills, Penna. The Parisian was distinctly a Dorflinger pattern, was extensively cut by them, and not copied or cut by any other establishment.

TRADE-MARK. Too early for trade-mark.

4. STRAWBERRY-DIAMOND AND STAR

The Strawberry-Diamond and Star is a very important pattern for it shows the transition of the strawberry-diamond from the commonly accepted English form to the later standard American motif.

In English and Irish patterns, the strawberry-diamond is a four-sided cut motif varying in size from 1½ inches down to a ¼-inch square. This slightly raised square or rectangle is crosshatched with tiny fine lines making miniature diamonds on the larger field. In the Early American patterns the strawberry-diamond motif retains this character as shown on the Bakewell pieces. During the Middle Period the motif was made smaller as the depth of its sides became greater until it lost its original character, becoming simply a small diamond with one X or single cross on top.

In 1886, Walter A. Wood, a partner with Tom B. Clark in the T. B. Clark Company, designed a variation of the strawberry-diamond, the cross-cut diamond, and fan motifs. In Wood's Strawberry-Diamond and Star pattern the progression of the strawberry-diamond motif is plainly visible. He uses a pattern of four diamonds, two of them the old strawberry crosshatched with tiny lines in a multiple cutting and the other two the modern X cutting with two diagonals added. These diagonals were later dropped. [Cf. Strawberry-Diamond and Fan (Pattern 18).] The pattern designed by Wood was not extensively cut.

CLASSIFICATION.

1. Dishes, 5-inch square, shallow
2. Nappies, shallow sides, 6, 7, 8-inch square; 7 by 4½ inches oblong; 7 inches round
3. Plates, 8½ and 10-inch (perhaps some 7-inch square plates were cut)
4. Saucedishes, 4 and 5-inch, shallow
5. Tumblers, 5-ounce mineral, 8-inch whisky or finger, star bottoms

VARIATIONS.

Cornell. Produced by Maple City Glass Company, Hawley, Penna.

PLATE 81
Strawberry-Diamond and Star, Pattern 4
Reproduced from the files of the United States Patent Office

Strawberry-Diamond and Prism. Cut by J. Hoare and Company, Corning, N. Y.

Strawberry-Diamond and Scallop. From unidentified Brooklyn glasshouses.

Strawberry-Diamond and Fan. This most famous descendant became in its own right Pattern 18.

COLOR. Clear. Color unlikely.

ORIGIN. T. B. Clark and Company, Honesdale, Penna.

TRADE-MARKS. Cut before trade-marks were used.

5. LEIGHTON'S BOW-KNOT

Leighton's Bow-Knot was designed and patented in 1886 by one of the famous Leighton brothers instrumental in the development of the New England Glass Company during the Middle Period. At the time William Leighton, Jr. designed the Bow-Knot pattern, he seems to have been connected with the firm of Hobbs-Brockunier & Co. Although William Leighton, Sr. had perfected the lime glass formula which revolutionized the pressed glass industry in 1864, William Leighton, Jr. never lost his interest and enthusiasm for cut glass of fine quality, or for red, green, and yellow lead glass.

Leighton's Bow-Knot, first cut in 1887, is rare but worth any collector's search for it was cut on exquisitely fine metal. The heart-shaped bow described in Leighton's letters patent as "a scroll ornamentation resembling bunches of ribbons," proved too expensive to be practical and was later dropped from the pattern. The diagonal lines and the use of the Maltese cross were new to cut glass design in 1887.

CLASSIFICATION.

1. Berry bowls, 7, 8, 9-inch
2. Saucedishes, 4, 4½, and 5-inch

The pattern may have been cut in compotes, tumblers, and salts, but none are known at this time. It appears certain that no stemmed

W. LEIGHTON, Jr.
ORNAMENTATION OF DISHES OR VESSELS.
No. 16,994.   Patented Nov. 23, 1886.

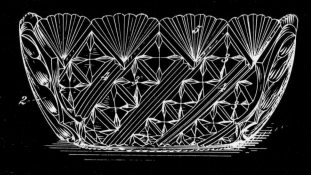

WITNESSES: INVENTOR,

Att'y.

PLATE 82
Leighton's Bowknot, Pattern 5
Reproduced from the files of the United States Patent Office

ware—goblets or wines—were cut with the bow-knot, although some may have been cut with the smaller Maltese cross.

VARIATIONS.

Miller's Maltese Cross. On the same day that Leighton took out patent papers for his Bow-Knot, J. E. Miller of Pittsburgh patented the Maltese Cross pattern. His patent was witnessed by a member of the old Bakewell family. There was no litigation but considerable controversy ensued. Miller's Maltese Cross does not have the heart-shaped motif later dropped by Leighton's Bow-Knot, nor has it the swirling effect of diagonal lines found in the standard, the figures being perpendicular to the base. The bowls are somewhat taller than Leighton's bowls and the tops are deeply scalloped in six or eight almost arched panels. Both patterns are rare, but they can be found in berry sets.

COLOR. Clear, also colors, probably only red and yellow; Miller's Maltese Cross was cut in clear only.

ORIGIN. *Leighton's Bow-Knot,* Hobbs-Brockunier and Company, Wheeling, West Virginia.
Miller's Maltese Cross, Phoenix Glass Company, Pittsburgh, Penna.

TRADE-MARKS. None.

6. MIDDLESEX

One of the last patterns ever cut by the old New England Glass Company, Middlesex is one of the most beautiful of all cut glass patterns. It is extremely rare and a collector's item since it is one of the first of the curved miter patterns ever cut.

It was designed and patented by William C. Anderson, a glass cutter at the New England Glass Company where Edward Drummond Libbey was his boss. Libbey had inherited the New England Glass Company when his father died in 1883. Although it was facing bankruptcy, Edward Libbey felt that if he could convert the

PLATE 83
Middlesex, Pattern 6
Reproduced from the files of the United States Patent Office

New England Glass Company to the new-style heavy lead, deeply cut tableware, he might be able to save it. He offered prizes for designs for cut glass, and Anderson's Middlesex was one of the first ones turned in. Later Anderson went to Toledo and became chief designer for Libbey.

Though it is possible that Middlesex was later cut in Toledo at the Libbey Glass Company, it is not one of the patterns listed in their 1890 catalogue. Probably all pieces of the Middlesex pattern were cut on New England Glass Company blanks before the furnaces were converted to gas, and have that singularly mellow softness to their brilliance not found in glass fused in gas-fired furnaces.

Middlesex is the first cut glass pattern on record to use the 8-point star in a repetitive design. The 8-point star was the forerunner of the 10 and 12-point star known as the hob-star because the intersecting points form a figure in the center of the star resembling a raised hobnail. The 10 and 12-point hob-star was much used in later Libbey patterns.

CLASSIFICATION.

1. Berry bowls, 7, 8, and 9-inch
2. Bonbon or olive dish, 5-inch, shallow
3. Celery vase
4. Compote, 7-inch, stemmed, no covers
5. Saucedishes, 4½-inch, shallow
6. Tumblers, small finger, straight sides, star bottom

Other pieces may have been cut in this pattern, probably some salt dishes and ice-cream plates.

VARIATIONS.

Lorimer, using the 8-point star with straight splits between, is neither so well designed nor so well cut as Middlesex, and should not be confused with the standard which has curved splits.

Sultana, a Dorflinger variation which drops the inner fan, adding a small star. Any pattern combining the simple 8-pointed star with double splits (such as the Lorimer) may be considered a variation of Middlesex. Several such variations were cut by the T. B. Clark

[199]

Company in Honesdale, Penna., but usually without the curved splits combined with the fan motif.

COLOR. Probably all pieces cut were clear glass since the New England Glass Company had stopped making colored glass by 1886. All Lorimer pieces are also clear.

ORIGIN.

Middlesex. New England Glass Company, Cambridge, Mass.; later possibly Libbey Glass Company, Toledo, O.
Lorimer. Maple City Glass Company, Hawley, Penna.

TRADE-MARK.

Middlesex. Unmarked because the New England Glass Company did not use trade-marks.
Lorimer. Small maple leaf trade-mark of the Maple City Glass Company (see Appendix IV).
T. B. Clark Company 8-point patterns are marked with the Clark circle (see Appendix IV).

7. ANGULATED RIBBON

This is often mistaken for an Early American or an English pattern. It has an old-style look about it that is charming in the few small bowls and saucedishes that have survived. There are probably a good many more pieces of Angulated Ribbon around than have so far been recorded, as it was popular and relatively inexpensive in its day. The patent papers describe it as "consisting of a circular band composed essentially of an angulated ribbon." Andrew Snow, Jr., the designer, was treasurer of the Mount Washington glassworks about 1890, according to Thomas A. Tripp of Fairhaven, Massachusetts, who was manager of that company at the time and afterward of its successor, the Pairpoint Glass Company. In Mr. Tripp's opinion, Angulated Ribbon was not cut extensively after 1890.

CLASSIFICATION.

1. Bowls, 7, 8, 9-inch, shallow

PLATE 84
Angulated Ribbon, Pattern 7
Reproduced from the files of the United States Patent Office

PLATE 85
Russian and Pillar, Pattern 8
Reproduced from the files of the United States Patent Office

2. Butter patties, 3-inch
3. Plates, 6, 7, 9-inch, slightly curved up at edge
4. Saucedishes, probably 4½ to 5-inch, shallow; none now known to exist.

VARIATIONS. None

COLOR. Clear glass.

ORIGIN. Mount Washington Glass Company and later the Pairpoint Glass Company, both in New Bedford, Mass.

TRADE-MARK. None.

8. RUSSIAN AND PILLAR

The Russian and Pillar pattern was one of that early group of swirl patterns which also included Leighton's Bow-knot. The standard was patented and designed by T. G. Hawkes in 1887, but was not cut extensively by him until several years later. Some collectors regard it as a variation of the Russian and it can be used with the Russian in service sets. However, it is a distinct pattern in itself and was so considered by its contemporaries.

The pillars of the pattern are particularly lovely on the fine Hawkes blanks, resembling in their smooth texture the pillars of the early Robinson decanter (Plate 45).

CLASSIFICATION.

1. Berry sets
2. Fruit bowls, 7 and 9-inch, deep tapering sides
3. Plates, 8½ and 12-inch
   Some wine glasses and goblets were cut in this pattern on order. These are rare.

VARIATIONS. *Crystal, Russian and Leaf,* and *Wheat* are all Hoare variations of the standard Russian and Pillar. Wheatstalks replace the pillars in the Wheat variation, and also on *Harvest,* another

PLATE 86
Grecian, Pattern 9
Reproduced from the files of the United States Patent Office

variation cut by Fry. Straus cut still another variation known as *Russian Swirl*. Toward the end of the Brilliant Period, a number of popular variations appeared on many types of blanks.

COLOR. Clear only.

ORIGIN. T. G. Hawkes Glass Company, Corning, New York. The Wheat variation was cut by J. Hoare and Company of Corning, N. Y., and Harvest was developed ten years later by the H. C. Fry Glass Company, Rochester, Penna.

TRADE-MARKS. Later cuttings of Russian and Pillar have the Hawkes trade-mark (see Appendix IV) but many were cut before adoption of the trade-mark. Wheat shows no trade-mark as the Hoare trade-mark had not yet been adopted.

9. GRECIAN

If Grecian were not so important as a specific design in its own time, it might be listed in later charts as a variation of the Russian pattern. The standard Grecian has a field of star and hobnail cutting with oval lozenge-shaped figures of clear glass, evenly spaced as radiants from a 10-point star bottom. Designed by T. G. Hawkes, it was cut in a full dinner service as one of two sets to be displayed at the Paris Exposition in 1889, where they won the international grand prize. Because of the Paris award, Grecian is of particular interest to collectors. It is comparatively rare.

CLASSIFICATION.

1. Bonbon or olive dish
2. Bowls, 7, 9, and 10-inch, sloping sides
3. Celery dishes
   a. boats
   b. vases, cut in 1889, earlier than the boats, but very rare
4. Compotes, 7, 9, 10-inch, on stems, cut feet, no covers
5. Finger bowls, 5-inch, straight sides
6. Goblets, round, with cut or plain stem; tapering, with cut stem

PLATE 87
Old-fashioned Hobnail, Pattern 10
Reproduced from the files of the United States Patent Office

7. Ice-cream dishes, 5-inch, rare
8. Nappies, 6 to 9 inches
9. Plates, 5 (rare), 6, 8½, 10-inch
10. Platter, 12-inch, slightly curved up on the edge
11. Salts, individual and table, globe and tub
12. Saucedishes, 4½-inch, shallow; 5-inch, deep
13. Sugar bowls, globular or square, with covers, no handles
14. Tumblers, finger, 2-ounce; straight, star bottoms, 5 to 8-ounce
15. Wines, saucer champagne, claret, and sherry, also small cordials; cut stems and feet
16. Vase, rose

VARIATIONS. Probably other glasshouses followed the practice of cutting clear figures through a Russian pattern background but only the Grecian by Hawkes shows the 10-point star bottom.

COLOR. Usually clear, but some small wines and cordials were cut in green and red to accompany larger services in clear glass.

ORIGIN. Designed and cut by the T. G. Hawkes Company, Corning, N. Y.

TRADE-MARK. Not yet adopted.

10. OLD-FASHIONED HOBNAIL

Although this figure is sometimes called the English Hobnail, it was never used as extensively in either England or Ireland as it was in America. Early glass cutters of the Middle Period and a few in the Early American Period made use of the six-sided hobnail motif, but its greatest use was after 1888 when glass manufacturers found the pattern both effective and inexpensive. Later hobnail pieces can be distinguished from those of the two earlier periods by the brilliance of the metal and the accuracy and depth of the splits. The hobnail is a fairly simple cutting, similar to the old block motif. Parallel horizontal splits are bisected by diagonal parallels forming the six-sided figure called hobnail from its resemblance to the hobnails used on the soles of old boots.

[207]

CLASSIFICATION.

1. Basket, 6 by 10 inches, flat with handles
2. Berry or center bowls, 8, 9, 10 and 12-inch, flat bottom; square, round, or oval
3. Bonbon or olive dishes, 5 and 6-inch round, 5-inch crescent, 7-inch oak leaf, 5 and 7-inch heart
4. Bread plate, 10-inch oval
5. Butter patties, 3-inch, flat and stemmed, square and round
6. Butter tub with plate
7. Canoe-shaped salted-nut dish
8. Celery dishes
   a. boats, flat or curved sides, 5 by 10½ inches
   b. vases, straight or stemmed
9. Champagne jug, 2-quart, straight, without cover, with handles
10. Claret jugs, 1-pint, 1½ pint, 1-quart with handles
11. Cologne bottles, 4, 6, 8-ounce narrow neck, square, globe, round
12. Compotes, 8, 9, 10-inch round, short or tall stem
13. Cruets, 6 or 8-inch, 6 or 8-ounce, tapering or globe
14. Decanters, 1-pint, 1½-pint, 1-quart; narrow or ring neck, globe
15. Finger bowls, 5-inch, 2½ inches deep
16. Goblets, tall and short stem, globe, tapering, and bell
17. Ice-cream platter, 7 by 12 inches, oblong
18. Mustard jar
19. Nappies, 7, 8, 9-inch; round, with handles; square, with or without handles
20. Pin trays, 4-inch, oak leaf, heart, and crescent
21. Plates, 7, 8½, 10, 12, 13-inch
22. Powder box with glass or metal tops
23. Punch bowl, 15-inch, with pedestal
24. Punch cups with handles
25. Rose bowl
26. Salts, table and individual, globe, square, and tub
27. Saucedishes, 4 and 4½-inch, shallow
28. Sherbets, stemmed or flat, with handles
29. Smelling-salts bottles

30. Spoonholder, flat, oval, 7½ by 3½ inches
31. Sugar bowls, standard, globe and tub, with or without covers, with or without handles; older pieces without handles
32. Sirup pitcher, globe, with or without silver top
33. Toothpick holders, square, round, flat, and stemmed
34. Tumblers, highball or iced tea, 10, 12-ounce; whisky or finger, 5, 6-ounce; champagne or mineral, 5-ounce
35. Vases, tall, straight, or stemmed
36. Water pitchers, straight or globe
37. Wine glasses, saucer champagne, hock, claret, Madeira, sherry, cocktail, and cordial

VARIATIONS.

Hob-in-Pillar-Panel, cut by T. G. Hawkes Glass Company, Corning, N. Y.
Hobnail and Fan, cut by all companies
Hobnail and Russian, cut by all companies

COLOR. Clear, green, ruby, amber. Colored pieces are very rare.

ORIGIN. Cut by all companies.

TRADE-MARK. Only a few pieces carry a trade-mark since this was considered a commercial pattern. Libbey Glass Company marked some pieces as did the T. G. Hawkes Glass Company after 1896.

11. DEVONSHIRE

One of the loveliest of all the early patterns, Devonshire shows the progression of design motifs from the earlier Irish forms to the more modern star, hob-star, and curved split. Thomas G. Hawkes, the designer, was a sixth-generation glass manufacturer and cutter who found it natural to adapt ancestral Irish motifs to the New World geometric arc forms. Devonshire uses alternate squares of old English strawberry-diamond, single star, fan, and pyramid-diamond. Though rather ornate, it is an effective pattern and was very popular—and expensive. Note the large hob-star in

PLATE 88
Devonshire, Pattern 11
Reproduced from the files of the United States Patent Office

the bottom. This was one of the first patterns to use the 24-point hob-star, always a mark of quality in cutting.

As in the case of many of the finer patterns, it is easier to find complete sets of Devonshire than of commoner designs. Possibly that is because the elaborate sets were brought out only on state occasions. As a complete service of Devonshire originally cost several thousand dollars, it was treasured to hand down as an heirloom. Today such a service could not be duplicated at three times the 1889 price.

CLASSIFICATION.

1. Bonbon or olive dishes, 5-inch, round, shallow; 4½ by 5-inch oblong; also, a less common type, 5 by 7-inch
2. Bowls, 7 and 9-inch, flat with slightly curved straight sides
3. Butter patties, 3-inch, rare
4. Celery vase, (frequently mistaken for Irish, and sold as Waterford, as they use the old English strawberry-diamond combined with the fan scallop)
5. Compotes, 5 and 7-inch, stemmed, no covers
6. Finger bowls, 4-inch, with slightly curved, straight sides
7. Goblets, round, with cut foot; tapering, with plain foot
8. Nappies, 7 and 9-inch
9. Plates, 6, 8½, 10, and 12-inch
10. Rose bowl, round
11. Salts, globe, table only
12. Saucedishes, 4½-inch, shallow
13. Sugar bowls, globe and square (cut on same shape blanks as Grecian), covers, no handles
14. Tumblers, finger, 2-ounce; 7-ounce, straight sides, star bottoms
15. Wines, saucer champagne, claret, sherry, small liqueurs, tapering or round
16. Vases, tapering, stemmed

VARIATIONS. *Tokio,* a later, less expensive copy of Devonshire cut by J. Hoare & Co. used continuous strawberry-diamond field instead of alternating star and strawberry-diamond. No other variations were attempted, probably because expense limited sale.

[211]

T. A. BAKER.

GLASSWARE.

No. 18,621.   Patented Sept. 25, 1888.

PLATE 89
Baker's Gothic, Pattern 12
Reproduced from the files of the United States Patent Office

COLOR. Clear glass, except for a few red or green liqueurs and small wines in which the bowls were colored and the stems clear

ORIGIN. Thomas G. Hawkes Company, Corning, N. Y.

TRADE-MARK. The small Hawkes trade-mark of a shamrock with a hawk on either side of the name, is found stamped with acid on the bottom of later pieces. Some early pieces are unmarked, as they were cut before the trade-mark was adopted.

12. BAKER'S GOTHIC

It was inevitable, after the curved split was adapted to glass design, that the Gothic arch should soon follow. Baker's Gothic, designed by Thomas A. Baker, designer and glass cutter for the T. B. Clark Company, was the first of the Gothic patterns. The Gothic arch between the points on all six sides of the star gives this pattern its name. It was cut extensively by the Clark company in complete sets and in a wide variety of shapes, as it was adaptable to almost any glass form. Note the 6-pointed star reaching to the very edge of the scalloped rim. This, together with the cross-hatched lozenges in the center, are the distinguishing features of the pattern. The true standard shows a star center in three of the central star lozenges, though not all authentic pieces cut by Clark follow this form minutely. However, if you find a piece of Baker's Gothic that does show these three starred centers, it is safe to assume that it was an early cutting, probably around 1890.

CLASSIFICATION.

1. Berry bowl, 9-inch
2. Bonbon or olive dishes, 5½-inch, with handle, 5-inch without handle
3. Celery vase
4. Champagne jug, 2-quart, straight sides
5. Claret jugs, 1 and 1½-quart, with stoppers and handles
6. Compotes, 5, 7-inch, stemmed, no covers; low stemmed 5-inch with dome cover, probably intended as butter dish

7. Goblets, bell, 6½-inch
8. Nappies, 7 and 8-inch, round
9. Plates, 6, 8½, and 10-inch
10. Punch bowl, 10-inch, rare
11. Saucedishes, 4½-inch, shallow
12. Sugar bowls with handles (probably later); round sugar bowl with cover, no handles
13. Tumblers, 8-ounce standard, straight, star bottom; no 12-ounce iced tea, but possibly some 5-ounce mineral tumblers
14. Water pitcher, 1-quart, flared
15. Wines, most plentiful in this pattern, saucer champagnes, claret, and sherry; a few cordials

Also such incidentals as candlesticks, toothpick holders, mustard pot with cover.

VARIATIONS.

Denrock, with three Gothic arches instead of six and star cuttings enclosed in arches with fan and chair bottom cutting between, a corruption of the old Baker's Gothic cut by the Maple City Glass Company, is not as well designed nor as sharp a pattern. Found in 5 and 6-inch nappies, with and without handles.

Gotham, a much later variation cut by J. Hoare and Company, Corning, N. Y., using alternate hob-star and crosshatched lozenge-shaped figures on pint decanters, celery boats, 7, 8, and 9-inch berry bowls so like the standard as to be almost interchangeable in sets.

COLOR. Clear only.

ORIGIN. T. B. Clark Company of Honesdale, Penna. Variations by Maple City Glass Company (Denrock) and by J. Hoare and Company (Gotham).

TRADE-MARK. Later pieces marked with Clark trade-mark (see Appendix IV).

13. FLORENCE

Designed by William C. Anderson for E. D. Libbey in 1889, this somewhat ornate pattern was one of the first to be cut extensively at the new Libbey Glass Company in Toledo, Ohio. One unique feature will quickly distinguish this pattern for the collector. In the bottom of each piece, including the stemmed ware, is a 12-point hob-star; the space between the points is filled in with a fan, making a fan and hob-star rosette.

CLASSIFICATION.

1. Berry bowls, 7-inch, with straight or tapering sides
2. Bonbon or olive dish, 6-inch, with and without stem and handle
3. Celery boat (later)
4. Claret jug, with handles and stopper
5. Compotes, 5 and 7-inch, short-stemmed; also one tall 6-inch compote with shallow dish
6. Cream jug, 6-inch, straight
7. Decanters, quart and pint, with and without handles
8. Finger bowls, 5-inch
9. Goblets, 6½ inch, tall; globe only
10. Ice tub, 9-inch
11. Ice-cream platter, oval
12. Nappies, 8 and 9-inch round
13. Pitcher, miniature 6-inch, excellent collector's item
14. Plates, 6 and 8½-inch, 10 and 12-inch oval bread plates
15. Punch bowl, 12-inch, with stand
16. Saucedishes, 5-inch, shallow
17. Sugar bowl, without cover or handles, straight and tapering
18. Sirup jug, no stopper
19. Tumblers, 5-ounce, called mineral or champagne tumblers; 8-ounce finger tumblers, short and star bottomed
20. Water pitchers, 1 and 2-quart
21. Wines, saucer champagne, claret, sherry wine, wine, cordial

Also such incidentals as mustard pot with cover, candlesticks, center bowl

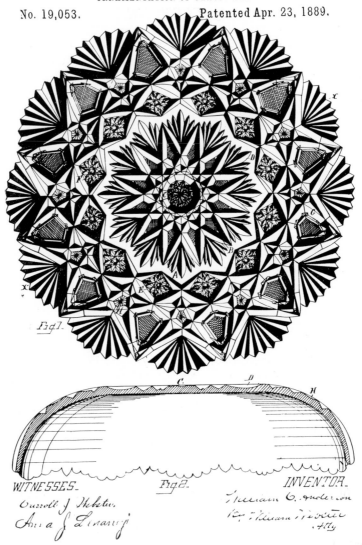

Fig.1.

Fig.2.

WITNESSES.

Carroll J. Hebster,

Anna J. Linarcy

INVENTOR.

William C. Anderson

By William Tirrell

Atty.

PLATE 90
Florence, Pattern 13

Reproduced from the files of the United States Patent Office

VARIATIONS. *Star,* cut by the same company ten years later, is the Florence redesigned, without the crosshatching, and with the fan scallop modified, making a very beautiful, expensive cutting highly esteemed by collectors. The 12-point star and fan rosette on the bottom is retained, and this figure identifies any variation of Florence, the first pattern to use it.

COLOR. Clear only.

ORIGIN. Libbey Glass Company, Toledo, Ohio.

TRADE-MARK. Any piece of Florence or Star, cut after 1892, bears one or other of the Libbey trade-marks (see Appendix IV).

14. LOUIS XIV

Louis XIV is most unusual. It was designed by Richard Briggs of Boston, Massachusetts, one of the country's foremost china and glass merchants, and patented by him in 1889. It was cut only on special order for his most select clientele, but the pieces have survived because they were preserved in heirloom sets.

Louis XIV is often taken for an imported pattern and sold as Baccarat because of the fleur-de-lis motif, but all glass of this pattern was cut by T. G. Hawkes exclusively for Richard Briggs' patrons. Some pieces were cut with family crests and coats of arms. Several sets were ordered for clubs and yachts, with a monogram substituted for one of the fleur-de-lis motifs. Only the very finest quality lead glass was used. Some few pieces were cased and cut through, some were gilded. Occasionally pieces of china were made in the same pattern to accompany the glass service. The shape of the plates and bowls is very modern, with only a slightly raised, almost flat border. Note the shading in the 10-point star, which is standard, although not all Louis XIV pieces show it. Most collectors are glad to have one plate or bowl in Louis XIV. A whole collection or service would be almost priceless in today's market.

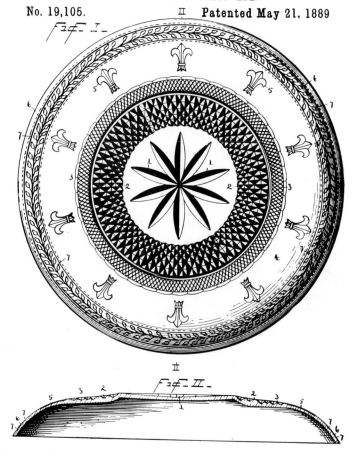

Witnesses
Norris A. Clark
Walter Allen

Inventor
Richard Briggs
By   Attorneys
Knight Bros

PLATE 91
Louis XIV, Pattern 14

CLASSIFICATION.

1. Berry bowls, 7 and 9-inch
2. Bonbon dish, 6-inch, no handles
3. Decanter, 1½-quart, ring neck, heavy base
4. Finger bowls, 5-inch
5. Goblets, 6½ inches tall, bell-shaped
6. Plates, 6, 8½, and 10-inch, some 12-inch
7. Saucedishes, 4½-inch, shallow
8. Tumblers, 5-ounce mineral; 8-ounce finger or whisky
9. Wine, saucer champagnes, claret, sherry, wine, cocktail, and cordial

No compotes were listed on invoices, though some may have been cut.

VARIATIONS. None.

COLOR. Clear with red, green, and sometimes yellow casing or flashing; rim frequently gilded.

ORIGIN. Cut only by T. G. Hawkes Glass Company, Corning, N. Y.; sold only by Richard Briggs, Boston, Mass.

TRADE-MARK. None, as all pieces were cut to order on Richard Briggs' design.

15. BRAZILIAN

The Brazilian Pattern was designed and patented by Thomas G. Hawkes in May of 1889, but it was not cut extensively until the next year. As a standard Hawkes pattern it was cut over a period of fifteen years, reaching the peak of popularity in the latter part of the Gay Nineties. It is an elegant pattern, very effective, brilliant, and expensive.

Pieces found and collected today will be heirlooms of tomorrow because of the high quality metal used in the blanks, the exquisitely fine cutting on the glass, and the effectiveness of the design.

Any collector interested in Brazilian should make careful note of

T. G. HAWKES.
ORNAMENTATION OF GLASSWARE.

No. 19,114.   Patented May 28, 1889.

Fig III.

Witnesses

Norris A. Clark

Walter Allen

Inventor

Thomas G. Hawkes.

By his Attorney:

Knight Bros

distinctive characteristics such as the alternate English strawberry-diamond and fan cutting around the scalloped edge of the plate and around the top of the goblet. Directly under each fan is a smaller replica. Directly under the strawberry-diamond is a lapidary or old single-star motif. The 13-inch plate has a 24-point star center.

CLASSIFICATION.

1. Berry bowls, 7 and 9-inch
2. Candelabra and candlesticks
3. Compote, 7-inch
4. Decanters, 1-quart, globe, and ring neck
5. Finger bowls, 5-inch only
6. Goblets, standard bowl with cut stem and scalloped star bottom
7. Nappies, 5, 7, 8, and 9-inch round
8. Plates, 6, 8½, 10, and 13-inch
9. Punch bowl, with pedestal
10. Rose bowls and center bowls
11. Saucedishes, 4½ and 5-inch, shallow
12. Tumblers, 5-ounce mineral, 7-ounce finger or whisky
13. Vases, tapering
14. Wines, saucer champagnes, claret, sherry, cocktail, and cordial

VARIATIONS. A variation of Brazilian was cut in a complete service for President Diaz of Mexico. As this was an elegant and popular pattern, it was imitated by many other cutting houses. Most of these imitations were ungraceful, and none but the standard Brazilian is worth collecting.

COLOR. Clear.

ORIGIN. T. G. Hawkes Glass Company, Corning, N. Y.

TRADE-MARK. Early pieces unmarked; pieces cut after 1895 carry trade-mark (see Appendix IV).

DESIGN.

S. O. RICHARDSON, Jr.
ORNAMENTATION OF PITCHERS, &c.

No. 19,165.   Patented June 18, 1889.

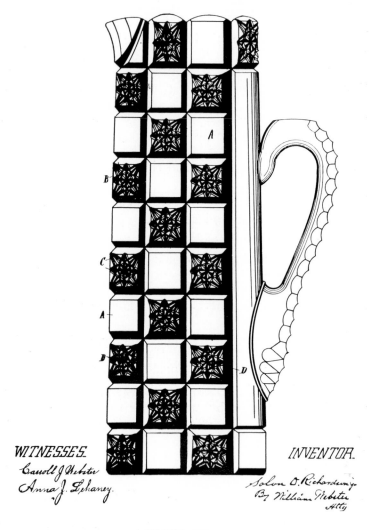

WITNESSES.

Carroll J. Webster

Anna J. Delaney.

INVENTOR.

Solon O. Richardson Jr

By William Webster

Atty

PLATE 93

Richardson's Pitcher, Pattern 16

Reproduced from the files of the United States Patent Office

16. RICHARDSON'S PITCHER

Richardson's Pitcher is a remarkable novelty in cut glass and worthy of a collector's search. It was designed by Solon O. Richardson, Jr., an important figure in the glass industry of the nineteenth century and particularly in the fortunes of the W. L. Libbey and Son Company, to whom he assigned the design. He was thoroughly versed in the technical aspects of glass tableware making as well as an early experimenter in making electric-light bulbs. The Libbey company, which had just set up shop in Toledo when Richardson designed his novelty, were losing money and had finished the year 1889 $3,000 in the red. Richardson believed that the company needed more and different patterns and Libbey was willing to try anything. While Richardson's letters patent suggest that the pattern can be cut on other similar glass articles, it is doubtful if it was actually cut on any ware other than 2-quart champagne pitchers and smaller jugs of similar shape, except for a few incidental pieces. It is a very effective, brilliant pattern, of alternate blocks and 8-point squared star with hob center. Needless to say, it is rare.

CLASSIFICATION.

1. Pitchers, chiefly, 2-quart champagne jugs; 1½-quart water pitchers; miniature cream pitchers, and other straight-sided vessels with no tops
2. Salts, square, cut in limited quantity
3. Sugar bowl, no handles or cover
Other incidentals are toothpick holders and possibly some square bowls with straight sides, but none have been found so far.

VARIATIONS. Too distinct a checker-board pattern to allow for variation. Even in its day this pattern was considered extreme by contemporaries and not copied extensively.

COLOR. Clear only.

ORIGIN. W. L. Libbey and Son Glass Company (later Libbey Glass Company), Toledo, O.

TRADE-MARK. Too early for trade-mark.

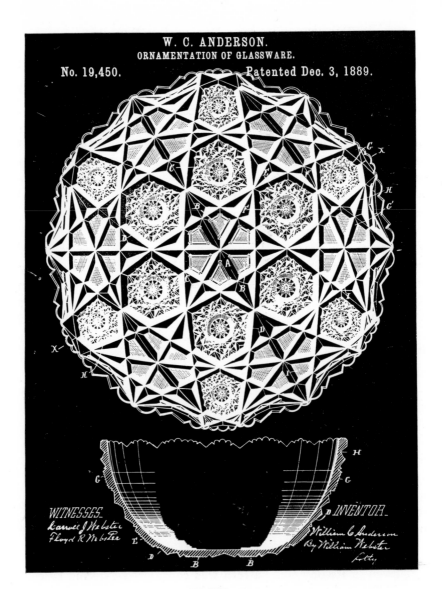

W. C. ANDERSON.
ORNAMENTATION OF GLASSWARE.
No. 19,450.   Patented Dec. 3, 1889.

PLATE 94
Stratford, Pattern 17
Reproduced from catalogues of the Libbey Glass Company

17. STRATFORD

The distinguishing characteristic of this pattern is not the 18-point hob-star so dear to the heart of the Libbey glass cutters, but the relatively simple hexagonal figure in which each of the six sides is intersected by a deep split and the areas between decorated by crosshatching. The stars in this pattern are incidental although they contribute greatly to it. Notice the lack of fan motif in the border and the faint suggestion of scallop.

The Stratford pattern was designed by William C. Anderson for Libbey soon after the firm moved from Cambridge to Toledo. It was one of the principal Libbey patterns prior to the World's Columbian Exposition in Chicago. Many bowls, goblets, and tumblers were cut in Stratford. Other pieces are a little more difficult to find.

CLASSIFICATION.

1. Berry bowls, 7, 9-inch
2. Bonbon or olive dishes, 5 and 6-inch, with or without handles
3. Champagne jug, 2-quart, straight
4. Claret jug, 1½-pint, stoppers to match, handles
5. Cream jug, small, globe
6. Compotes, 6-inch tall, 7-inch, tall or short-stemmed
7. Finger bowls, 4½-inch, 2 inches deep
8. Goblets, tapering and bell-shaped
9. Nappies, 7 and 9-inch
10. Plates, 7 and 8½-inch; also 10 and 12-inch special bread plate
11. Punch cups with handles
12. Saucedishes, 4½ and 5-inch, shallow
13. Sherbets
14. Tumblers, 5-ounce mineral or champagne, 8-ounce finger or whisky
15. Wines, saucer champagnes, claret, sherry, and cordial

VARIATION. Any variation of this pattern would come under a non-listed design heading. It could only vary in the star points or the

PLATE 95
Strawberry-Diamond and Fan, Pattern 18

*Reproduced from catalogue of the T. G. Hawkes Glass Co., also illustrated
by Libbey Glass Co., and J. Hoare and Co.*

number of crosshatched hexagonal figures. This is one of the patterns in which only the standard is important.

COLOR. Clear only.

ORIGIN. W. L. Libbey and Son Glass Company and Libbey Glass Company, Toledo, O.

TRADE-MARK. Earlier pieces not marked, since the trade-mark was not in general use until four or five years after the granting of this patent. Later pieces have Libbey trade-mark (see Appendix IV).

18. STRAWBERRY-DIAMOND AND FAN

A simpler adaptation of Strawberry-Diamond and Star (Number 4), this pattern combined a deep-sided square diamond, marked on top with an X, with fan scallops at the edges. More American glass was cut with the Strawberry-Diamond and Fan pattern than any other Brilliant Period pattern including its closest rival, the Russian. As one old glass cutter said, he could cut it in his sleep with his eyes closed and one hand under his head. Developed by manufacturers and glass cutters as a means of keeping up with competition in a fast-growing business, Strawberry-Diamond and Fan was well received by American women. They liked the relative simplicity of the cutting and the fact that a whole service of Strawberry-Diamond and Fan could be bought for a fraction of the cost of a service of Chrysanthemum or Grecian or Florence, or any of the more ornate combinations of stars and definitive cutting.

It is the easiest pattern to collect in sets at the present time. Care should be taken, however, to collect only fine pieces. Since the pattern was so extensively cut over such a long period of time, there are good and bad pieces. Young apprentice cutters were sometimes put to work on the Strawberry-Diamond and Fan design. Since the pattern is easy to find, select pieces that are sharply cut, in which the lines are true. Watch for the 24-point star center. Though not essential to the pattern, this is a sign of quality.

CLASSIFICATION. The number and shapes of pieces cut in the Strawberry-Diamond and Fan pattern are practically limitless. The partial list given below indicates which pieces are most easily collected.

1. Berry bowls, 6, 7, 8, 9, 10-inch
2. Butter patties, 3-inch, flat and stemmed
3. Celery dishes
   a. boat, flat, in various shapes; square with handles
   b. vase, straight, stemmed goblet type
4. Champagne jug, 2-quart, straight
5. Claret jugs, pint and quart, with handles and stoppers
6. Cologne bottles, narrow neck, square, globe, and round
7. Compotes, 6, 7, and 8-inch common, covered or uncovered, taper or flat
8. Cream jugs, globe, straight, standard
9. Cruets, 6 and 8-inch globe; 6 and 8-ounce taper
10. Decanters, quart, globe, flat-bottom steamboat type, or Rodney; also ring neck
11. Finger bowls, 5-inch, 2½ inches deep
12. Goblets (less common), globe, bell, and taper; some with long stems
13. Nappies, all sizes
14. Plate, 6, and 8½, 10, 12, and 13-inch
15. Salts, globe, tub, square, table and individual
16. Saucedishes, 4½ and 5-inch, with or without handles; 5 by 9 inches, square
17. Sherbets, low, stemmed; punch cups with handles
18. Sugar bowl, with or without cover or handles
19. Tumblers, all sizes, 5-ounce mineral or champagne, 7 and 8-ounce whisky
20. Wines, saucer champagnes, claret, sherry, cocktail, cordial

Incidentals include candlesticks, center bowls, punch bowls, toothpick holders, sirup pitchers, vases, bowls, mustard pots, and many others.

VARIATIONS. While there are obvious variations of the Strawberry-Diamond and Fan, the standard is so plentiful that it only should be collected in services. The standard varies only as to quality, center star, and number of fan scallops on the border.

COLOR. Common in clear glass, also cut in red, green, and yellow. Colored cut glass is always more rare than clear, and Strawberry-Diamond and Fan colored pieces are very effective.

ORIGIN. It is almost impossible to credit any single piece without a trade-mark stamp to a specific glasshouse. Every one of the houses cutting glass in the last years of the nineteenth century cut the Strawberry-Diamond and Fan pattern.

TRADE-MARK. Many pieces have trade-marks, but many more do not. Lack of a trade-mark does not mean that the piece is an old one, since many of the later trade-marks were only paper stickers that washed away after the first using. Early cuttings had no trade-marks. Aging shows in way the points of the diamonds wear down and round off, as do the scallop edges of the fan.

19. MACBETH

This rare pattern was designed and patented by Daniel Forbes, a cutter who worked for the George H. Hibbler shop in Brooklyn. It is probably one of the best organized and composed of all the Brilliant Period patterns. Notice that the scallops are determined by the radiants of the fans. The only star in the design is the central or base motif. The crosshatching on these pieces is particularly fine. Any collector should be proud to own even one piece of Macbeth; it is extremely doubtful whether a complete set could ever be collected.

CLASSIFICATION.

1. Berry bowls, 7 and 9-inch
2. Finger bowls, 5-inch diameter, 2½ inches deep
3. Nappies, 7 and 9-inch, probably a few square; none now known
4. Plates, 6 and 8½-inch
5. Saucedishes, 4½ and 5-inch, shallow

D. FORBES.

ORNAMENTATION OF BOWLS OR DISHES.

No. 19,642. Patented Feb. 11, 1890

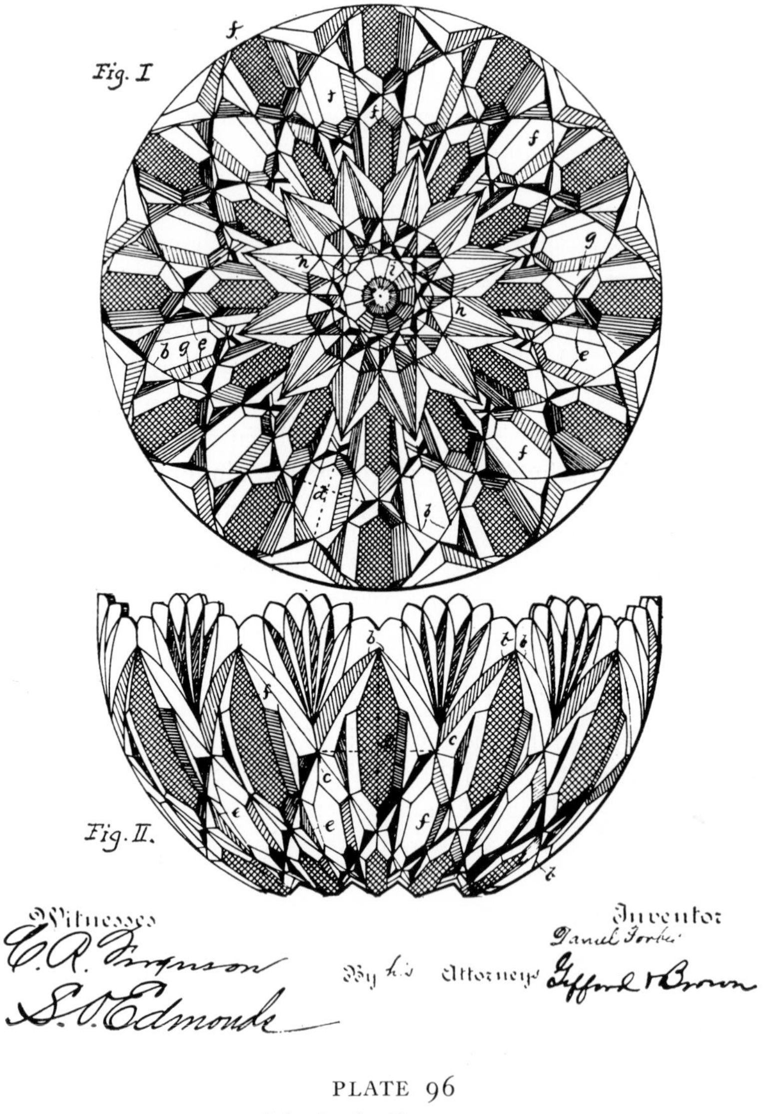
Fig. I
Fig. II.
Witnesses
Inventor
Daniel Forbes
By his Attorneys Gifford & Brown

PLATE 96

Macbeth, Pattern 19

Reproduced from the files of the United States Patent Office

No jugs, goblets, or wines were cut in the Macbeth, so far as is now known.

VARIATIONS. None.

COLOR. Clear only.

ORIGIN. George H. Hibbler, Brooklyn, N. Y.

TRADE-MARK. None.

20. *VENETIAN*

The Venetian pattern is another unusual pattern designed by T. G. Hawkes. While not widely cut, it has a distinct individuality which more than repays the collector's diligent search. This is the first pattern to make use of the Greek cross in cut glass design, and is easily recognized by the teardrop radiants in the center motif which are crosshatched and alternated with the fan motif. The fan scallops around the edge are deep and well defined.

CLASSIFICATION.

1. Berry bowls, 7 and 9-inch, sides very straight, almost perpendicular to the bases
2. Bonbon or olive dish, no handles
3. Celery boat, 4½ by 11 inches
4. Compote, 7 by 7 inches, no cover
5. Cruets, 6 and 8-ounce, straight sides, lapidary stoppers
6. Finger bowls, 5-inch, straight sides
7. Goblets, tapering only
8. Nappies, 8 and 9-inch
9. Plates, 8½ and 12-inch
10. Saucedishes, 4½ and 5-inch, shallow
11. Tumblers, 5-ounce mineral and 8-ounce whisky
12. Wines, saucer champagnes, claret, sherry, and cordial

VARIATIONS. Many glasshouses soon began using the teardrop radiants or the Greek cross. The most common variation was the Venice

No. 19,865.   Patented June 3, 1890.

Fig. I.

Fig. II.

Witnesses: Inventor:
J. Ydepfer.   Thomas G. Hawkes.
Walter Allen   By Knight Bros.
                                              Attorneys.

PLATE 97
Venetian, Pattern 20

pattern cut by J. Hoare & Co. The similarity between the standard and the Venice lies in the prominent use of crosshatching and the confusing similarity in the shape of the blanks used. This similarity arises in a number of Hawkes and Hoare patterns due to the fact that during this period both companies were buying blanks from the Corning Glass Company. While exclusive patterns such as the Louis XIV were made to order with specified metal content, standard blanks were supplied to all cutting houses. Hence the similarity in metal and form. Only the cutting and pattern varied.

COLOR. Clear only.

ORIGIN. T. G. Hawkes Glass Company, Corning, N. Y.

TRADE-MARK. Early pieces carry no mark. Some later pieces show Hawkes trade-mark (see Appendix IV).

21. CHRYSANTHEMUM

The Chrysanthemum pattern of T. G. Hawkes shows the influence of the curved split in cut glass design, a relatively new motif in 1889. It also shows the use of the small hob-star in the pattern itself. This was one of the first patterns to make use of the 20-point star as a design motif. Until this time the star of many points, or the hob-star had been used principally as a central figure.

In his patent papers, Hawkes says, "The leading features of my design consist of the large central figure having radial leaves and the flowers between the outer portions of the leaves, thus forming what I call the 'chrysanthemum' design . . . leaves extending radially from a common center, having cross cut blades and ovate stalks. Between the leaves are flowers having central rosettes."

Chrysanthemum was one of the two Hawkes cut glass patterns to win the grand international prize for cut glass at the Paris Exposition in 1889. It was patented the following year, and became very popular, although it was expensive.

[233]

T. G. HAWKES
ORNAMENTATION OF GLASSWARE.

No. 20,257   Patented Nov. 4, 1890

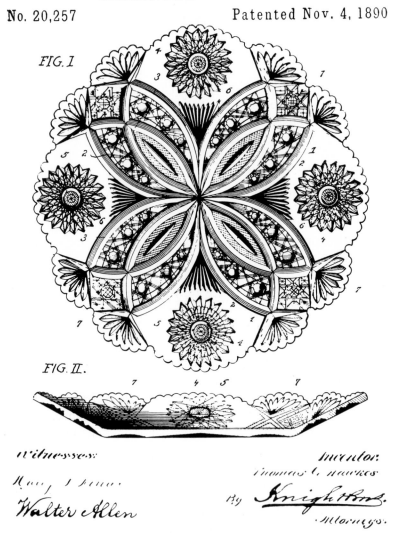

FIG. I

FIG. II.

Witnesses:

Inventor:
Thomas G. Hawkes

By *Knight Bros.*
Attorneys.

PLATE 98
Chrysanthemum, Pattern 21
Reproduced from the files of the United States Patent Office

CLASSIFICATION.

1. Berry bowls, 7, 8, 9-inch
2. Butter patties, 3-inch, flat
3. Celery vase
4. Champagne jug, 2-quart, no stopper
5. Claret jug, 1½-pint, with stopper
6. Cologne bottles, square, globe, and round
7. Compotes, 6 and 7-inch, none covered
8. Cruet, 6-ounce, 6 inches tall
9. Cream jug, globe only
10. Decanter, 2-quart, matching stopper
11. Finger bowls, 4½ and 5-inch across, 2½ inches deep
12. Goblet, 6½-inch, globe only
13. Nappies, 5 and 6-inch
14. Plates, 6 and 8½-inch; also a large 13-inch. More plates were cut in this pattern than any other shape.
15. Punch bowl, 15-inch, with stand
16. Salts, globe only
17. Saucedishes, 4½-inch, shallow
18. Sugar bowl, globe without handles, cover
19. Tumblers, 5-ounce mineral or champagne, 7-ounce whisky
20. Water pitcher, straight
21. Wines, saucer champagnes, claret, sherry, wine, cordial

Incidentals: Other pieces may have been cut as vases and rose bowls, small pin trays and short-stemmed compotes, but the Hawkes inventories do not show these pieces.

VARIATIONS. The *Libbey Chrysanthemum,* a much later pattern, came to the market at least fifteen years after the original. It is overornamented and shows the tendency toward the decline of the period to combine totally dissimilar motifs. This variation uses the notched prism liberally; the leaves, instead of being a conventionalized system as in the standard, are realistic. Realistic flower cuttings were to follow the geometric patterns of the Brilliant Period, and the Libbey Chrysanthemum gives a preview of this trend. The flower in the variation has only 18 points in the star, contrasted with the twenty points of the standard Chrysanthemum.

PLATE 99
Wedgemere, Pattern 22
Reproduced from the catalogue of the Libbey Glass Company

COLOR. Clear only.

ORIGIN. T. G. Hawkes Glass Company, Corning, New York; Libbey Chrysanthemum by Libbey Glass Company, Toledo, O.

TRADE-MARKS. Early Chrysanthemum unmarked. Later cuttings marked with Hawkes trade-mark. All Libbey variations marked with Libbey trade-mark (see Appendix IV).

22. WEDGEMERE

The Wedgemere, designed by W. C. Anderson for Libbey, is one of the patterns which shows development or adaptation within itself. As can be seen from the standard patent-office illustration, the Wedgemere started following the motif of concentric circles then popular in fine cut glass. The outline of the patented design is angular, adaptable to square-shaped pieces. However, as the century drew to a close, the Wedgemere became one of the Libbey luxury cuttings, exhibited with its sister pattern, the Kimberly. The concentric circles in the pattern now become less distinct, and the fan appears at the end of the radiants which show a more pronounced cane pattern in the later stemmed ware than in the original design.

Probably the most distinguishing feature of Wedgemere is not in the pattern so much as in the blanks on which it was cut. The flaring stems of the wine glasses and goblets are unique, elaborately cut and show both cut knops and flutes. Wedgemere is neither as well organized nor as consistent as its sister pattern, Kimberly, but it makes a most attractive table service, especially the stemmed ware.

CLASSIFICATION.

1. Berry bowls, 7, 8, 9-inch
2. Bonbon or olive dish, 4½-inch
3. Butter patties, 3-inch, flat and stemmed
4. Celery boat and vase
5. Champagne jug, 2-quart, straight, no top
6. Claret jugs with matching stoppers

7. Compotes, 6 and 7-inch, stemmed
8. Cruets, 6 and 8-ounce, matching stoppers
9. Cream jugs, on stems, and straight
10. Decanters, quart and pint, globe and narrow neck
11. Finger bowls, 5-inch
12. Goblets, standard globe 6½ inches tall
13. Nappies, 5, 6, 7, 8, and 9-inch
14. Pitchers, straight and globe
15. Plates, 6 and 8½-inch, also 10 and 13-inch, some oval
16. Saucedishes, 4½-inch
17. Sherbet cups with handles
18. Tumblers, 5-ounce mineral, 6-ounce champagne, 7-ounce whisky
19. Wines, tall hock, saucer champagnes, claret, sherry, plain wine, and cordial

Incidentals: Probably everything from candlesticks and cologne bottles to spoonholders were cut in Wedgemere. The pattern is so diversified, however, that unless the collector has a very clear idea of the standard, a service does not seem unified when assembled in quantity.

VARIATIONS. Any star cane, and fan combination with concentric circles may be classified as a Wedgemere variation. Stemmed ware, however, must have flaring cut feet.

COLOR. Clear; some red cordials were made, but they are rare.

ORIGIN. Libbey Glass Company, Toledo, O.

TRADE-MARK. Earlier pieces unmarked. Libbey Glass Company trade-mark (see Appendix IV) on most pieces.

23. KIMBERLY

The Kimberly, a sister pattern of Wedgemere, was designed for Libbey by William C. Anderson in 1892. As it was cut extensively, full table services can be collected. From the patent-office record, it will be seen that the standard Kimberly consists of six 16-point stars spaced between the points of a center 6-point star device. The

Fig. 1.

Fig. 2.

Witnesses·
Carrol J Webster
Grace E. Lehany

Inventor:
William C Anderson
By William Webster
atty

PLATE 100

Kimberly, Pattern 23

Reproduced from the files of the United States Patent Office

center field of the central star is crosshatched. Small fans are used only at the tip of the larger star. In later cuttings (notably the large punch bowl cut in the early years of the twentieth century after the pattern had already been on the market for ten years) the larger hob-star has been increased to a 20-point hob-star. The ice-cream platter shows a combination of the larger and smaller hob-star, but the pattern retains its essential character in all pieces and all years.

Catalogues quote the manufacturer's price for the punch bowl at $130 f.o.b. Toledo; it retailed in New York City at $250. The ice-cream set was quoted at $120 at the manufacturer's; the platter alone probably cost the customer $50.

Some writers discussing the Kimberly in later years (and it was, like the Russian, much publicized) like to refer to it as named after the famous Kimberley mines because it resembles a diamond in its cutting. This is a fairly pat explanation that helps fix the pattern in a collector's mind, but it does not happen to be true.

It will be noticed that the African city is spelled with two e's, the Libbey pattern with only one. The Kimberly pattern was actually named for Charles G. Kimberly, a wholesale dealer in crockery, glass, and Rockingham ware, in New Haven. Just why this merchant was so honored is not now known. It may be that Kimberly came to the rescue of E. D. Libbey financially. It was not an unusual practice for wholesalers to "tide over" manufacturers as was the case when Richard Kinder of New York helped Benjamin Bakewell get on his feet in Pittsburgh in 1808. Mr. Kimberly may have suggested the star-within-the-star pattern to Anderson, Libbey's chief designer, as Briggs suggested Louis XIV to Hawkes. Or it may be that Libbey simply named the star pattern for Kimberly in appreciation of an unusually big order. Be that as it may, the Kimberly pattern was named for a Connecticut Yankee, not for the great Kimberley diamond mines of British South Africa.

CLASSIFICATION.

1. Berry bowls, all sizes, 7, 8, 9, 10-inch
2. Bonbon or olive dishes, with or without handles

3. Butter patties, 3-inch, flat and stemmed
4. Champagne jug, 2-quart straight
5. Claret jug (early) with handle and matching stopper
6. Celery vases, straight and stemmed (boats cut later)
7. Cologne bottles, square, round, globe; narrow and open neck, with matching or lapidary stoppers
8. Compotes, in all sizes 5, 6, 7, 8, 9, and 10-inch, with or without tall cut stems; some stems show air twists, some knops, some plain flutes
9. Cruets, 6 or 8-ounce, tapering or globe
10. Cream jugs, stemmed and globe, straight
11. Decanters, quart and pint, tapering and globe, narrow or ring neck
12. Finger bowls, 4½ and 5-inch, 2 and 2½ inches deep
13. Goblets, globe standard, cut knop stem under side of foot cut with radiant blaze, not star bottom
14. Ice-cream platter and dishes
15. Nappies, 7, 8, 9, and 10-inch, round and square
16. Plates, 6, 8½, 10, and 12-inch
17. Punch bowls, with or without pedestals
18. Salts, globe, tub, and square; table and individual
19. Saucedishes, 4½ and 5-inch
20. Sherbet cups
21. Sugar bowl, with handles, no cover
22. Tumblers, 6-ounce finger
23. Water pitchers, straight or globe
24. Wines, saucer champagnes, claret, sherry wine, wine, cordial
Incidentals include candlesticks, mustard jars, powder boxes (later). This was such a popular pattern that almost any shape was used at one time or another.

VARIATIONS. Many variations were cut by companies that did not mark their ware and were less careful with their cutting. In collecting Kimberly, it is important to collect only the Libbey standard or their later Kimberly with the 20-point hob-star. Any star within a star pattern which resembles the Kimberly but shows other variations such as the addition of cane cutting or strawberry-diamond cutting should be rejected. Note that the standard pattern does not come clear to the top of stemmed ware or finger bowls and that the fan pattern is subordinate. [N.B. The Hawkes pattern, Kimberley (spelled with two e's), which was put out about the same time, bears no similarity to the Libbey pattern.]

COLOR. Clear. Some pieces of stemmed ware were cut in colored or cased glass, principally the still wines or the cordials. Some few colored goblets were cut, probably in either red or green, but these are very rare.

ORIGIN. William C. Anderson design and patent assigned to W. L. Libbey and Son Glass Company, Toledo, O.; later cut by Libbey Glass Company.

TRADE-MARK. Early pieces unmarked as they were cut before the adoption of the trade-mark. Many later pieces carry one or another of the Libbey trade-marks (see Appendix IV).

24. RATTAN

Rattan was designed by John S. O'Connor and clearly shows the influence of his own earlier Parisian (Number 3) which started the trend toward curved splits in cut glass design. Rattan combines the 20-point star medallion with an elaboration of the simple chair bottom motif, elliptical fields of crosshatching with pronounced fan scallops. The patent-office record of the pattern does not do it justice. Flattened out as it is on the drawing it looks overornamented, but cut on shallow glass dishes, berry sets, and nappies, it is a particularly striking pattern. The rattan cutting, crosshatched fields and fan scallops decorate the sides while the central star with its field of bordering smaller stars makes a most effective bottom decoration.

While O'Connor had left Dorflinger's to go into business for himself by the time he patented Rattan, it is probable that he was still using Dorflinger blanks in his cutting shop. Consequently, the quality of Rattan pieces would be hard to distinguish from that of Dorflinger standard patterns.

PLATE 101

Rattan, Pattern 24

Reproduced from the files of the United States Patent Office

CLASSIFICATION.

1. Berry bowls, 7 and 9-inch
2. Finger bowls, 4½ and 5-inch
3. Ice-cream dishes, 4½-inch, shallow
4. Nappies, 6, 7, 8, 9, and 10-inch
5. Saucedishes, 5-inch, shallow

Rattan was probably not cut in any other shapes or in complete services.

VARIATIONS.

Marguerite, cut by the United States Glass Company, Pittsburgh, Penna.
Pebble, by J. Hoare and Company, Corning, N. Y.
Rose of Sharon, Kiefer Brothers (address unknown)

These and like variations of Rattan, which combine the chair bottom motif with stars and crosshatched fields, should not be confused with O'Connor's standard which is a much more simple cutting than it appears on the patent record.

COLOR. Clear only.

ORIGIN. John S. O'Connor, in business for himself in White Mills, Penna.

TRADE-MARK. None.

25. *SIX SEA SHELLS*

Six Sea Shells, one of the prettiest of the nineteenth-century patterns, looks older than it really is. It was first cut as a definitely composed pattern in 1892 when Walter A. Wood designed it for the T. B. Clark and Company of which he was a partner. Wood refers in his patent papers to the six shells as being lancet-arched forms. They are, more simply, the familiar fan motif made narrower and longer. The spaces between these motifs are cut with two smaller replicas separated by a conventionalized Greek cross. The center is a 6-point star.

DESIGN.

—o—

W. A. WOOD.

ORNAMENTATION OF GLASSWARE.

No. 21,466.   Patented Apr. 12, 1892.

Attest
Walter Donaldson

William Hall

Inventor
Walter A Wood

by Elli Spear
Atty.

PLATE 102

Sea Shells, Pattern 25

Reproduced from the files of the United States Patent Office

CLASSIFICATION.

1. Berry bowls, 9 and 10-inch, with straight 2½ and 3-inch sides
2. Butter patties, 3-inch diameter
3. Compote, 6-inch, with short stem
4. Finger bowls, 5-inch, 2 inches deep
5. Nappies, 7, 8, 9-inch
6. Plates, 6 and 8½-inch, perhaps 10-inch
7. Saucedishes, 5-inch, shallow

No stemmed ware is known to have been cut in the Six Sea Shell pattern, but it may have been cut more extensively than is now known.

VARIATIONS. *Zenda,* cut by J. Hoare and Company, Corning N. Y., uses English and strawberry-diamond motif alternately between shells instead of Greek cross.

COLOR. Clear.

ORIGIN. T. B. Clark Company, Honesdale, Penna.

TRADE-MARK. None.

26. CORONET

Coronet is one of the Gothic patterns. It plainly shows the concentric circles, later used successfully by the same designer, T. G. Hawkes, in the very popular Nautilus pattern. The Coronet was designed particularly for a set of angular blanks sold by the Corning Glass Company to several local cutting shops, including those of T. G. Hawkes and Walter Egginton. The blanks were made principally in ice-cream sets and were surprisingly popular during the later years of the nintenth century. It is still possible to collect the Coronet pattern in dishes only. One of the amusing vagaries of collecting is that although the Coronet is one of the least attractive of all the fine Hawkes patterns, it is the one most in demand by collectors since its angular shape pleases the taste of decorators specializing in Victorian interiors. The small-sized dishes are some-

DESIGN.

T. G. HAWKES.

ORNAMENTATION OF GLASS VESSELS.

No. 21,705.   Patented July 12, 1892.

Witnesses: Inventor:
Harry S. Asher.   Thomas G. Hawkes
Walter Allen   By. Knight Bro
                                         Attorneys.

PLATE 103

Coronet, Pattern 26

Reproduced from the files of the United States Patent Office

times used as ash trays, which is a sacrilege since the heat of ashes and burning cigarettes is sure to crack the glass in time, and the old pieces are too rare to be so abused.

CLASSIFICATION.

Ice-cream sets, consisting of 10-inch platter and smaller individual ice-cream dishes to match.
Not cut in stemmed ware.

VARIATIONS.

The *Lattice* pattern designed and cut by Walter Egginton of Corning. The small dishes are interchangeable in the sets, being identical in shape. Egginton did not cut his Lattice pattern until a year after the Hawkes Coronet had become popular, and then in much smaller quantity, so that the Lattice cutting on the angular ice-cream platters is very rare indeed.

COLOR. Clear only.

ORIGIN. Distinctive angular blanks by Corning Glass Company. *Coronet* cut by T. G. Hawkes Glass Company, Corning, N. Y. *Lattice* cut by Walter Egginton, Corning, N. Y.

TRADE-MARKS. None, cut before Hawkes adopted a trade-mark.

27. COLUMBIA

Just what elephant tusks had to do with the World's Columbian Exposition (Chicago, 1893) is not clear but certainly the tusklike motifs in combination with a hob-star are the distinguishing features of this Libbey design for the World's Fair pavilion. Like its sister pattern, the Isabella, the Columbia sold like hot cakes and both are to be found in cologne bottles, butter dishes, decanters, and salt dishes from the Mississippi River through the Middle West and on out to the West Coast. The plates are all scalloped, and the tusk motifs are in the pillar cutting which is, perhaps, the highest form of the cutter's art. Examples of the Columbia pattern,

PLATE 104
Columbia, Pattern 27
Reproduced from the files of the Libbey Glass Company

especially in stemmed ware, are not so plentiful as those of the Isabella because it required more time and higher skill to cut the Columbia, and when the great crowds began streaming through the Libbey exhibit at the World's Fair, the souvenirs had to be of patterns that could be cut quickly.

CLASSIFICATION.

1. Berry bowl, 9-inch
2. Butter dish with cover
3. Celery vase
4. Cheese dish with cover
5. Cologne bottles 4, 6, and 8-ounce, globe and square
6. Cream jug, globe
7. Cruets, 6 and 8-ounce with handles
8. Decanters, 1½-pint and quart, globe
9. Dishes, 4 and 4½-inch
10. Finger bowls, 5-inch
11. Goblets, standard (rare)
12. Nappies, 7, 8, and 9-inch
13. Pitchers, round and globe
14. Plates, 6 and 10-inch
15. Salts, globe, table, and individual
16. Sherbet cups
17. Spoonholders, straight and horizontal
18. Tumblers, 5-ounce mineral, 7-inch standard, star bottom
19. Wines, claret, sherry, wine, cordial
Incidentals. Probably other unusual pieces were cut as the souvenir trade was brisk in this pattern.

VARIATIONS. The tusk-shaped prisms inverted with the chair bottom motif were used in a later variation called *Eleanor,* which is a lighter cutting by J. Hoare and Company, not so well designed as the standard.

COLOR. Usually clear although some cased pieces were made early in the year of 1893. A green cologne bottle is rare; a red cased butter dish is a collector's item.

ORIGIN. Libbey Glass Company, Toledo, O.; Variation Eleanor from J. Hoare and Company, Corning, N. Y.

TRADE-MARK. Libbey Glass Company (see Appendix IV).

28. ISABELLA

The Isabella is another of the Gothic patterns popular in the Gay Nineties. In flatware and saucedishes it is often mistaken for a Middle Period pattern because of the quaint square shape of the dishes. This pattern, however, was designed by William C. Anderson as one of the featured Libbey patterns for the World's Columbian Exposition (Chicago, 1893). There were 1,763,000 visitors to the Libbey glass exhibits at the Exposition. Each visitor received a little spun-glass bow on the end of a stickpin. The sale of paperweights and pin trays in the Isabella and Columbia patterns was phenomenal. There was scarcely a Middle Western home that did not proudly display on the parlor whatnot a square-cut saucedish in the Isabella pattern, or a butter dish in the Columbia design. Collectors who live west of the Mississippi River should have no difficulty at all in finding dessert sets in the Isabella pattern. The pattern does not lend itself to tumblers very well.

CLASSIFICATION.

1. Berry bowls, 7, 8, 9-inch, square shapes preferable and fairly common
2. Butter patties, 3-inch square and flat
3. Candlesticks
4. Compote, 7-inch, short-stemmed with square top
5. Goblets, 6½-inch (rare)
6. Mustard pot, with top
7. Nappies, 7, 8, and 9-inch square
8. Pitchers, ½-pint, 1-pint, 1½-pint, 1-quart, and 3-pint, all globe shaped
9. Plates, 6, 7, 8½, and 10-inch square
10. Salts, square

[251]

DESIGN.

—o—

W. C. ANDERSON.
ORNAMENTATION OF GLASSWARE.

No. 22,098.

Patented Jan. 3, 1893.

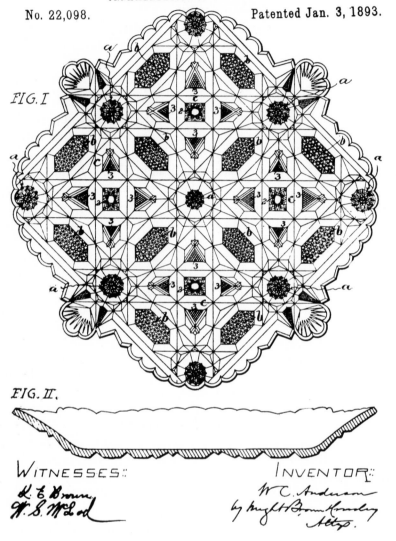

FIG.I

FIG.II.

WITNESSES::

L. E. Brown,
W. S. McLeod

INVENTOR::

W. C. Anderson
by Knight Brown Knindly
Atty.

PLATE 105

Isabella, Pattern 28

Reproduced from the files of the United States Patent Office

11. Saucedishes, 4½-inch, shallow, sometimes square or with owner's initials engraved in the center (rare)
12. Sugar bowl, square, no lid
13. Toothpick holder, square to match salts
14. Tumblers, 7½-ounce whisky, red with overlay, or cased, with owner's initials (collector's items)
15. Wines, standard wine shapes cut, but not extensively; uninteresting as pattern seems lacking in unity

VARIATIONS. None.

COLOR. Clear. Some whisky tumblers red with overlay, some cased; cordials also sometimes red. A few red berry sets were cut for the Fair, and gilded. Collectors should be careful to see that the pieces offered in this red ware are cut pieces, as pressed imitations were made later by other companies.

ORIGIN. Libbey Glass Company only.

TRADE-MARK. All marked (see Appendix IV).

29. BRISTOL ROSE

According to the letters patent of the designer, Thomas Singleton, Jr. of New Bedford, Massachusetts, the rose figure is the most important motif in the Bristol Rose pattern. This was the first cut glass pattern to make use of the 32-point star with its raised rosette center, and it is certainly a distinguishing characteristic of this pattern. But the most singular thing about the Bristol Rose and the easiest way to tell it from imitations is by the 7-point star center, and the repetition of the number seven in the border rose motifs and in the smaller buds at the star points. Almost all cut glass patterns follow the even number scale . . . six points, twelve points, twenty-four points. A few patterns designed for plates and shallow bowls use multiples of five, but seven is very rare indeed. Apart from the fact that the Bristol Rose is a very attractive pattern, it is of interest to collectors because of this odd number in the star points. It was a slow pattern to cut, and expensive to produce.

[253]

T. SINGLETON, Jr.
ORNAMENTAL GLASS DISH.

No. 22,287.   Patented Mar. 14, 1893.

Fig. 1.

Fig. 2.

PLATE 106
Bristol Rose, Pattern 29
Reproduced from the files of the United States Patent Office

CLASSIFICATION.

1. Berry bowls, 7, 8, and 10-inch
2. Celery vase
3. Compote, 7-inch stemmed (rare)
4. Cream jug (rare)
5. Nappies, 7-inch
6. Plates, 8½-inch
7. Saucedishes, 4 and 5-inch shallow
8. Tumblers, 7-ounce whisky

Stemmed ware may have been cut in Bristol Rose, but none is now known.

VARIATIONS. *Marion,* cut by Pairpoint later, is a variation on Bristol Rose, with only 24 points (or sometimes 26) to the hob-star, and a 6-point star with or without fan tips. No known variations ever used the 32-point star or the 7-point star center of the standard.

COLOR. Clear.

ORIGIN. Singleton's design patent was assigned to the Mount Washington Glass Company, New Bedford, Mass. After the company was consolidated with the Pairpoint Glass Company, the less intricate variation, Marion, was introduced.

TRADE-MARK. None.

30. *GOLDEN WEDDING*

Golden Wedding is one of the curved split patterns developed by Benjamin Davies, designer for Straus in New York. These patterns were all fairly popular in the Eastern market, though none of them is very pretty, or too well designed. The Golden Wedding is typically overornamented, lacking unity like other Straus patterns, but it is prettier in glass than in a reproduction.

Many collectors hunt for this ornate pattern simply because of its oddity and because it is a Straus pattern never copied. The six

PLATE 107
Golden Wedding, Pattern 30
Reproduced from the files of the United States Patent Office

circular figures around the edge are formed by curved splits that become question marks when seen from the reverse side.

CLASSIFICATION.

1. Berry bowl, 9-inch
2. Celery boat, 11 by 4½ inches
3. Saucedishes, 4½ and 5-inch, shallow, some with handles
4. Tumblers, 8-ounce straight
Probably no goblets, wines, or finger bowls were cut.

VARIATIONS. None.

COLOR. Clear only.

ORIGIN. Cut only by L. Straus and Sons, New York City.

TRADE-MARK. None.

31. *BERGEN'S WHITE ROSE*

There is very little of a rose about this pattern which lacks any of the leaf or realistic cutting of the later period patterns. Why its designer, James D. Bergen, felt that it resembled a rose is obscure to modern collectors. It is included here as an example of the fine patterns cut by the Bergen Company during the last years of the nineteenth century.

Bergen's White Rose is typical of the highly conventionalized, well organized and geometric patterns of this designer. Lucky indeed is the collector who finds goblets or any stemmed ware in Bergen's White Rose pattern, for they are rare and have a modern, almost mosaic quality to the central band cutting which is most beautiful.

CLASSIFICATION.

1. Berry bowl, 9-inch
2. Finger bowls, 5-inch, 2½ inches deep, very fine metal
3. Goblets, globe

[257]

DESIGN.
—o—
J. D. BERGEN.
GLASS VESSEL.

No. 23,317.   Patented Mav 29, 1894.

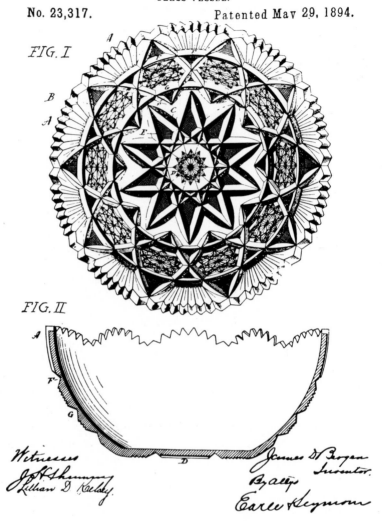

FIG. I

FIG. II

Witnesses
James D Bergen
Inventor.
By attys
Earle Seymour

PLATE 108

Bergen's White Rose, Pattern 31

Reproduced from the files of the United States Patent Office

4. Nappies, 7 and 9-inch
5. Plates, 6 and 10-inch, some 8½-inch
6. Salts, table and individual
7. Saucedishes, 4 and 4½-inch, perhaps 5-inch
8. Sherbet cups
9. Sugar bowl, round, no handles but cover
10. Tumblers, wide-bottom, 7-ounce, finger (rare)
11. Wines, claret, sherry, cordial, perhaps some saucer champagnes, though doubtful

VARIATIONS. None.

COLOR. Clear.

ORIGIN. J. D. Bergen Company, Meriden, Conn.

TRADE-MARK. Early pieces have none. For later markings, see Appendix IV.

32. *CORNING*

The Corning may have been cut as early as the Centennial in Philadelphia (1876) but as the pattern was not officially recorded in patent records or catalogues before 1895, it must be placed toward the last of the nineteenth century in a chronological listing. Exclusively a Hoare cutting, the Corning pattern was named quite as much for the Corning Glass Company which supplied the blanks, as for the city in which both manufacturer and cutter were located. It became a very popular pattern.

The Corning pattern is a pleasing arrangement of straight splits, which when cut in a border form small squares, decorated with small single stars, and larger squares in which a 16-point hob-star is centered. The central star on the bottom of bowls, plates, and the feet of stemmed ware, shows fan motifs between the points. In this respect the pattern resembles Libbey's Florence, but as the border patterns are so very different, there is no likelihood of confusion between the two.

PLATE 109
Corning, Pattern 32
Reproduced from a catalogue of J. Hoare and Company

CLASSIFICATION.

1. Berry bowls, 7, 8, 9, and 10-inch, square straight-sided, also round
2. Butter dish and cover
3. Butter patties, 3 inches square and flat, very interesting
4. Candlesticks
5. Celery vase, square and straight, unusual
6. Champagne jug, straight
7. Center bowl
8. Cheese dish and cover
9. Claret jug with stopper
10. Cologne bottles, old ones square, later ones round globe
11. Compotes, old ones square on short stems, later tall, round, with cover
12. Cream jugs, globe and straight
13. Decanters and carafes, pint and quart, globe
14. Finger bowls, 5-inch, straight sides very effective with the somewhat square border to match berry bowls and saucedishes
15. Goblets, 6½-inch standard, uncommon
16. Plates, 7, 8, 9, 10-inch, round and square
17. Punch bowl
18. Rose bowl
19. Salts, square with stems
20. Saucedishes, 4½ and 5-inch, shallow, square to match berry bowls, easy to find
21. Sherbets, flat and round, with handles and on stems
22. Spoonholder
23. Sugar bowl, square with cover, no handles
24. Sirup pitchers
25. Toothpick holder
26. Tumblers, 5 and 7-ounce short, wide-bottom (rare)
27. Wines, saucer champagnes, claret, sherry, wine, and cordial

VARIATIONS. *Oriental* and *Meteor,* both cut by the same company as the standard.

COLOR. Clear only.

PLATE 110
Croesus, Pattern 33
Reproduced from a scrapbook of the T. G. Hawkes Glass Company

ORIGIN. J. Hoare and Company, Corning, N. Y., cut on Corning Glass Company blanks.

TRADE-MARK. Some marked with Hoare trade-mark (see Appendix IV), but by no means all.

33. CROESUS

Croesus is one of the earliest patterns to use the chair-bottom motif. Blocks of chair-bottom are combined with three fans as a border above swirled pillars and smaller notched prisms. While the pattern combines several different motifs the effect of the design is unified and graceful. It is an expensive pattern and one that was never cut extensively by any other company but its originators, the J. Hoare Company of Corning.

CLASSIFICATION.

1. Berry or center bowls, 7, 8, 9, 10-inch round
2. Bonbon or olive dishes, 5 and 6-inch round
3. Carafe, 1-quart
4. Nappie, 14 by 8 inches, oval
5. Punch bowl, 10 inches high, with pedestal, 20 by 13 inches oval
6. Punch cups with handles
7. Saucedishes, 4 and 4½-inch shallow
8. Wine glasses, saucer champagne, hollow-stem champagne, hock, claret, Madeira, sherry, cocktail, and cordial

VARIATION. In the larger pieces the Croesus border was combined with the Russian cutting instead of this swirled pillar and notched prism. The border is so distinctive that the two patterns may be used together, but the Russian cutting does create a variation known as *Croesus with Russian Field*.

COLOR. Clear only.

ORIGIN. Exclusive with J. Hoare and Company, Corning, N. Y.

TRADE-MARK. None.

[263]

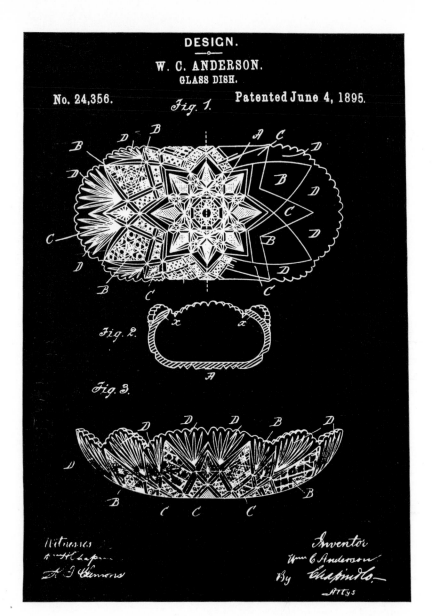

DESIGN.

W. C. ANDERSON.
GLASS DISH.

No. 24,356.

Fig. 1.

Patented June 4, 1895.

PLATE III
Imperial, Pattern 34
Reproduced from the files of the United States Patent Office

34. *IMPERIAL*

The Imperial pattern was cut extensively by Libbey during the closing years of the nineteenth century. The original idea as conceived by William C. Anderson was to have an 8-point star as the center of the design, with the points built up by shield cuttings to form a larger star. This idea is preserved in the larger pieces. It is noticeable in the celery dish illustrated, but gets completely lost in the stemmed ware or smaller pieces. Anderson combined the single-star motif with the cane figure and the intersecting squares described in his letters patent as "cut in representation of outwardly divergent ensiform leaves, whereby a suggestion of Egyptian ornamentation is derived."

The pattern reproduction is of interest to collectors as it shows the earliest use of the celery boat. Libbey afterward used this same blank for many celery boats in other patterns, but before the Imperial was cut in 1895, celery dishes were either tall slender vases, or outsize stemmed goblets. The sides of the celery boat pictured in the Imperial pattern curl over toward the center. Earlier patterns were cut on similar blanks at a later date.

CLASSIFICATION.

1. Berry bowls, 7, 8, 9-inch
2. Bonbon dish, 4½-inch
3. Butter patties, 3-inch, flat and stemmed
4. Candlesticks
5. Celery boats, some with curled-in sides
6. Claret jug, globe
7. Cologne bottle, 6-ounce
8. Compotes, 7 and 8-inch, short and tall stems
9. Cruets, 6 and 8-ounce, lapidary stopper, handle
10. Decanters, pint and quart
11. Finger bowls, 4½-inch, 2 inches high
12. Goblets, standard 6½-inch
13. Mustard pot

14. Nappies, 5 to 10-inch
15. Plates, 6, 8½, and 10-inch
16. Salts, stemmed individuals; round or globe, table size
17. Saucedishes, 4½-inch
18. Toothpick holder
19. Tumblers, 7½-ounce, star bottom
20. Water pitcher, globe
21. Wines, saucer champagne, claret, sherry wine, wine, cordial

VARIATIONS. None.

COLOR. Clear only

ORIGIN. Libbey Glass Company, Toledo, O.

TRADE-MARK. Libbey trade-marks (see Appendix IV).

35. PRINCESS

The Princess is a fairly common pattern that was cut over a period of approximately fifteen years so that a luncheon service can be collected without much trouble.

Princess was one of the last patterns W. C. Anderson designed for Libbey. Until November 12, 1895, Anderson had been assigning all his patterns to the Libbey Company as a matter of course. However, by the time the Princess was patented, Anderson had decided either to sell his designs outright or collect a royalty on all cuttings from his patterns. Evidently his relations with Libbey remained amicable, however, as J. D. Robinson, assistant general manager of the Libbey Glass Company, was one of the witnesses to Anderson's patent application for the Princess in 1895.

The distinguishing characteristics of the Princess pattern are the alternating English and American strawberry-diamond points between the fan scallops with a bow-knot cut through the crosshatching on the points. The hob-star, then so popular in all cut glass patterns, particularly with Libbey, is only used as a center motif in this pattern.

[266]

W. C. ANDERSON.
GLASS DISH.

No. 24,874. Patented Nov. 12, 1895.

Fig 1.

WITNESSES.

Carroll J. Webster

Bertha M. Schwager

INVENTOR.

William C. Anderson

By William Webster
Atty.

PLATE 112

Princess, Pattern 35

Reproduced from the files of the United States Patent Office

CLASSIFICATION.

1. Berry bowls, 7, 8, 9, and 10-inch, straight sides
2. Bonbon dish, covered
3. Butter patties, 3-inch flat
4. Candlesticks
5. Celery boat, 11 by 4½ inches, with curved sides
6. Center bowls
7. Champagne jug, 2-quart, straight
8. Claret jug
9. Cologne bottles, 6 and 8-ounce globe
10. Compotes, 7-inch, short-stemmed, 6-inch tall
11. Cruets
    a. 6-ounce narrow neck, cut handle, lapidary stopper
    b. 4-ounce short-necked oil cruet
12. Decanters, narrow-necked globe, with or without handles
13. Finger bowls, 5-inch, straight sides
14. Goblets, standard 6½-inch, cut stem and modified knop
15. Mustard pot
16. Nappies, 7, 8, and 9-inch
17. Pitcher, globe
18. Plates, 6 and 8½-inch, also 10 and 12-inch; some oval bread and cookie plates
19. Punch bowl
20. Salts, globe, individual and table
21. Saucedishes, 5-inch
22. Sherbet cups with handles
23. Spoonholder
24. Sirup pitcher
25. Toothpick holder
26. Tumblers, standard 7-ounce finger, 5-ounce champagne
27. Wines, saucer champagne, claret, sherry, wine, cordial
28. Vases

VARIATIONS. *Libbey Harvard* is a variation of the Princess, not of the standard Harvard (Pattern 36). This variation, cut on blanks similar in shape to those used for the standard, also alternates the English and American strawberry-diamond between fan scallops;

but it uses a clear field without the bow-knot or crosshatching. The Libbey Harvard also introduces a small single diamond as part of its design. The stemmed ware of the variation has a broken cutting where the stem is joined to the bowl, unlike the standard. Less well designed and less costly than the standard, Libbey Harvard may be used to fill in Princess sets so long as the collector knows the difference. Standard cuttings of Princess originally cost a third to a half more than Libbey Harvard, and the same ratio should hold today. Three other variations acknowledged their debt to the standard pattern by name:

Dorflinger's Princess, designed by James O'Connor and cut by C. Dorflinger & Sons, White Mills, Penna., 1893

O'Connor's Princess, designed by A. E. O'Connor and cut by John O'Connor, Hawley, Penna., 1895

Pairpoint Princess, designed by Thomas Singleton, Jr. for the Pairpoint Glass Company, New Bedford, Mass., 1894

COLOR. Clear.

ORIGIN. Libbey Cut Glass Company, Toledo, O.

TRADE-MARK. Libbey trade-mark (see Appendix IV).

36. HARVARD

The Harvard pattern is one of the standard chairbottom patterns. It consists of a series of squares covering the entire surface area of the dish or plate. The raised center of each square resembles a hobnail, crosshatched in alternate squares in the standard. This pattern should not be confused with the old Russian pattern. In the Harvard, the squares are set apart from one another usually by two lines, sometimes by two straight lines and a wavy line.

Although the Harvard pattern is not so old as the Russian, or earlier star patterns, it is older than the prism cuttings and older than any of the pinwheel cuttings.

CLASSIFICATION.

1. Berry bowls, 7 and 9-inch
2. Butter patties, 3-inch flat

PLATE 113
Harvard, Pattern 36
Reproduced from a scrapbook of the T. G. Hawkes Glass Company

3. Celery boat or vase
4. Cologne bottles, square and globe-shaped
5. Compote, 7-inch stemmed and with flaring feet
6. Cream jug, straight-sided, fluted top
7. Cruet, 8-ounce, tall
8. Decanters, pint and 1½-pint, square
9. Finger bowls, 5-inch
10. Goblets, standard, (rare)
11. Nappies, 5 to 9-inch
12. Pitchers, tapering and globe-shaped
13. Plates, 6, 8½, and 10-inch
14. Saucedishes, 5-inch square
15. Tumblers, 5 and 7-ounce, (rare)
16. Wines, saucer champagnes, claret, sherry, cocktail, cordial

VARIATIONS. This pattern of simple squares readily lent itself to variation, and many leading glasshouses used the basic design with adaptations. Thus, the elevated square was cut in a single star motif in the Kohinoor, by J. Hoare and Company, Corning, N. Y. In others, alternate squares were polished in plain hobnails.
Rochester Harvard, one of the first patterns cut by the H. C. Fry Glass Company, Rochester, Penna., is distinguished by the remarkable sharpness of the cutting which makes for exquisite brilliance when held to the light. Among other patterns to be regarded as Harvard variations are:
Bird-in-a-Cage was cut by H. P. Sinclaire Glass Company, Corning, N. Y.
Corning Harvard and *Kohinoor* were cut by J. Hoare and Company, Corning, N. Y.
National was cut by Krantz Smith and Company, Honesdale, Penna.
Panel was cut by T. G. Hawkes Glass Company, Corning, N. Y.
Quilt Block was cut by T. B. Clark Company, Honesdale, Penna.
Trellis was cut by Walter Egginton, Corning, N. Y.

COLOR. Clear usually, but color used occasionally as this was an effective pattern to cut through casing. The J. D. Bergen Company cut Harvard variations through red and green casings.

ORIGIN. In the absence of patents earlier than 1909, it is hard to say which of the leading glass companies cut the first Harvard pattern. In my own opinion, the honor should go to the Pairpoint Corporation, New Bedford, Mass.

TRADE-MARK. Some Harvard pieces are marked, but the majority are not.

37. NAUTILUS

The Nautilus was the first pattern to introduce the notched prism in cut glass design. The notched prism principle persisted far into the twentieth century because it was easier to cut than the hob-star and could be produced much less expensively. The Nautilus design by Thomas G. Hawkes, however, is not one of the inexpensive patterns. It was carefully designed and executed, adapting its design to the shape of the blank used. It is an important pattern because it shows the transition of style from the Gothic patterns of the late nineteenth century to the straight split cuttings of the early twentieth century. The Nautilus is rare but can still be collected in dessert sets.

CLASSIFICATION.

1. Berry bowl, 9-inch
2. Bonbon or olive dishes, irregular shapes
3. Plates, odd
4. Saucedishes, 5-inch, shallow

VARIATIONS. The Nautilus was copied extensively, but collectors should select only the standard, easily distinguished by the shape of the pieces and the three concentric rings.

COLOR. Clear only.

ORIGIN. T. G. Hawkes Glass Company, Corning, N. Y.

TRADE-MARK. On some pieces (see Appendix IV).

Fig 1

Fig 2.

Witnesses :
Herbert Bradley
Walter Allen

Inventor
Thomas G. Hawkes
By Knight Bros
Attorneys

38. PRISM

Pattern stealing was common practice among glass manufacturers and cutters. By the close of the nineteenth century competition was so keen that efforts were being made by all manufacturers to cut costs. Since the principal cost in the manufacture of cut glass then as now, is the hand labor involved, any pattern that reduced this factor became a target for competitive imitation.

When the Nautilus pattern was introduced by Hawkes, W. C. Anderson of the Libbey Glass Company was only one of many designers who were quick to see the advantage of using the prism motif. Anderson designed a pattern in 1897 which was later modified by Libbey as the Prism pattern. Soon everyone had a Prism pattern, all being cut at a much lower cost than had been possible with the many-pointed hob-star.

CLASSIFICATION.

1. Bonbon or olive dish, 6-inch with handle
2. Bowls, 6 to 10-inch, straight, flaring, or square sides
3. Butter patties, 3-inch flat
4. Candlesticks
5. Celery dishes, vase and boat, straight sides, flaring, or curved
6. Center bowls
7. Cologne bottles, globe and square
8. Compotes, 7-inch, tall and short stem
9. Cruets, 4, 5, 6-ounce, short stemmed
10. Decanters, globe and tapering
11. Finger bowls, 5-inch
12. Goblets, 6¼ inches high, plain border around top
13. Ice-cream platter
14. Loving cups
15. Pitchers, 1-pint and 2-quart, globe-shaped with fluted tops
16. Plates, 6, 8½, 10, and 13-inch
17. Punch bowl without pedestal
18. Rose bowls and rose jars
19. Salts, stemmed and globe

PLATE 115
Prism, Pattern 38
Reproduced from a catalogue of the Libbey Glass Company

20. Saucedishes, 5-inch flat
21. Sherbet cups with handles
22. Spoonholder, in shape of celery boat, but smaller
23. Sugar bowl, with handles, no covers
24. Sirup pitcher
25. Tumblers, 8-ounce standard, wide bottom
26. Vases
27. Wines, saucer champagnes, claret, sherry, cocktail, and cordial

VARIATIONS. Variations using the Prism cutting and the name were put out by many leading glasshouses at the turn of the century, usually in combination with a star or other conventionalized border motif. Prism became almost a universal pattern. At least two prism patterns developed were distinctive enough to warrant selection as independent standards, namely White House (Pattern 39) and Bull's-Eye (Pattern 44).

COLOR. Clear only.

ORIGIN. The Libbey Glass Company cut this particular Prism pattern as the standard.

TRADE-MARKS. Some pieces are trade-marked, others not (see Appendix IV).

39. WHITE HOUSE

This simple notched prism pattern developed into a standard. Unlike Bull's-Eye (Pattern 44) and variations of Prism (Pattern 38) White House uses no large figure in combination with the notched prism. It was not an expensive pattern to cut and it remained popular for many years. Men particularly like the tailored simplicity of the notched prism and bead combination. This may account for the fact that when President Truman ordered a new service of cut glass to replace the old Russian service at the White House in 1947, a modern adaptation of this old White House pattern was selected for the service by the Thomas G. Hawkes Glass Company who executed the order.

[276]

PLATE 116
White House, Pattern 39
Reproduced from the files of the Crockery and Glass Journal

Plates in this pattern have a small central simple star (not to be confused with the hob-star motif). This star is definitely subordinate and not a basic motif in the pattern.

The White House is another fine pattern for the collector just beginning to assemble a service of cut glass, as the pattern was cut by so many houses that it is comparatively easy to find matching pieces.

CLASSIFICATION.

1. Bonbon or olive dish, 6-inch
2. Bowls, 4½ to 8-inch, graceful sides
3. Butter dishes
4. Cheese plate with cover
5. Cologne bottle, narrow neck, 6-ounce
6. Compote, 7-inch, tall stem
7. Cruets, with or without handle, lapidary stopper
8. Decanters, Rodney and globe
9. Goblets, tapering and standard
10. Nappies, 7, 8, 9, and 10-inch
11. Pitchers, straight 1 and 2-quart globe
12. Plates, 6, 8, 10 and 12-inch, other odd plates
13. Rose bowls
14. Salts, globe
15. Saucedishes, 4½ and 5-inch shallow
16. Sherbet and custard cups with handles
17. Sugar bowl, handles, no cover
18. Sirup pitchers
19. Tumblers, 5, 7, and 8-ounce, heavy and tapering
20. Vases
21. Wines, claret, wine, saucer champagne, pousse café, cordial, cocktail, and sherry

VARIATIONS. I would consider a variation of this standard any design that uses the prism with or without notching, with or without beading, provided it is not combined with any other larger figure, such as the bull's-eye or star. In some variations the prisms are

notched and the beading subordinated; in others, the notching follows a pronounced, sometimes intricate small pattern of its own. *Brunswick* and *Modern White House* were both cut by T. G. Hawkes Glass Company, Corning, New York.
Hindoo was cut both by J. Hoare and Company at Corning, and by the T. B. Clark Company, Honesdale, Penna.
Pluto was also cut by T. B. Clark Company.
Prism and Bead was cut by Bawo and Dotter, New York City.
Tasso was cut by J. D. Bergen Company, Meriden, Conn.

COLOR. Clear.

ORIGIN. Both United States Glass Company, Pittsburgh, Penna., and A. H. Heisey and Company, Inc., of Newark, O., cut a prism pattern called White House. Which of them originated the Notched Prism and Bead standard pattern is anybody's guess.

TRADE-MARK. Not all pieces were marked, and not all trade-marks have stayed on the glass; but there are some marked pieces (see Appendix IV).

40. CORINTHIAN

Every glasshouse cut a Corinthian pattern. The name was nearly as universally used as "Russian" or "Strawberry-Diamond and Fan." Unfortunately there was no such uniformity of design. Almost every cutter helped himself to a fairly florid pattern and called it Corinthian. I have taken as standard the Libbey Corinthian, not because it is any better than some of the others, notably the Bergen or Clark Corinthian, but because it was cut so extensively that fairly complete services may be assembled. Furthermore Libbey used very interesting and "collectible" blanks for its Corinthian pattern. The Corinthian card-table, or ice-cream set listed was the first of its kind to be cut and sold as a unit. Notice the heart, club, spade, and diamond nappy, or individual ice-cream dish. The rather boat-shaped bowl could be used for fruit or ice cream and the 9-inch plate for cookies or cake. Such sets can still be assembled.

[279]

PLATE 117
Corinthian, Pattern 40
Reproduced from a scrapbook of the T. G. Hawkes Glass Company

The pattern is fairly simple to identify in its standard form. The 16-point hob-star is the central motif. This figure appears in the center of each piece, forming the center of a Greek cross. The arms of this cross are decorated by triangles of crosshatching, with terminating points of strawberry-diamond separated by smaller boxed 16-point stars. The description makes the pattern sound more intricate than it actually is. When you see the stemmed ware or bowls from the side, they appear to be only alternate points of boxed 16-point hob-star and strawberry-diamond cuttings. The Corinthian was never cut in any but the finest glass. A covered Corinthian butter dish sold for $30.00 at jewelers in New York, Chicago, and Pittsburgh in 1900.

CLASSIFICATION. Like so many of the later Libbey patterns Corinthian was cut so extensively and on so many different types of blanks that it is possible to give only the partial list below. Collectors may find other pieces not listed which are none the less authentic Corinthian standard, possibly all the more valuable for their rarity.

1. Berry bowls, 6 to 10-inch oblong, round, and square
2. Bonbon or olive dishes, 4½ and 5-inch, round and square
3. Butter patties, 3 inches, on stems, fine for miniature collections
4. Celery boat
5. Cheese dish with cover
6. Cologne bottles, globe, round, and square, also long-necked globe
7. Compotes, short and long-stemmed, with or without air twists
8. Cruets, 4-ounce oil, vinegar to match
9. Decanters, pint and quart, with long necks, some with handles
10. Finger bowls, 5-inch
11. Goblets, standard, 6½ inch
12. Honey jar
13. Jelly tray, square
14. Mustard pot
15. Nappies, heart, spade, diamond, and club, flat-sided to match saucedishes
16. Pitchers, tall and short, globe and tapering, all sizes

17. Plates, 6, 8½, 10 and 12-inch round, oblong, and square
18. Punch bowl with pedestal
19. Rose bowl
20. Salts, globe and standard, individual and table
21. Saucedishes, heart, spade, diamond, and club, matching nappies
22. Sherbet cups, stemmed
23. Spoonholder
24. Sugar bowl with handles, no top
25. Tumblers, 5-ounce champagne or mineral; 8-ounce standard
26. Vases, tapering
27. Wines, saucer champagnes, claret, sherry, wine, cordial

VARIATIONS. *Delft,* which substitutes two small stars for the large star in alternate fields, was cut by J. Hoare and Company, Corning, N. Y.
Elmira Corinthian is almost identical with Delft, except for three small splits between the strawberry-diamond and large hob-star.

COLOR. Clear only.

ORIGIN. Libbey Glass Company, Toledo, O.

TRADE-MARK. Libbey trade-mark (see Appendix IV).

41. HAWKES' ABERDEEN

Thomas G. Hawkes was one of the few designers who specifically named his pattern in his letters patent. He follows this rule with the Hawkes' Aberdeen, one of the better popular patterns of its day: "The leading features of my design consist of a large double cross or asterisk figure covering the body of the dish, having radial pointed arms, a central rosette at the crossing of the arms forming the body of the figure, crosshatching on the arms and double lines extending lengthwise of the arms, thus representing leaves having stems, checkered cutting at the inner ends of the arms, and foils between the arms having rosettes, thus forming what I call 'Aberdeen' design."

DESIGN.

T. G. HAWKES.
GLASS VESSEL OR DISH.

No. 25,386.   Patented Apr. 14, 1896.

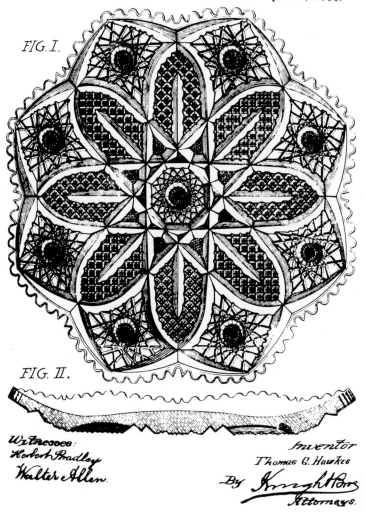

FIG. I.

FIG. II.

Witnesses:
Robert Bradley
Walter Allen.

Inventor
Thomas G. Hawkes
By *Knight Bros*
Attorneys.

PLATE 118
Aberdeen, Pattern 41

Reproduced from the files of the United States Patent Office

The Aberdeen is not so plentiful as some other patterns but it rewards the collector by its sturdy design and interesting flat shape in plates and saucedishes.

CLASSIFICATION.

1. Berry bowls, 7 and 9-inch
2. Butter patties, 3-inch
3. Nappies, 7, 8, and 9-inch
4. Plates, 6, 8½, 10 and 13-inch
5. Saucedishes, 4½ and 5-inch

Other pieces may have been cut in this pattern, but such pieces are rare. Collectors of Aberdeen will have more success concentrating on dessert sets.

VARIATIONS. As in the case of any heavily cut standard, this pattern was copied later in less expensive cuttings. The Hawkes' Aberdeen checkering on the points of the central figure is particularly fine. This distinguishing characteristic of the pattern is not found in variations.

COLOR. Clear only.

ORIGIN. T. G. Hawkes Glass Company, Corning, N. Y.

TRADE-MARK. Some pieces carry the Hawkes' trade-mark (see Appendix IV).

42. VICTORIA

The Victoria, less common than some of its contemporaries, is listed here as an example of cutting done by the Imperial Cut Glass Company of Philadelphia. The pattern was designed and patented by Joseph B. Hill, chief designer for Imperial and himself a subject of the Queen of England. He had learned his trade in English cutting shops and his design shows the somewhat stilted and old-fashioned form still being followed in England at the end of the nineteenth century. The radiant splits in the center are typical and

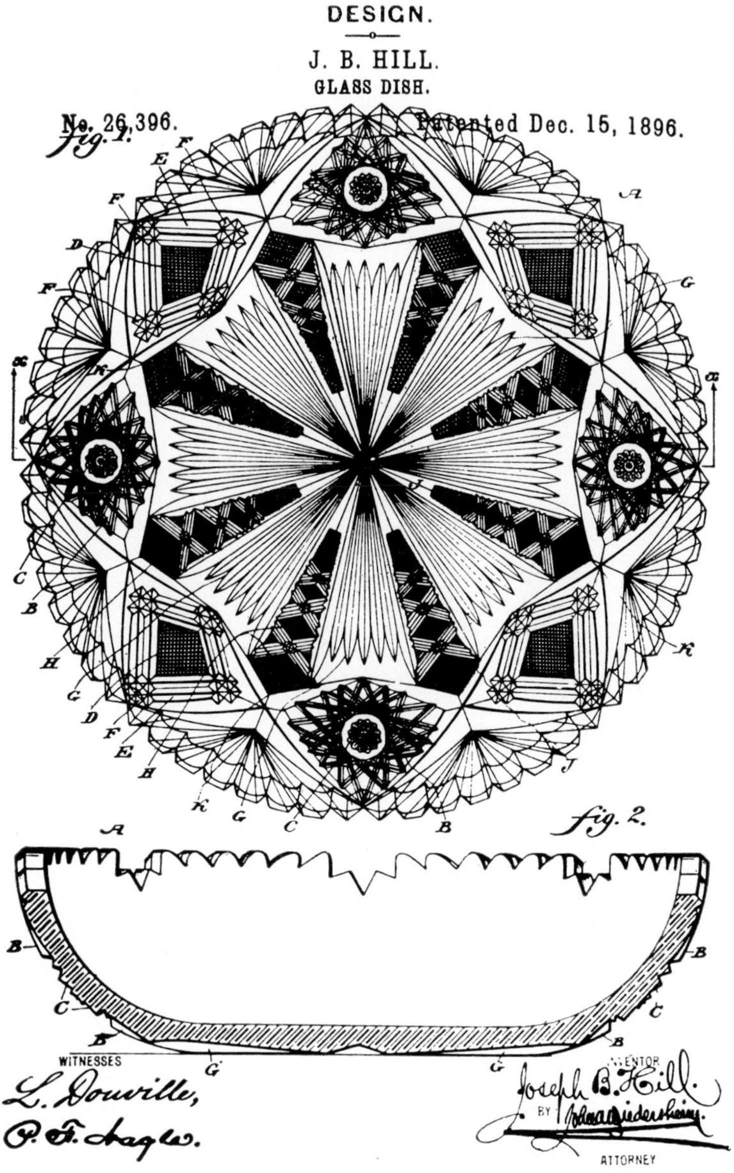
DESIGN.
J. B. HILL.
GLASS DISH.
No. 26,396.
Patented Dec. 15, 1896.
Fig. 1.
Fig. 2.
WITNESSES
L. Douville,
P. F. Nagle.
INVENTOR
Joseph B. Hill.
BY
ATTORNEY

PLATE 119

Victoria, Pattern 42

Reproduced from the files of the United States Patent Office

DESIGN.

H. SCHREIBER.
GLASS DISH.

No. 27,321.　　　　　　　Patented July 13, 1897.

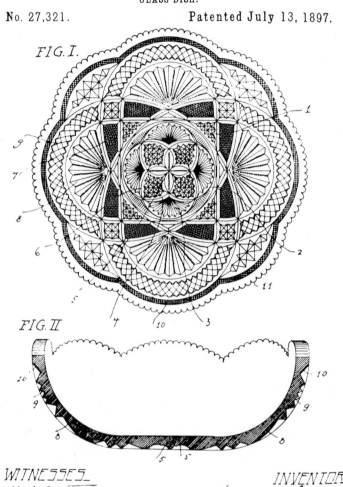

FIG. I.

FIG. II

WITNESSES
H. H. Marin
Maud Schumacher

INVENTOR
Herman Schreiber
By William Webster
atty

PLATE 120

Dunkirk, Pattern 43

Reproduced from the files of the United States Patent Office

the minute crosshatching of the checkered areas is more reminiscent of the later English patterns. Because of the crosshatching on the bottom, most of the Victoria pieces at first glance appear to be unpolished. They are, however, rare and any collector should be proud of a dessert set in this pattern.

CLASSIFICATION.

1. Berry bowl, 9-inch
2. Nappies, 5, 6, and 7-inch
3. Saucedishes, 4 and 5-inch, sloping sides
Perhaps other pieces were cut in the Victoria pattern, but none are now known.

VARIATIONS. *Pittsburgh Victoria* was cut by the United States Glass Company about 1900.

COLOR. Clear only.

ORIGIN. Imperial Cut Glass Company, Philadelphia, Penna.

TRADE-MARK. None.

43. DUNKIRK

The Dunkirk is another of the rare patterns that will repay the collector for the diligent search necessary to find proof pieces. Just as the Victoria reflects the English background of its designer, the Dunkirk has a distinctly Continental flavor although it was designed and patented in America. Herman Schreiber of Dunkirk, Indiana, designed the Dunkirk for his employers, the Ohio Flint Glass Company in 1897. It was cut more extensively than the Victoria and like it has often been mistaken by collectors for a Middle Period pattern.

CLASSIFICATION.

1. Berry bowls, 7 and 9-inch
2. Bonbon or olive dishes, 5 and 6-inch

[287]

DESIGN.

—o—

A. SNOW, Jr.

GLASS RECEPTACLE.

No. 28,178.   Patented Jan. 18, 1898.

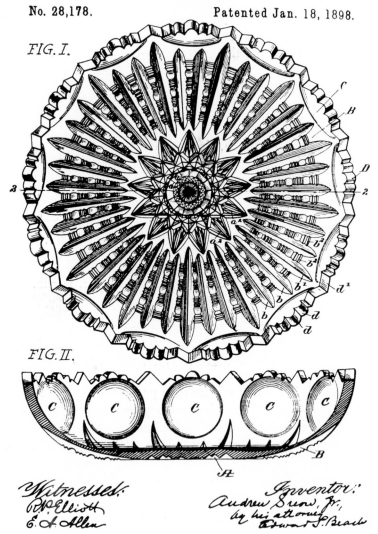

FIG. I.

FIG. II.

Witnesses:
W. P. Elliott
E. A. Allen

Inventor:
Andrew Snow, Jr.,
by his attorney
Edward S. Beach

PLATE 121

Bull's-Eye, Pattern 44

Reproduced from the files of the United States Patent Office

3. Cream pitcher, small
4. Nappies, 7 and 8-inch
5. Plates, 6 and 8-inch
6. Salts, small
7. Saucedishes, 4 and 4½-inch
8. Tumblers, 5-ounce, wide bottom finger

Probably no stemmed ware cut, either goblets or wines; possibly some covered dishes and perhaps a few straight-sided water pitchers, none now known.

VARIATION. None.

COLOR. Only clear so far as is known.

ORIGIN. Ohio Glass Company, Bellaire, O.

TRADE-MARK. None.

44. BULL'S-EYE

The Bull's-Eye pattern is a good selection for a collector interested in accumulating a dinner service or a luncheon set. So many companies cut the Bull's-Eye pattern in different shapes that it is comparatively plentiful. Moreover, variations on the standard only contribute to the effectiveness of the Bull's-Eye service, making the table setting more interesting.

Basically, this is a prism pattern to which the designer, Andrew Snow, Jr., added the bull's-eye figure on the sides of dishes and bowls. From the collector's point of view Pairpoint pieces stamped "Patented Jan. 18, 1898" are the most desirable. Some fine Bull's-Eye pieces were also cut by J. G. Bergen and L. Straus. The standard is a combination of the prism pattern and the old English roundelet which came to be known in this country as the bull's-eye . . . not as elegant a name perhaps, but more expressive. The roundelet or bull's-eye got its form from the old German kugel or as the Irish sometimes called it, the "puntie" after the mark left by the pontil iron. The tumblers are heavy and well designed and much in demand for present-day use as old-fashioned glasses.

[289]

CLASSIFICATION.

1. Berry bowls, all shapes, 7, 8, 9, 10-inch, punch bowls and standards
2. Bonbon or olive dishes, square and round
3. Brandy or whisky jug, square stopper
4. Butter dish, covered
5. Butter patties, 3-inch flat and stemmed
6. Celery boat and vase
7. Champagne jug
8. Cheese dish, covered
9. Claret jug, large
10. Cologne bottles, squat and globe, square and oblong, tapering
11. Compotes, 7 by 7 and 6 inches, covered and stemmed
12. Cream pitcher, miniature to match 1-quart pitcher, straight and globe
13. Cruets, 4, 5, 6-inch oil and vinegar, very common
14. Decanters, 1-quart and 1½-quart, tapering, globe and ring neck; also pint claret decanter with handle
15. Finger bowls, 5-inch, 2½ inches deep
16. Goblets, standard, 6½ inches
17. Nappies, 7, 8, 9-inch
18. Pitchers, 1 and 2-quart, straight and globe
19. Plates, 6, 8, and 10-inch, also odd sizes
20. Saucedishes, 4½-inch, shallow
21. Sugar bowl, handles, no cover
22. Toothpick holder
23. Tumblers, 5 and 7-ounce, short with wide bottom
24. Wines, saucer champagnes, claret, sherry, cocktail, and cordial

VARIATIONS. Any design incorporating the bull's-eye motif with the prism is a variation on this standard. Benjamin Davies designed such a variation for L. Straus and Sons of New York City, putting the bull's-eye in the bottom of the bowl or dish. J. G. Bergen Company also cut some fine Bull's-Eye pieces. *Navarre,* by T. G. Hawkes Glass Company, is another good one.

COLOR. Clear.

ORIGIN. Pairpoint Corporation, New Bedford, Mass. (design by Andrew Snow, Jr.)

TRADE-MARK. Some pieces of the standard Bull's-Eye are marked with the Mount Washington or Pairpoint trade-mark and patent number. However, there are good cuttings on this pattern that are not marked. If your pieces are marked, compare with trade-mark list (see Appendix IV).

45. PINWHEEL

The pinwheel or buzz, as many glassmen prefer to call the figure, was not cut until the twentieth century, and while some pieces which show this motif are fine glass of good design, the pinwheel is identified by connoisseurs with the decline of Brilliant period design. Most of the pieces with the pinwheel as part of the pattern are overornamented, clumsy in shape, and lacking in definite design.

The Pinwheel pattern of 1899 was simply a 12-point swirling star with fan motifs following the direction of the star points. The original design by Patrick H. Healy and the blanks used for it are well designed and graceful. Healy assigned his pattern to the American Cut Glass Company of Chicago, which was an out-cutting subsidiary of the Libbey Glass Company. William C. Anderson joined the American Cut Glass Company about 1900, and the company continued to produce very fine cuttings on Libbey blanks.

Many collectors have started Pinwheel collections including all variations of Pinwheel cuttings. This is a good plan for beginners, as it makes it fairly simple to assemble a pattern, but the novice should be on the lookout for pressed blanks in the Pinwheel pattern. The Pinwheel and the pressed blank were popular at the same time, the former with customers, the latter with dealers. A collection of the Pinwheel pattern, cut on fine blanks of good design and metal, is desirable and choice. But the collector should be guided by the practicality of the piece, its shape, balance, and beauty, quality of metal, and sharpness of cutting. Avoid overornamentation and pressed blanks. Never pay as much for any Pinwheel cutting as you would for the earlier hob-star patterns such as the Kimberly, Florence, or Chrysanthemum.

PLATE 122

Pinwheel, Pattern 45

Reproduced from the files of the United States Patent Office

CLASSIFICATION.

1. Berry bowls, 7, 8, 9, 10-inch
2. Butter patties, 3-inch
3. Celery boat
4. Cologne bottles in all shapes, standard, globe, and odd
5. Compotes, in all sizes and lengths of stem, air twisted stems in some
6. Cruets, all sizes and shapes
7. Decanters, in all sizes, globe and straight
8. Finger bowls, all sizes
9. Goblets, globe, tapering, bell, in endless variety
10. Nappies, 7, 8, 9-inch
11. Pitchers, all sizes and shapes, some good and some bad design
12. Plates, 6, 8½, 10, and 12-inch
13. Sherbet or punch cups, in all shapes and sizes, some stemmed
14. Saucedishes, 4½ and 6-inch
15. Sugar bowl with handles
16. Tumblers, in all sizes, mostly star bottom, standard 8-ounce
17. Wines, in all sizes, saucer champagne, twisted and hollow stem, sherry, claret, wine, cordial, and Monte Carlo (later)

VARIATIONS. Later Pinwheel patterns dropped the central star and became a series of tangents to a central hobnail. Endless variations of the Pinwheel appeared, some good, others hasty and overornamented. Most common are:
Cut Buzz, by United States Glass Company, Pittsburgh, Penna.
Highland and *Whirlwind,* both cut by Quaker City Cut Glass Company, Philadelphia, Penna.
Marvel, by Maple City Glass Company, Honesdale, Penna.
Pinwheel and Star, by J. Hoare and Company, Corning, N. Y.
Twenty-Two, by Pairpoint Corporation, New Bedford, Mass.

COLOR. Clear.

ORIGIN. American Cut Glass Company, Chicago, Ill., out-cutting subsidiary of Libbey Glass Company.

TRADE-MARK. Some are marked and some are not (see Appendix IV).

PLATE 123
Comet, Pattern 46
Reproduced from the files of the Libbey Glass Company

46. COMET

The Comet pattern is very easy to identify. Many patterns have fanciful names that betray some element of whimsy in the imagination of the designer. But the Comet pattern could have no other name. It was first cut by the Hoare company. Afterwards, toward the end of the Brilliant Period, it was cut by almost all of the Eastern cutting houses with the exception of the Hawkes and Bergen glass companies.

Halley's comet had been predicted but had not yet appeared in the sky when the Hoare company began cutting the Comet pattern. The fortunes of the glass business were waning at the time. The glass cutters were grumbling about wages and hours, and strikes threatened on all sides. Glass workers had always been highly organized and their power had long been one of the major concerns of the industry. The Comet pattern was one of those designed to cut costs. But the glass workers, by nature superstitious, took the comet as a sign of foreboding. The comet that appeared in Europe in 1456 had caused such terror there that the Christian Church added the following lines to its daily prayers, "Lord, save us from the Devil, the Turk, and the comet." Some waggish member of the glass union recalled the prayer in 1900 and it became one of the grim jokes of the trade, the portent being that the heyday of cut glass was practically over, as indeed it was.

CLASSIFICATION.

1. Berry bowls, 7, 8, 9, and 10-inch
2. Celery vase or boat, 11 by 4½ inches
3. Decanters, quart and pint, also carafes
4. Finger bowls, 5-inch
5. Goblets, globe, tapering, bell, but very light metal and very sketchy cutting; doubtful if many have survived.
6. Nappies, 7, 8, and 9-inch
7. Plates, 6 and 8½-inch, 10 and 12-inch
8. Salts, globe, individual
9. Saucedishes, 5-inch

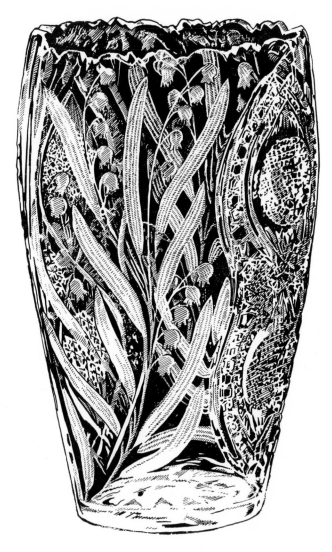

PLATE 124
Lily-of-the-Valley, Pattern 47
Reproduced from the files of the T. G. Hawkes Glass Company

10. Tumblers, 7-ounce star bottom
11. Whisky jugs, with stoppers
12. Wines, same metal as goblets, very fragile, saucer champagnes, claret, sherry, cocktail, and cordial

Probably many incidental pieces, such as center bowl, punch bowl, and candlesticks.

VARIATIONS. Many variations of the Comet were cut by different companies, but large or small, border or single, the pattern remained the Comet.

COLOR. Clear only.

ORIGIN. The J. Hoare and Company, Corning, N. Y.; later cut by many other companies.

TRADE-MARK. Some pieces are trade-marked, others are not (see Appendix IV).

47. LILY-OF-THE-VALLEY

The Lily-of-the-Valley pattern is important to collectors for two reasons. It is one of the first, and therefore a forerunner of the vogue for, realistic cuttings in cut glass. Secondly, the Lily-of-the-Valley pattern is one of the authenticated Fry pieces and any piece of Fry glass is now collectible.

Henry C. Fry took out the first patent for a cut glass pattern ever issued, in 1868. However, he did not patent the Lily-of-the-Valley, and it was cut by other companies but never on such fine metal or with such exquisite cutting. The quality of Fry glass is comparable to the early Steuben, made under the Hawkes-Carder owership in 1905, and to the later Libbey and present-day Steuben engraved ware. Not only is the quality of the metal exquisite, showing high lead content, purity of silica, and proper balance of other ingredients, but the Fry system of fusion has never been surpassed.

CLASSIFICATION.

1. Berry bowls, 8, 9, and 10-inch
2. Brandy jug, 1½-pint

PLATE 125
Plain Flute, Pattern 48
Reproduced from the catalogue of the Libbey Glass Company

 3. Claret jug, 1½-pint
 4. Cologne bottles, 4, 6, and 8-ounce
 5. Compote, 7-inch
 6. Finger bowls, 5-inch
 7. Goblets, 6½-inch bell-shaped
 8. Jelly dish, 5-inch shallow
 9. Nappies, 7 and 9-inch
10. Plates, 6 and 8½-inch
11. Saucedishes, 4½-inch
12. Tumblers, 8-ounce standard
13. Whisky jug, 1-pint
14. Wines, hollow-stem champagne, claret, sherry, cocktail, cordial

Incidental pieces: As Fry made a practice of cutting individual pieces and incidental gift pieces, almost anything from a slender bud vase or rose bowl to an ice bucket may be found in the Lily-of-the-Valley pattern.

VARIATIONS. Though there were other applications of the realistic cutting of Lily-of-the-Valley, the Fry pattern is the standard and can be recognized by the brilliance and ring of the metal.

COLOR. Clear only.

ORIGIN. H. C. Fry Glass Company, Rochester, Penna.

TRADE-MARK. The Fry trade-mark was not always applied. Many fine examples of Lily-of-the-Valley are unmarked.

48. PLAIN FLUTE

The Plain Flute cut by the Libbey Company is a modern application of the old Colonial Flute. It is not likely to be confused with the old Colonial Flute because the more modern pieces have a brilliance and sparkle and keenness in their cutting that is absent in the older pieces. The Plain Flute was cut in a full line of almost everything that could be cut at all and enjoyed a tremendous vogue for a few years. It was widely used in fine hotels and clubs, and many pieces can be found with individual monograms and crests engraved on one or more of the fluted sides. Plain Flute was never an expensive pattern. But for modern collectors it has a distinct charm and value for use with modern china, pottery, and table settings.

CLASSIFICATION. A complete classification of Libbey Plain Flute is out of the question. The pieces cut in the greatest number are listed for the guidance of collectors.

1. Bowls, 7, 10, and 12-inch
2. Cologne bottles, large, small, thin neck
3. Compote, no cover
4. Cruet, oil
5. Decanters, all sizes and shapes
6. Finger bowls, straight, or rounded, with 6-inch plate
7. Goblets, standard, straight stem
8. Lemonade cup and plate (called "custard cup" in earlier patterns)
9. Nappies, 9 and 10-inch
10. Pitchers, globe and straight
11. Plates, 6, 7, and 12-inch
12. Saucedishes, 5, 6, 7-inch
13. Sherbet, now called "punch glasses" in this pattern, stemmed, with or without handle
14. Tumblers, in numerous sizes since this was also a bar-ware pattern
15. Wines, hollow-stem saucer champagne, cocktail, crème de menthe, number 2 cocktail, number 2 crème de menthe

Incidentals include a cigar jar, also a grapefruit glass and an oyster cocktail glass, the first time these pieces have been added to the standard service.

VARIATIONS. Itself a variation of the old Colonial Flute, Plain Flute is a standard modern pattern.

COLOR. Probably clear only.

ORIGIN. Libbey Glass Company, Toledo, O.

TRADE-MARK. See Appendix IV.

49. *KAISER*

The Kaiser is another modern application of the old Colonial Flute, resembling the Plain Flute. The main difference from the older pattern is in the shape of the vessels. It was an inexpensive pattern and was widely sold in the Middle West. Kaiser is collectible in sets and makes a most interesting pattern to use with Early American furniture or Colonial reproductions in maple and other light woods. It is easily recognized by its more modern shape, and there is little likelihood of confusion with the authentic colonial-flute cuttings of the Early American Glass Period or the Middle Period because of the high brilliance of the Kaiser metal and the absence of age marks on the bottom and edges of the cut flutes.

CLASSIFICATION.

1. Berry bowls, 7, 8 and 9-inch
2. Celery vase or boat
3. Cologne bottles, long narrow neck
4. Decanters, 1-pint, 1½-pint, and 1-quart
5. Finger bowls, 5-inch
6. Goblets, all sizes as this was essentially a bar-ware pattern. The small goblet and the large goblet each retailed for approximately $10.00 a dozen
7. Nappies
8. Pitcher
9. Plates, 6 and 8-inch
10. Saucedishes
11. Sherbet or custard cup with handle
12. Tumblers, 2½, 3½, 4½, 6, 7, and 8-ounce in short and tall shapes, for bar-ware
13. Wines, champagne, wine, cocktail, cordial, claret, pousse café, saucer champagne, and number 2 cocktail

Incidentals mostly related to the gentle art of conviviality, including odd decanters, bitters bottles, bar bottles, water carafes in several sizes without stoppers, small cruets and jugs.

PLATE 126
Kaiser, Pattern 49
Reproduced from the catalogue of the United States Glass Company

VARIATIONS. There are no variations of the Kaiser. Any flute pattern—including the Plain Flute and the Kaiser—may be said to be a variation of the old Colonial Flute.

COLOR. Clear, yellow and amber.

ORIGIN. United States Glass Company, Pittsburgh, Penna.

TRADE-MARK. None.

50. CORNFLOWER

As the Brilliant Period came to a close and deep miter cuttings became disorganized, diffuse and clumsy, many glass shops failed and manufacturers began a search for some new design to bolster up the failing market.

From 1905 until 1910 a number of realistic floral and fruit patterns were designed and cut. Many of these show fine workmanship. Some are copper-wheel engravings polished out with acid. The shapes of the glass pieces are usually modern.

The Cornflower, designed by R. H. Pittman, was cut by T. B. Clark and Company. It shows the use of the realistic leaf cutting, the old application of the conventionalized flower, cut with the triple miter stone. The shape of the plate is modern and the treatment of the design is new. Although this pattern was not patented until a flurry of patent activity in 1909, it was being cut some time before this.

These floral and fruit patterns signify the end of the Brilliant Period. Glass was cut until World War I shut off essential materials. But the metal was generally inferior after 1905. The majority of the glass cutting houses had gone out of business in 1904. The best of the later pieces were the floral patterns, but these were cut only in incidental pieces with a limited quantity of stemmed ware and tumblers. Whatever cutting was done in the old style found scant market for the old patterns; and the new deep miter patterns were so inferior and trivial that they are not worth collecting. However, a fine collection of plates can be assembled from late Brilliant

PLATE 127
Cornflower, Pattern 50
Reproduced from the files of the United States Patent Office

Period floral patterns in either 6 or 8½-inch size. They make a useful collection and an interesting one. There is considerable variety in pattern.

CLASSIFICATION.

1. Berry bowls, 7 and 9-inch
2. Compote, 7-inch
3. Finger bowls, 5-inch
4. Goblets, standard
5. Nappies, 7 and 9-inch
6. Plates, 6, 8½, 10 and 12-inch
7. Saucedishes, 4½ and 5-inch
8. Tumblers, 5-ounce mineral or finger, 8-ounce standard
9. Wines, saucer champagnes, claret, sherry, cordial

Incidentals include bottles, pin trays and smelling salts

VARIATIONS. None of this specific pattern, although there is some similarity among all the flower patterns of the latter days of the Brilliant Period.

COLOR. Clear.

ORIGIN. T. B. Clark and Company, Honesdale, Penna.

TRADE-MARK. See Appendix IV.

PLATE 128

*The Merry-Go-Round Bowl represents the finest American craftsmanship to-
day. Designed by Sidney Waugh for Steuben Glass, it was presented by
President and Mrs. Harry Truman to H.R.H. Princess Elizabeth, on the
occasion of her marriage. (Photograph, courtesy Steuben Glass)*

◇ ◇

CUT GLASS, TODAY AND TOMORROW

TODAY American cut and engraved glass reflects more than two hundred years of expert craftsmanship. Modern American glass is made from scientifically pure ingredients—ground quartz rock, lead oxides, potash, and other minerals, as the formula dictates—fused under modern methods of controlled heat. The resulting fine metal is fashioned by expert workmen in the traditional ways of offhand or handmade glass. Patterns are combinations of the old motifs adapted to the simplicity of modern design. Miter splits, panels, flutes, bull's-eye, and fringe motifs are still used, but in combinations that do not interfere with the basic and unified impression of the article itself. More expensive pieces are decorated with copper-wheel engraving in the manner of the artists of the Early American and Middle periods.

It is in subject matter that modern engravings differ from old ones. Early engravings were usually concerned with serious historical scenes or fanciful interpretations of mythological subjects. Modern engravings are distinguished by wit and humor and have an undeniable American style, a most distinguishing trait (Plate 128).

Today fine glass is being made in considerable quantity in other lands and while much of it is very beautiful, many experts maintain that *American glass is superior to any other of contemporary manufacture*. The quality of our metal is as unique today as it was a hundred years ago when manufacturers discovered the superior sands of the Berkshire and Juniata areas, and our methods of pyrometric control of fusion result in a practically flawless lead glass. The evolution of American design has been steady and sound. Our glass is well proportioned and simply designed, our engravings show humor, originality, and imagination. But our glass is expensive. *Little of the glass imported from Czechoslovakia, Sweden, Holland, and France can compare in quality with our finer pieces but it does compete in price.* Because of lower wage scales modern European glass can be made, cut, exported, and sold here for less than our fine domestic glass, and still return a profit to the foreign manufacturers. Our rate of pay to glassmakers in 1964 was five times that of 1891, and American retail prices are proportionately higher.

THE T. G. HAWKES GLASS COMPANY

The fact that fine glass is still made in America is due to the tenacious faith of an old man and the stubborn vision of a young one, both seventh-generation members of world-renowned glass families. Samuel Hawkes, president of the T. G. Hawkes Glass Company, and Arthur Amory Houghton, Jr., president of Steuben Glass works, were directly responsible for the first place American cut and engraved glass holds in the contemporary markets of the world. Mr. Hawkes kept the spark of perfectionism alive during the years when other manufacturers of fine tableware were letting it die. Mr. Houghton kindled the spark into the steady flame of American glass design.

Founded in 1880 by a descendant of the Hawkes family of Dudley, England, and the Penrose family of Waterford, Ireland, the T. G. Hawkes Company is the only one of the old companies to continue cutting glass through the years. Hawkes metal is of uniform quality and brilliant luster. Each finished modern piece is acid stamped with the Hawkes trade-mark, the shamrock enclosing two small hawks on the larger pieces, a small H for the stemmed ware. Modern Hawkes patterns are combinations of traditional miter-cut motifs like the prism and block of the modern White House pattern. Other pieces are engraved, sculptured, or cut in the French Baccarat technique known in America as rock-crystal cutting.

When the company was started in 1880, Thomas Hawkes bought

PLATE 129

TOP AND BOTTOM: *Finger bowl and stemmed ware, White House service,
ordered from the T. G. Hawkes Glass Co. by Franklin D. Roosevelt in 1938
to replace the more expensive Russian pattern. The engraved coat of arms is
simplified (cf. Plate 68).* CENTER: *Twelve-inch intaglio plate by Hawkes.*
(Smithsonian Inst.)

blanks from the Corning Glass Company, founded in 1868 by his good friend Amory Houghton, Senior. In 1903 Mr. Hawkes decided to make his own blanks according to Waterford formulas long treasured by his family. For this purpose he organized the Steuben Glass Works with his son, Samuel, and Frederick Carder of Stourbridge, England, as partners. From 1903 until 1918 blanks were made at the Steuben works for the cutters and engravers of the Hawkes Company. During World War I the Steuben works became a subsidiary of the Corning Glass Company.

MODERN STEUBEN GLASS

For the first time in its history the Corning Glass Works attempted production of finished cut glass at the Steuben works. The company operated at a loss until 1933 when, after repeated reorganization, Arthur Amory Houghton, Jr., great-grandson of the founder of the Corning Glass Works, assumed management and control of the Steuben division at Corning. Following a policy of making only fine handmade modern glass in which form and pattern were specifically designed for the medium of lead crystal, young Houghton developed Steuben glass to a point of perfection which has made it world famous.

The Gazelle Bowl was designed by Sidney Waugh and produced in 1935. This piece marks the beginning of the Houghton experiment in fine American cut and engraved glass. In 1935 the first Steuben exhibition was held at the Knoedler Gallery in New York and in 1937 Steuben glass received the Gold Medal at the Paris Exposition. Not all the glass is engraved and relatively few pieces are panel or flute cut. By far the most successful pieces have been those designed by Sidney Waugh, among them the Merry-Go-Round Bowl (Plate 128), the Mariners' Bowl, and the goblets depicting the Seven Deadly Sins (Plate 130).

LIBBEY GLASS

The Libbey Glass Company has a longer history of fine cut and engraved ware than any other glass company now in production.

PLATE 130

LEFT: Envy, engraved goblet, 7½ inches high, from the set, Seven Deadly Sins, designed by Sidney Waugh for Steuben. RIGHT: Mariners' Bowl, also by Waugh for Steuben. The composition of the glass, hand-fashioning and delicate shading of the engraving are modern developments of age old techniques. (Steuben Glass)

As the direct descendant of the old New England Glass Company it has a heritage of designs and patterns from which to choose modern adaptations. In 1940 the company began cutting a service of tableware called Modern American. It included various types of stemware, decorative bowls, trays, vases, centerpieces, candle holders, plates, and dishes. While most of it was plain crystal, some was decorated with stone-wheel cutting and copper-wheel engraving and followed the fine traditions of the Leighton family who cut and engraved similar glass for Libbey's parent company more than a hundred years before.

Although the patterns cut on the modern tableware were simple, as in the Saint Louis or Dutch Diamond motif shown in the Libbey table service (Plate 131), the pattern was withdrawn after World War II because of costs. In 1940 the Hermitage pattern sold for $24 a dozen in cocktail and wine glass sizes. Libbey is now producing two lines of tableware, "The Premier" and the "Thriftee." Modern patterns include Bamboo and Vienna, both cut with decorating. Windswept is hand cut. Less expensive Libbey patterns combine hand cutting with machine abrasion.

OTHER CONTEMPORARY CUTTING SHOPS

The most reliable figures obtainable gave fewer than two hundred and ten cutters and engravers employed in the glass industry at mid-century. This was fewer than were at work in one good-sized cutting shop fifty years ago when there were over a thousand such workrooms in operation. There are few apprentices learning the art and trade. While more glass is being cut now than in the years following World War II, the amount of tableware coming to the market is negligible compared to the quantities produced in the early years of the century.

Companies cutting tableware at the present time are Bryce Brothers Company, Mount Pleasant, Pennsylvania; Fostoria Glass Company, Moundsville, West Virginia; Libbey Glass Company, Toledo, Ohio; Steuben Glass Company, Corning, New York; Lotus Glass Company, Barnesville, Ohio; Susquehanna Glass Com-

PLATE 131

Saint Louis or Dutch Diamond set of modern tableware from Libbey. Discontinued after World War II. Such a set of goblets of fine lead metal, cut with this relatively simple motif retailed in 1940 for $24.00 a dozen. (Libbey Glass Co.)

pany, Columbia, Pennsylvania; Tiffin Art Glass Company, Tiffin, Ohio; Imperial Glass Company, Bellaire, Ohio; Seneca Glass Company, Morgantown, West Virginia.

For the most part modern cut tableware is stemmed and of light metal with simple surface decoration. Mr. Robert S. Holt, president of Bryce Brothers Company, describes their patterns as being "florals and geometrics applied to various patterns." Modern costs of manufacture simply make glass of heavier metal impractical and all but one of the contemporary glass houses has ceased making it altogether.

Some of the larger china and glass stores maintain a small cutting shop where initials or commemorative messages may be engraved on glass of good quality. Penrose Hawkes, a descendant of the Penrose and Hawkes families of Old Waterford, Ireland, maintains the Hawkes Crystal Shop in Corning, New York, where engraved ware is being made and sold in the remodeled show room of the T. G. Hawkes Glass Company.

Visitors to the Steuben Glass Center in Corning, New York, may see master engravers, the last of a great and noble craft, at work on the glass heirlooms of tomorrow.

THE FUTURE OF AMERICAN CUT GLASS

Fine American cut glass will probably always be expensive. Ingredients are expensive and labor costs high. Each piece before cutting is either free blown or mold blown. In 1950 there were 8,888 blowers employed in America. For a forty-hour week they received an average of $2.21 an hour. Many blowers could earn $100 a week. This is piece pay and the work is slow. A blower cannot be hurried. Glass cools at a definite rate and can only be worked at specific temperatures.

Cutters and engravers earned from $1.40 to $3.00 an hour— three times the average wage of 1891, and even then a nine-inch berry bowl sold for $35. Now the same bowl would have to sell for $100 retail to be profitable. It costs more to produce cut glass now than ever before. In 1947 an appraiser put a replacement value of

[314]

PLATE 132

Flamingo, *one of a series of twenty-one plates for which designs were adapted by Steuben artists from drawings of John James Audubon. Diameter, 10½ inches. In September, 1964, a full set of these plates retailed for $6,300. (Steuben Glass)*

$24,000 on the twenty-four-inch punch bowl which "Rufe" Denman cut for the Libbey Glass Company to display at the St. Louis Exposition in 1904. The twenty-one Audubon plates engraved by Steuben (Plate 132) retail for $6,300 for the set. One dozen Hawkes crystal goblets in a relatively simple cutting cost more than $100. These present-day costs include first quality material and highly skilled labor. As long as such costs exist our cut glass will remain a luxury and as a luxury it will be appreciated.

Meantime our younger glassmen are evolving a distinct style. Fine glass, like any other art craft, is a product of its environment. American glass of the middle years of the twentieth century reflects the times just as the somewhat precious cuttings of the 1830s were compatible with bracelet waists, Cabriolet bonnets, shoulder shawls, and sleeve extenders. The deep miter cuttings of the Gay Nineties were full of glitter, sparkle, and rich ornamentation. Modern glass is free of furbelows, sincere in design, and forthright in decoration.

Past generations of American glassmen took the old lead formulas of early English and Irish glassmakers and with American ingenuity found ways to refine the ingredients, measure the minerals, and most important of all, control the heat of fusion in furnaces. The craftsmanship of American glass, including the art of fashioning glass at 1,400 degrees Fahrenheit, has been passed on from father to son to grandson. The simplicity, the solid sturdy design of American glass today is the mid-twentieth century peak of an evolution which began in 1771 with Henry William Stiegel.

The development of American glass has been halting, but always one or two steadfast men have kept to the course of sincere and honest workmanship and design. It would now appear that American art-craftsmanship is once again on the threshold of a brilliant era in that most compelling of craft mediums—glass. And as an early sage of the glass industry, Antonio Neri, remarked some three centuries ago, "If the metal is as good as it can be . . . and the workmanship as good as it should be . . . and the design a mirror of tomorrow . . . the glass is the best there ever has been or is ever likely to be."

PLATE 133

Vase, 11 inches high, designed by Marie Laurencin for Steuben Glass. The design is reminiscent of engravings of the Middle Period which were influenced by continental traditions. (Steuben Glass)

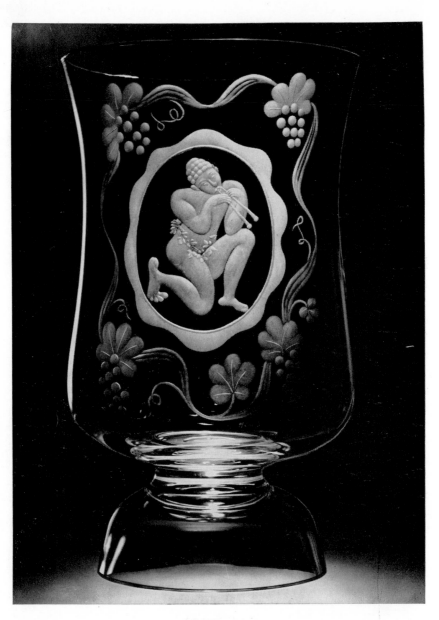

PLATE 134

*Vase, 15 inches high, designed by Henri Matisse for Steuben Glass. While
this piece and that on plate 133 are interesting as curiosities, they do not, in
the opinion of many collectors, have the important relation to the development of art craftsmanship in glass that is evidenced in the distinctly Amer-
can tradition of design exemplified by Sidney Waugh. (Plates 128 and 130)*

◇ ◇

CANDLESTICKS, CANDELABRA, CHANDELIERS

GLASS candlesticks were considered rather a precious trifle when they were first made in England in the seventeenth century. Until that time metal candle holders had served the purpose. The frivolous innovation was frowned on by the sturdy citizenry. However, before long glass candlesticks, candelabra, and chandeliers became a symbol of elegance and aristocracy. They have somehow managed to maintain their high social standing ever since.

It takes time and a full purse to assemble a representative collection of cut glass candlesticks for they are fairly rare. Many of the earliest ones made in America about 1825 were molded with square step bases, only the cup or bobêche was curved and cut in scallops. The prisms which hung from the bobêche were made of fine clear or colored glass which was cut and polished. After 1830 candlesticks were cut in flute, panel, and step cuttings and they were always ornamental rather than practical. The prisms of the early candlesticks were the button or jewel head pendeloque or spear type, and the candlesticks were sometimes twelve inches high. As the century progressed the candlesticks became shorter, broader, and more ornate; the prisms grew longer, and the colors brighter.

Deming Jarves at Sandwich specialized in luster-enameled cut candlesticks with crystal bobêches and prisms. These ornate candlesticks were called lusters and were made in pink, yellow, blue, or green glass with opal, opaque, or colored overlay. Cut glass prisms hung around the bobêches and sparkled in the candlelight. These are the lusters that have been extensively copied in modern Czechoslovakian glass. It is possible that similar lusters were made in other glasshouses since Pittsburgh, Wheeling, and Brooklyn companies made ornamental candlesticks and were known to have their own recipes for fine opaque glass suitable for casing and overlay.

Square molded candlesticks came into vogue in 1880 with the Brilliant Period and followed it through to the end. They were made in all heights from three to twenty inches. Many sets of candlesticks were made in many types of cutting. Then toward the end of the period, around 1905, inferior glass was molded into tall square candlesticks. These were sold in great quantity to country stores and drugstores to be used as supports for glass shelves. Some have sketchy crosshatching or superficial etching. Intrinsically they are of slight value, but collectors find them interesting and the better ones make effective table settings with modern glass and china.

A representative collection (Plate 135) of cut glass candlesticks might include handmade examples of early panel cutting; some candlesticks with scalloped bottoms (F, G, H, and I), some with bobêches and prisms, fine Sandwich lusters and flute-cut sticks (C) in clear colors, yellow, green, or red; one or two short-stemmed candlesticks (D and E) with loop handles; representative engraved candlesticks from the Middle Period; cut pieces (A and B) from the later Brilliant Period; and several square-molded and cut-over candlesticks from the late nineteenth century. Since candlesticks were frequently made to order after individual designs, unique pieces should be included wherever possible. In any case, a comprehensive collection should include examples from all three periods in all types of workmanship and with all methods of decoration.

CANDELABRA

Rarer than the candelabrum itself is the owner of a prism glass, multibranched, spear-hung and jewel-chained candlestick who does not firmly believe that it was manufactured by George Penrose himself at Waterford before the turn of the eighteenth century. Very likely more prism candelabra were imported into this country

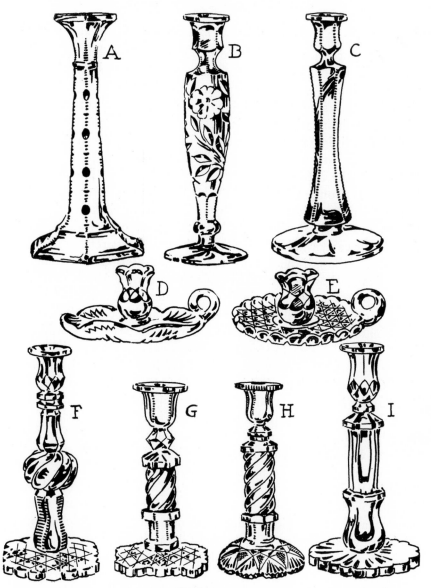

PLATE 135

*Crystal candlesticks: (A. and C.) Flute-cut with notching. Brilliant Period.
(B.) Intaglio cutting in floral design. Late Brilliant Period. (D. and E.) Flat
candlesticks similar to those cut at Sandwich during Middle Period. (F. G. H.
and I.) Very rare American copies of early Waterford candlesticks. (Reproduced from Hawkes' files)*

than other pieces of Irish glass (except tumblers) and it is true that Irish factories continued to make prism lighting fixtures long after their export of tableware had ceased. However, many very fine candelabra were also cut in America. William Gillinder's Franklin works in Philadelphia made a specialty of candelabra which were hung with cut prisms.

Before Gillinder there were the Fisher brothers in New York making fine cut candelabra and the Eichbaums in Pittsburgh specialized in the cutting of prisms and jewel chains. The New England Glass Company and the Wheeling houses also made prism candelabra. American designs were similar to those of imported pieces, but until family records, catalogues, or drawings can be found, our early candelabra will for the most part remain unknown.

Not so the girandoles of the Middle Period, the Paul-and-Virginias as they were called by contemporaries. About 1840 these mantel pieces were much in fashion. They were made of bronze, brass, and French gilt and mounted on marble bases. The figures represented Columbus, Lancelot, George and Martha Washington, Paul Revere, Robin Hood, Pocahontas, and the Crusaders. Most of the prisms for them were cut in Brooklyn, New York and Meriden, Connecticut. The fashion was at fever pitch when the novel, *Paul and Virginia,* was enjoying great popularity so manufacturers made many bases depicting this romantic pair. The figures at length became so common that girandoles, no matter what their subject, were known as Paul-and-Virginias (Plate 136).

Many candelabra from America were exhibited at the World's Fair in Paris in 1856 and at the New York Industrial Exhibition in 1854. The trend then in lighting fixtures was toward the stiff almost awkward design which culminated in the candelabrum exhibited by the Mount Washington Glass Works at the Centennial Exhibition in 1876. While candelabra of similar design may not appeal to collectors, the Mount Washington example is typical of the Middle Period. Such candelabra are rare, and documented pieces command a high price.

During the Brilliant Period, candelabra were made by the T. G. Hawkes Glass Company, the Libbey Glass Company, C. Dorflinger and Sons, and L. Straus and Company. Pieces of this time are usu-

PLATE 136

Girandole mantel set. American, about 1845. Sets were made with many figures. Columbus, Lancelot and Elaine, George and Martha Washington, and Paul and Virginia were favorites. (Mrs. Lida Snowden Henesey)

ally of fine metal with deep cutting. They too are rare. Later ones from the J. D. Bergen Company have cut glass bases and silver mountings. They are not so rare as the earlier candlesticks but are equally desirable and expensive.

An interesting collection might include a candelabrum from each of the important glasshouses in each period, or simply different bases of the Paul-and-Virginia type.

CHANDELIERS

Probably one out of ten cut glass chandeliers hanging in American homes and now labeled Waterford ever saw Ireland. At least nine times as many chandeliers were made in America in the Early Period as were imported from across the ocean. Chandeliers were difficult to transport and shipping space was needed for the smaller commodities on which the duty was lower and the profit higher. Furthermore, Bakewell's and other glass companies in Pittsburgh and Wheeling soon learned that the market was good for cut glass chandeliers particularly in the fine houses of Baltimore, Charleston, Savannah, Mobile, New Orleans, and Saint Louis. The cost of transporting carefully boxed chandeliers from Pittsburgh down the Ohio River, thence to the Mississippi, and around into eastern seaports was not high in comparison to transoceanic shipping. And local glass was duty free.

The earliest of these lighting fixtures now known is the Lafayette chandelier which hangs in the Pennsylvania Room of the Carnegie Library in Pittsburgh (Plate 137). As a result of a somewhat confused family record its history is not clear. While it is undoubtedly the chandelier that hung in the parlor of the old Mansion House in Pittsburgh during Lafayette's visit in 1825 and probably the very one that lighted the receiving line at the reception for the visitor, it could also either be the same chandelier or an exact duplicate of the six-candle fixture that Peter William Eichbaum made in 1810 for the Masonic hall in Kerr's Inn, Pittsburgh.

Eichbaum was running a hotel of his own at the time, having retired from active duty in the old Pittsburgh Glassworks. How-

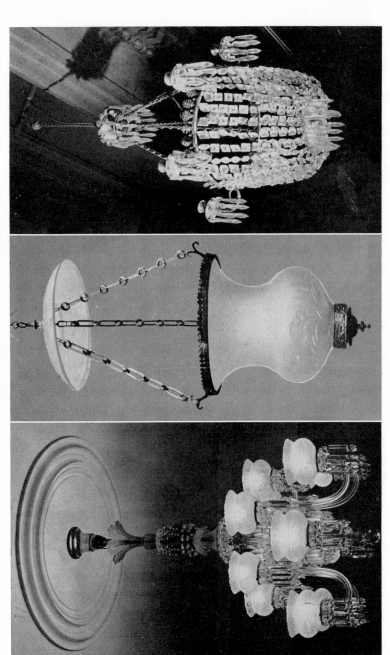

PLATE 137

LEFT: *Gas fixture, clear and frosted glass, from an old house in Geneva, N. Y. American, about 1845.* CENTER: *Hanging lantern with smoke bell, New England, but taken to China on a sailing vessel. (Both J. A. Lloyd Hyde)* RIGHT: *First chandelier known to be American-made. Six branches for candles. Probably Peter William Eichbaum about 1804. (Carnegie Library, Pittsburgh)*

ever, his old friend and former associate, General James O'Hara, was enthusiastic over starting a chandelier business in Pittsburgh, not so much for financial gain as because he had a taste for the elegance of crystal chandeliers and felt that their manufacture would be good publicity for the Pittsburgh glass factories. General O'Hara persuaded William Price, (who had been apprenticed to a brass founder and apparently knew brass better than glass) to make the brass frames and the chains. The glass was fine pot metal made at O'Hara's own Pittsburgh glassworks and the cutting was done by Eichbaum in his shop at The Sign of the Indian Queen.

There is record of at least seven chandeliers having been made in the early years of the nineteenth century in Pittsburgh. The largest was the twenty-candle fixture which was donated by General O'Hara to the First Presbyterian Church of Pittsburgh and hung there in 1804 when the church was built. A smaller six-candle chandelier made by Eichbaum for the lodge rooms of Ohio Lodge Number 113 in Kerr's Inn, was probably donated to the Masons by General O'Hara. It is probable, too, that another of the same small six-candle chandeliers was made for Eichbaum's hotel, The Sign of the Indian Queen, and later either sold or lent by them to the Mansion House, or to friends who lent it to the Mansion House, thus saving it for posterity. Whether the one now known is the twin of the Kerr six-candle fixture or the identical one may never be known, but it fits the description precisely. The piece was designed by Eichbaum, who was a German. The shape and arrangement of the jewel chains is German and very different from English and French designs then in use. However, the decoration of the brass crown reflects the English background of the brass founder, William Price. This is the earliest known American-made chandelier.

As time went on American designers followed the English and Irish forms of chandeliers in vogue in Europe. Plate 137 pictures a smoke bell made in New England and transported to China on a sailing vessel. Blue tinct is almost always pronounced in imported chandeliers. American pieces are usually of fine prismatic quality and good clear metal. Furthermore, it is to be remembered that a house built in 1812 had either a domestic chandelier or

PLATE 138

Chandelier made by William Gillinder at the Franklin works in Philadelphia, 1876. Frosted center piece and cups are typical of Gillinder chandeliers of this period. Originally made for electricity and one of the first so designed. (Mrs. S. N. Benham)

none, since there were no imports from Ireland in that war year.

William Gillinder's chandeliers of the Centennial period were elaborate and show much sandblast decoration (Plate 138). These are rare because glass so decorated was not strong enough to support the pendent prisms and chipped or cracked with the years. The one illustrated is not in perfect condition, but it is a fine example of an American chandelier of the late Middle Period. Originally designed for an electric fixture, it has never been rewired or changed in any way.

◇ ◇

LAMPS

FOR THE collector, cut glass lamps are an excellent specialty and
the possibilities are wide. America controlled the lamp market
during the nineteenth century and sent so many thousands of whale-
oil, Argand, Astral, and kerosene lamps to the ports of the world
that collectors' pieces of undeniable American origin sometimes
turn up in foreign lands.

Probably no other item of glassware was made in such volume
and variety. Yet collections of lamps are not so common as those of
bottles, decanters, and goblets and there are still a reasonable number of fine cut glass lamps to be found on dealers' shelves and at
auctions. Of course lamps of quality metal and distinguished workmanship are rarer than everyday lamps and consequently command
higher prices. Good examples of Early American flute cutting,
copper-wheel engraving, and other cut decoration are found on
lamp bases, shades, and particularly on the crystal pendeloques.

Although candlesticks, candelabra, and chandeliers were used in
wealthy households in America and Europe before and after the
1800s, lamps were the utilitarian equipment of the middle class.
Authors and poets wrote by lamplight, scholars, doctors, and law-
yers studied by lamps, preachers prepared their sermons by the
light of lamps, and many a mother burned what was literally mid-
night oil to finish a wedding dress. This does not imply that lamps
were not also put to use in mansions. Planters and bankers kept
their accounts by lamplight, too. In other words, the candelabra,
the chandelier, and the candlestick were, during the nineteenth
century, ornamental devices for special occasions, holidays, and

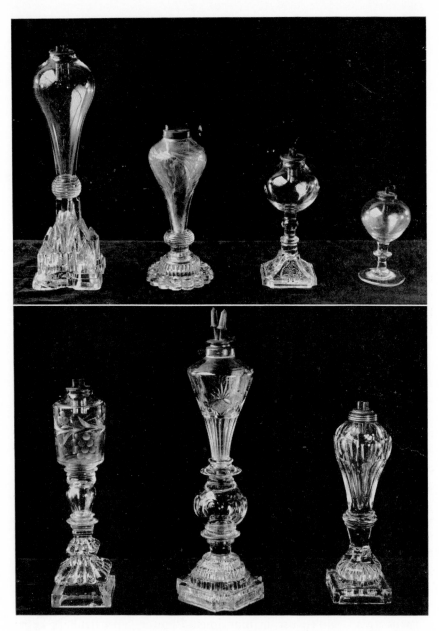

PLATE 139

when company came. It was the lamp of standing or hanging design that provided the practical means of illumination. The same general rules of design development that apply to desk and mantel lamps also apply to hanging lamps of the same period.

Different fuels were in use during the nineteenth century and these are of interest to the collector since fuel determined the type of lamp. No exact chronology is possible. Whale oil was in use long after the perfection of kerosene, and kerosene lighted many houses after others on the same street had converted to gas or even to electricity. Fuels came into use in approximately this order: from 1775 to 1845 common whale oil, sperm oil, seal oil, lard oil; between 1845 and 1850, camphene; about 1855 to 1860, kerosene; and from 1880 to 1900, natural gas and electricity.

WHALE-, LARD-OIL, ARGAND LAMPS

The early whale-oil lamp is a simple device which looks much like a kerosene lamp except that the top of the oil font is fitted with one or two small wick tubes (Plate 139). These whale-oil lamps were made extensively in Massachusetts by the New England and the Boston and Sandwich glass companies. Sometimes Sandwich lamps are found with shades but more often the shades have been broken. The bases are frequently made of colored lead glass, cased, cut, or engraved.

Lamps for sperm oil or spermaceti and seal oil were similar to those using the common whale oil. The earliest whale-oil or seal-oil lamps made of metal were without chimneys. The wicks were simple stringlike affairs which protruded at the top of the lamp through wick tubes. Even when there were two wicks the effect of the whale-oil lamp was dim indeed.

Lard-oil lamps were used in western or inland communities where whale oil was not available. Few lard-oil lamps were cut.

Seeking to increase the light of the whale-oil lamp, M. Aimé Argand, a Swiss engineer from Geneva, invented a relatively simple device in 1783 and revolutionized the illumination of the world. The wick of the Argand lamp is woven round like a sleeve and slipped over a hollow metal tube. The end of the tube which is lowered into the whale oil is closed at the bottom. The metal is perforated at the top admitting a current of air to circulate through this tube and aid combustion in the wick at the points of perforation. So remarkable was this sudden illumination of the dark that newspapers of the day advised readers accustomed to the soft glow of candles to use eye shades.

Argand lamps, which are now rare, have large oil fonts directly beneath the wick, and they cast a broad shadow on the desk or table immediately below. The oil fonts are usually made of metal. Only the shades are of cut glass. Like the Astral, Solar, and the later kerosene lamp shades, they are vase-shaped with a hole at the top for the chimney and at the bottom a flaring rim from which prisms are frequently suspended.

America, quick to seize upon the new and practical idea of the Argand lamp, immediately began manufacturing. But Argand lamps used only spermaceti as fuel and this fatty substance, found in the heads of sperm whales, was more expensive than common whale oil. In 1800 two Americans, White and Smithhurst, patented a lamp on the same principle that would burn common whale or seal oil. These lamps had globe fonts some of which were cut and mounted on cylindrical metal columns with marble bases. They are frequently sold as true Argand lamps although they are a variation on the original principle. Fine examples may still be found for they are not as rare as the larger and heavier Argands.

ASTRAL LAMPS, CAMPHENE, AND SOLAR LAMPS

The Astral (Plate 140) lamp was another improvement on the Argand principle and it was America's favorite from the time of its invention early in the nineteenth century until after kerosene came into common use following the commercial production of petro-leum. The Astral lamp has a ring-shaped reservoir so placed that shadow is not cast directly below the flame. It was invented by Benjamin Thompson of Woburn, Massachusetts, who was made Count Rumford by the Elector of Bavaria for his services in physics and illumination.

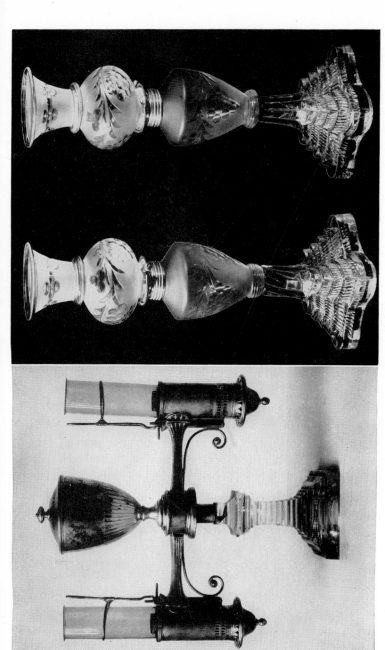

PLATE 140

LEFT: *Early Astral lamp, said to have been used by Washington at Mount Vernon. Base in step cutting. Oil reservoir is in center, above wick level of two burners. (Smithsonian Inst.)* RIGHT: *Early whale oil lamps, frosted shades, cut fonts, probably Sandwich. A matched pair with shades is rare. (Edison Inst.)*

The true Astral has the oil font at the side, above the wick burner and shade which are mounted over a small cylinder at the end of a horizontal arm. Oil is fed by gravity into the small cylinder below the wick burner. There are double and single-arm Astral lamps and for mantel decoration some elegant sets were made with a center lamp of two bars, one on either side, and two single-arm lamps for the ends. These mantel lamps are usually of metal. They were similar to the small whale-oil lamps and had shades from which cut prisms dangled. In time any tall table lamp with a slender central column supporting an oil font set close under the wick burner was called an Astral lamp, but the true Astral has the horizontal bar with one or two wick burners.

After 1850 lamps using a highly explosive combination of camphor and turpentine became popular. Camphene lamps were dangerous because their inflammable fuel was ignited by the slightest spark, but they were so fashionable that many women risked the danger of explosion and fire carrying the small cut glass hand lamps from room to room. Camphene lamps were particularly popular for bedroom and boudoir. Many such lamps were not much bigger than a mustard pot.

The cutting is usually a combination of the old strawberry-diamond, bull's-eye, or block motifs. The tops are of metal and snugly fitted over the top of the oil font. There are usually two wick tubes which vary in length from one inch to three inches extending out from the top. There may be only one, however. Usually these tubes are fitted with small caps attached to the metal top by short chains. These caps were supplied to snuff the flame since it was hazardous to blow out a flame over the camphene font. Anyone who has ever smelled a whale or lard-oil lamp knows why the ladies of the mid-nineteenth century preferred the pleasant odor of the dangerous camphene.

Solar lamps were invented by Cornelius and Company of Philadelphia in 1843. They are an adaptation of the Argand lamp principle. All such lamps are marked with the Cornelius trade-mark and patent date. Early examples burned whale oil or sperm oil, later styles used kerosene for fuel. Solar lamps have round wicks, bulblike chimneys, globe or flaring shades which are cut or sand-

PLATE 141

Pair of glass kerosene lamps. Fonts are crystal glass with ruby overlay engraved with grape design. Fonts are joined to opaque-white, pressed glass bases by lacquered and gilded brass couplings. American, about 1860. (Smithsonian Inst.)

blasted usually in floral decoration on colored glass. Shades are frequently hung with crystal cut prisms.

Kerosene replaced whale and lard oil and the camphene lamps because it was less expensive than spermaceti, less inflammable than camphene, and burned without the disagreeable odor of the animal fats. Early kerosene lamps followed the style of the later Argand lamps, that is, a round, colored glass fuel font mounted on a metal column over a marble base. Later kerosene lamps (Plate 141) were made to resemble the early nineteenth-century whale-oil lamps, in which a blown glass font was mounted while still hot on a molded glass base. Toward the end of the nineteenth century the Brilliant cuttings were used—Russian, hob-star, and other deep and curved-split motifs.

LAMP SHADES AND CHIMNEYS

The first lamp shades to be made in America were those draft protectors commonly associated with candlesticks and called hurricane shades. Such shades were made at the New England Glass Company as early as 1820 to be used on whale-oil lamps. They have been made from that time to this and are in common use in the twentieth century on electric lights.

The flaring shade often associated with a student lamp was first used on the Argand lamps and was cut in America in great quantity and variety after 1830. Such shades were made of colored glass, often sandblasted to deflect the glare and were decorated by shallow wheel cutting. Often they were hung with prisms in spear and pendeloque types. Globe shades made to cut down the greater brilliance of the kerosene flame, are of later manufacture, very few having been made before 1860. Some of the earlier examples are also hung with prisms.

The lamp chimney is said to have been the accidental invention of a man who placed a bottle over a flame to heat the liquid in it. The liquid boiled away, the bottom split off the bottle, and the cylinder that remained slipped down over the flame. To everyone's surprise it did not break. Henceforth glass chimneys proved so

PLATE 142

Shade for kerosene lamp, about 1860. Frosted and cut. (N.-Y. Hist. Soc.)

much more satisfactory than the iron ones then in use that they were soon generally adopted. Lamp chimneys are rarely cut except for hurricane shades which are in effect, chimneys.

MANUFACTURERS

Both the New England Glass Company and the Bakewell Glass Company made whale-oil lamps on the two-wick principle before 1820, but since all early whale-oil lamps look very much alike and the style of manufacture was the same, identification with factory or even locality is at this late date almost impossible unless there is documentary evidence. The fact that two cut glass lamps look alike and have similar bases and shades does not always mean that they came from the same glasshouse.

Of interest to the collector is the advertisement of the Bakewell, Page and Bakewell Company for November 20, 1827: "Astral or Sinumbral lamps on pedestals or for suspension, also Tuscan, Vase, Mantel and Chamber Lamps, in addition to their usual stock of plain and cut flint glass."

The colored and cut whale-oil lamps accredited to the Boston and Sandwich Glass Company were made at about this time. One point regarding these lamps has baffled collectors. The fonts appear to be of much better metal than the bases. It is now believed that in order to meet competition short cuts were used at the Sandwich glass factory and later copied by the Brooklyn and Pittsburgh glass houses. Lamp bases or feet were molded from common clear glass in square and step molds. Globe fonts were blown from fine lead glass in white and colors onto the hot molded bases while still in a viscose condition. After annealing the lamps were decorated by application to a moving wheel.

Type of lamp should be the first consideration of the collector. For a cabinet, lamps that have been converted to electricity are of slight value, no matter how rare the glass or how beautiful the shade or prisms because the old burners can not be replaced. There are, incidentally, some "electrified" lamps on the market which have baffled collectors who did not know their origin. When John

Dorflinger of White Mills, Pennsylvania, bought the stock of the old C. Dorflinger glassworks he found shelves of apothecary bottles which he sold to New York lampmakers for bases. These pieces were of course old genuine Dorflinger, and some of them of very beautiful red, blue, or green glass with elaborate cutting and gilding. The bottles were made for display in drugstore windows. For those collecting cut glass bottles they are interesting and now demand many times their original value from collectors of "apothecary furniture" but they should not be included in a collection of old lamps. The same would be true of cut glass vases which have been converted to lamps. These do not belong in a collection of lamps but in one of vases and then only after being reconverted. Vases and bottles that have been drilled to make holes for wiring are seldom prized by a collector of cabinet pieces.

A representative collection of cut glass lamps might include: an example of a whale-oil lamp, perhaps one known to have been made at the New England Glass Company, and another known to have come from the Boston and Sandwich Glass Company; a camphene burner; and an Astral lamp with cut shade; some Argand lamps from the earliest period (1800) to the Solar type base and shade (1843). Care should be taken in selecting lamps to examine font, shade, and prisms for modern substitutions: an Astral lamp which still has its original shade and prisms is worth considerably more than an Argand lamp from an even earlier period with a newer shade or with prisms from a modern Czechoslovakian glass factory.

PLATE 143

UPPER, LEFT: *Pair of brandy decanters with flute cutting and bands of sharp-diamond motif. New England Glass Co., 1817–1830. (Mrs. S. N. Benham)*
RIGHT: *Whisky tumbler and decanter, cut from pattern that won the gold medal at Franklin Institute in 1827 for Bakewell Co. (Philadelphia Mus.)*
LOWER: *Brandy decanters owned by Henry Clay.* LEFT: *Perhaps by Isaac Duval;* RIGHT: *Bakewell. (Smithsonian Inst.)*

❖ ❖

CHAPTER XV

DECANTERS, COLOGNE BOTTLES, CONDIMENT SETS

PROBABLY the first glass vessel ever made was a bottle and decanters, jugs, cruets, and cologne bottles still comprise the largest category in cut glass. The Rodneys were the first decanters to be brought to this country and copied here (Plate 41). These were the ordinary bottles without neck rings. They were made of indifferent metal and decorated with simple wheel engraving. While Rodneys were relatively common in their day, they are prized by modern collectors as interesting examples of early glass.

The decanters made by Benjamin Bakewell in the 1820s are round, sturdy, and generally well cut (Plate 143). The Robinson decanter (Plate 45) which follows the cylinder shape in vogue in England in 1827 is one of the finest American decanters of this period. The heavy, flute-cut decanters, some with steeple stoppers (Plate 58), were much in style in 1840 and can still be found in a variety of shapes, sizes, and metals. Decanters following the shape of champagne bottles came later (Plate 6). Decanters with star-cut bottoms were made after 1830. In America definite styles in bottles disappeared after the beginning of the Brilliant Period when, contrary to the rule in England and Ireland, shapes so varied that they were no longer an indication of age.

A wide variety of shapes, patterns, and stoppers make decanters most interesting to collect. (See Plate 144.) The Daisy cordial (A) was cut during the later years of the period. The popular Croesus pattern was a favorite for claret decanters (B). A variation of the Russian decorates a barrel decanter (C) which probably lacks the original stopper. Another claret decanter (E) is cut with a straw-

PLATE 144

Decanters: (A.) Intaglio daisy cutting. (B.) Croesus pattern. (C.) Barrel type. All typical of Brilliant Period with cut neck rings and lapidary stoppers. (D.) Globe, Russian pattern. (E.) Claret pitcher, strawberry-diamond and panel motifs. (F.) Grape pattern, cut intaglio. (From scrapbooks of T. G. Hawkes Glass Co.)

berry-diamond field, while a similar decanter (D) is cut in the true Russian pattern. An intaglio cutting in the Grape pattern (F) is representative of the finer work of the late years of the Brilliant Period.

DECANTER RINGS AND OTHER DECORATION

Some collectors put emphasis on the importance of neck rings on decanters. On English and Irish glass these are some indication of origin. The triple ring was most frequently used at Waterford. Cork glasshouses favored the feather ring, and the triangular cutting originated at Belfast. These are only general indications and cannot be taken as evidence for positive identification. In American glass they mean little except, perhaps to suggest the locality in which the particular glassworker was apprenticed. The New England Glass Company made fine feather rings on many of their decanters. Bakewell used three rings. Those on the Curling decanters (Plate 51) are "trailed," that is, applied in the Venetian manner—superimposed while hot on hot metal.

The cutting on Irish decanters between 1780 and 1850 follows a trend from panel cutting to large diamonds and then to splits and festoons; arching came next with nailhead diamonds. The strawberry and crosshatched diamonds were popular contemporaneously, followed by flute cutting. Finally, panel cutting in combination with splits and hollow prisms leading into the diminutive or miniature solid field cutting.

Earlier decanters, that is, those made before 1820, have plain ground bottoms, sometimes showing a round indentation where the pontil was cracked off and the scar polished. After 1820 the bottoms were cut, first in a wheel of intersecting splits, later in a star. Plain-bottom decanters were cut after 1820, but the star splits were not used on the bottoms of vessels before 1820, either in Ireland or America.

PLATE 145

LEFT: *Decanter, 15 inches, with Saint Louis or Dutch diamond cutting on neck, sharp diamond-band decoration. Shield inscribed C. Belonged to family of Commodore Isaac Chauncey. New England Glass Co., 1860.* CENTER: *Heavy lead glass decanter, Early American Period. (Both N.-Y. Hist. Soc.)* RIGHT: *Brandy set, Sweeney, Wheeling, W. Va., about 1840. (Oglebay Inst.)*

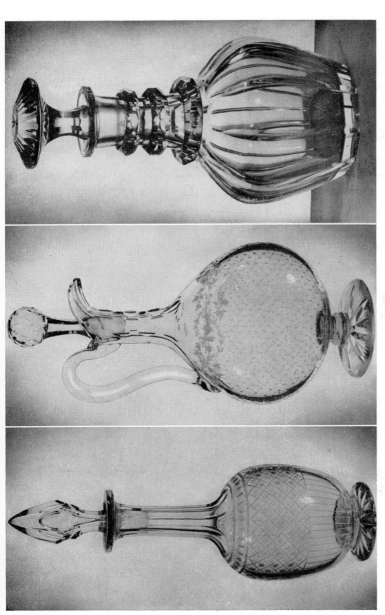

PLATE 146

LEFT AND CENTER: *Decanter and claret jug engraved and cut by Christian Dorflinger, Greenpoint Works, Brooklyn, 1860.* RIGHT: *Decanter variously accredited, George and P. C. Dummer, Jersey City, about 1845, or John L. Gilliland, Brooklyn works, of the same period. Fine quality metal, split cutting. (N.-Y. Hist. Soc.)*

PLATE 147

Cologne bottles, Brilliant Period. (A.) Globe-shaped, hobnail motif. (B.)
Swirled Panel. (C.) Globe-shaped, Richelieu pattern. (D.) Intaglio daisy.
(E.) Unusual flaring type, strawberry-diamond motif. (F. and G.) Engraved.
(H. and I.) Catsup bottle and cruet. (From catalogue of J. Hoare and Co.)

COLOGNE BOTTLES

In 1875 when the great vogue for cut and fancy bottles saved many a company from bankruptcy, all sizes and shapes were made for perfume and cologne. (See Plate 147.) Globe colognes were very popular. The hobnail motif is used on A and the Richelieu on C. Cylinder bottles dominated the style during the middle of the Brilliant Period. The swirled Panel pattern was used on a bottle five inches high, not including the stopper (B). Pillar and diamond cuttings decorate a four-inch globe cologne bottle. Light surface engraving was used on a bottle with a peaked stopper (D) and cutting combined with light engraving on another (F).

An unusual bottle with a flared bottom (E) combines strawberry-diamond and gothic-panel cuttings. The butterfly and daisy bottle (G), though fairly common, is decorative and certainly collectible, as are many other cologne and perfume bottles.

CONDIMENT SETS

The Brilliant Period may well be called the condiment period. Every well-set table carried an array of the spicy attributes of the kitchen neatly done up in cut glass bottles of suitable design. Catsup bottles were short, usually not over six inches, with handles, and broad lips (Plate 147, H). Vinegar and oil cruets were usually cut in pairs sometimes of equal size, sometimes with the oil cruet somewhat larger than the vinegar. Tabasco bottles were not over five inches high.

One cruet (Plate 147, I) indicates what befell fine American cut glass toward the end of the Brilliant Period. In an effort to meet competition, manufacturers and cutters strained their imaginations to the breaking point. In this cruet there are visible ten different motifs. Furthermore the bottle is square, the foot is molded and out of balance, and the stopper is overornamented. Collectors value such pieces only as oddities and points of comparison for the fine pieces in their collections.

[347]

PLATE 148

UPPER, LEFT TO RIGHT: *Cologne bottles. Strawberry-diamond combination, Middle Period; two Early block-cut bottles; globe-shaped and sharp-diamond field from Brilliant. (Mrs. John M. Feeney)* LOWER, LEFT TO RIGHT: *Rare, old bottle with Saint Louis cutting; two engraved bottles; two of aquamarine glass, panel-cut from Middle Period. (Author's Collection)*

PLATE 149

UPPER: *Cruets from Brilliant Period. (Mrs. John M. Feeney)* LOWER, LEFT:
*Salt shakers, Boston and Sandwich Glass Co., 1825–1830. (Mrs. S. N. Ben-
ham)* RIGHT: *Double perfume bottle or gemel, 5½ inches high. Clear blown
lead glass, New England Glass Co., engraved by Louis Vaupel in 1870s.
(Brooklyn Mus.)*

◇ ◇

BOXES, BASKETS, KNIFE RESTS

D URING the Brilliant Period every possible article was made of cut glass and some impossible ones, too. Nothing escaped. Toilet sets and tableware, mantel and desk appointments, even umbrella stands were decorated under the influence of the moving wheel. Today the smaller items are fun to collect, since ingenuity produced them in so many different forms. From 1880 until 1910 glass boxes were made in a variety of shapes, sizes, and patterns and for many purposes. There were jewel, glove, handkerchief, salve, puff, powder, and hairpin boxes, and also hair-receivers. Although modern collectors now use the larger boxes for candy, and the square or oblong ones for cigarettes, most cut glass boxes were originally designed as boudoir accessories (Plate 150).

The first piece (A) is an oval jewel box, measuring five by seven inches, cut in chair-bottom, hob-star, and fan motifs with sterling silver mountings. The blank for it was made by the Union Glass Company and the cutting was done by J. Hoare and Company. Another large jewel box (B) of later date is eight inches in diameter, and though without silver fittings, is prized by collectors. Footed puff boxes are rare. One I saw with an intaglio Daisy pattern suggests that it was cut during the closing years of the Brilliant Period. The one pictured (C) which shows a combination cutting of strawberry-diamond, half flute, and notched prism motifs is earlier. While both pieces are interesting in a collection, this is the better one and would cost from three to four times as much to reproduce today as the box with the intaglio Daisy.

The Nassau pattern, a late combination of chair-bottom and

[350]

PLATE 150

Glass boxes. (A.) Oval jewel box, 5 by 7 inches. (B.) Jewel box, Nassau pattern. (C.) Footed puff box, rare. (D.) Jewel box, Nassau pattern. (E.) Strawberry-diamond and bull's-eye motifs. (F.) Puff box. (G. H. and I.) Clermont pattern. (From scrapbooks of T. G. Hawkes Glass Co.)

daisy cuttings, was much used on boxes. A jewel box (D) is illustrated in this pattern. Nassau was also cut in handkerchief, glove, powder, and salve boxes, cologne bottles, and dresser trays.

Puff boxes in the Gotham pattern were cut in several sizes, from three and five up to eight inches. One square puff box was cut in bull's-eye and notched prism. Another, which we have chosen to illustrate (E) is of good design cut in strawberry-diamond and bull's-eye. It measures six inches across, three and one-half inches high. Another is a puff box, (F), very late Brilliant Period. The cutting is hob-star-and-fan and the box measures four and one-half inches.

Collectors frequently find boxes of varying sizes all of one pattern and fitted with silver tops. Two such salve boxes (G and H) are illustrated with a puff box (I) to match cut in the Clermont pattern. These were cut on Pairpoint glass blanks and fitted with silver covers by Gorham. All pieces illustrated are clear crystal. Colored cut glass boxes are extremely rare since colored glass was not popular during the years when cut glass boxes were fashionable.

BASKETS

The idea of making baskets of glass did not originate in America. The early Venetians tried their skill at delicate glass replicas of woven cane and reed baskets, but as early as 1827 glassmakers in Sandwich and Cambridge were making baskets for their own amusement or as presents for their families. Today such baskets are collectors' items. It was not until the Brilliant Period that manufacturers produced glass baskets commercially. They were very popular. From 1890 until 1905 a cut glass basket filled with seasonal garden flowers was a usual centerpiece for fashionable luncheon and dining tables. A number of these baskets are illustrated on Plate 151.

The baskets with vaselike stems and flaring tops are perhaps the most common. One I know has an interesting fan cutting of miter splits combined with a large English strawberry-diamond. It is twelve inches high not including the handle. An example of step

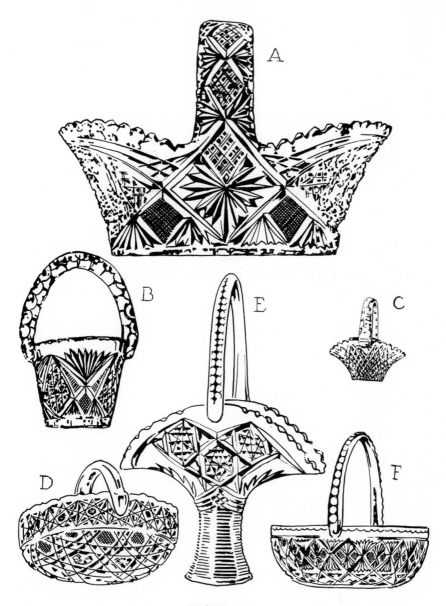

PLATE 151

Cut glass baskets relatively common fifty years ago are rare today. (A.) Fine type with flat handle. (B.) Small, bucket-shaped. (C.) Strawberry-diamond cutting. (D.) Gotham pattern. (E.) Prized shape for centerpiece. (F.) Flat basket for fruit. (From catalogue of J. Hoare and Co.)

cutting, or horizontal prism, is illustrated (E) on a similar basket.

Flat baskets (A, D and F) were also made for flowers or fruit and were fashioned in a variety of shapes. The Gotham pattern was cut on baskets of different sizes the nine-inch one illustrated (D). Oblong baskets with straight sides and flat handles were also prized. They are rare now in any cutting. Smaller baskets were cut for bonbons and lump sugar. For these the strawberry-diamond is the most common cutting (C). Small bucket-shaped baskets (B) are the rarest and the most valuable.

KNIFE RESTS

Knife rests make a collection more easily housed than larger, heavier pieces of cut glass. From 1850 to 1900 many were cut, some of them in patterns to match larger services. They were made in all sizes from small individual ones, sometimes used as place card holders, to large rests intended for the carving knife and fork. The finest knife rests are those in which quality metal has been cut with precision and in exact motifs.

Although knife rests probably were not made before 1850, they came into such vogue at that time that they are to be found in colored and cut glass of all descriptions. A representative collection has been made by Ruth H. Fenstermacher of Warren, Pennsylvania (Plate 152). Probably the oldest piece in the collection is Number 1 in Row D. Number 13 in Row E is also old with unpolished engraving on the bar. The crystal glass rests with lapidary cutting (Numbers 1, 2, and 3 in Row C), are relatively common, but the lapidary-cut knife rests in colored glass are rare. Numbers 6, 7, and 8 in Row E are respectively vaseline, blue, and amber. A few of the pieces, Numbers 12 and 16 in Row A; 6 in Row B, and 10 in Row E are of pressed glass. Number 1 in Row E is made of metal.

Many of the leading cut glass manufacturers of the Brilliant Period are represented in Miss Fenstermacher's collection and many of the more popular motifs can be identified. Notched-prism was used to decorate Numbers 1 and 2 in Row A. The hob-star motif is represented on Number 13 in Row C and Number 5 in

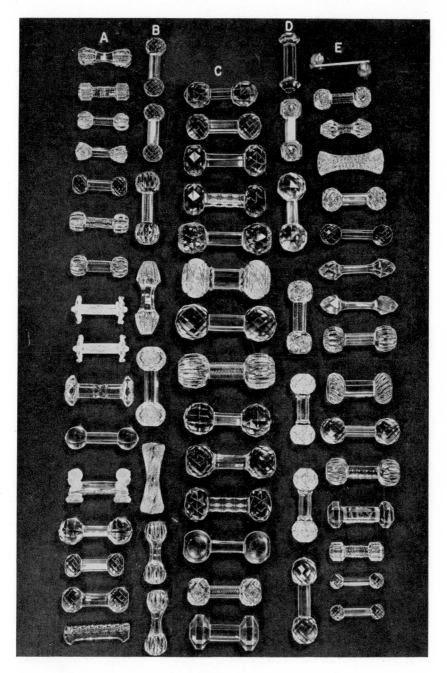

PLATE 152

Knife rests collected by Ruth H. Fenstermacher of Warren, Pennsylvania.
Collection includes lapidary cuttings, Hob-Star, Notched Prism, and engraved
patterns.

Row E. The sixth rest in Row C is an unusually fine cutting in Swirled Panels, a variation of Russian and Pillar, Pattern 14. Numbers 5 and 6 in Row D also show beautiful and rare cuttings.

OTHER ARTICLES

Other articles such as inkwells, paperweights, and doorknobs were made of cut glass, but since the patterns rarely varied from the straight flute and lapidary cutting there is not sufficient variety in these categories to form the basis for an exclusive collection. Major collections of paperweights will include several with lapidary cutting with the wheel used only to facet the surface of the glass and lend brilliance to the central subject rather than to contribute to the decoration. Such cutting is most frequently found on millefiori and silhouette medallion paperweights.

Cut glass doorknobs and tiebacks were also fashionable at the turn of the century but these, like the paperweights, were simply faceted pieces of crystal glass. Occasionally a lucky collector finds a doorknob on which the individual panels have been engraved in unpolished motifs or with a monogram. These are too rare to make a specific collection.

◇ ◇

CHAPTER XVII

CARE OF CUT GLASS

C UT GLASS should be washed carefully in tepid water with a mild soap or detergent. Make a stiff lather and work it carefully into the cutting with a soft brush. (A soft tooth brush is ideal for the purpose.) Rinse with clear water of the same temperature. Place pieces at once on a soft cloth, free of lint, and dry and polish with a brisk firm motion.

Cabinet pieces are sometimes cleaned with alcohol applied with a cotton swab. This method is usually adopted when glass is very old, rare, or showing signs of deterioration such as small cracks or separations between handle and vessel, or splitting and chipping on scalloped edges. Care should be taken never to lift such pieces by the handles.

Do not use ammonia in the water used for washing glass and avoid the use of strongly alkaline soaps. Ammonia may make the glass gleam because of its quick drying action but there is danger of its attacking the surface of the glass and causing surface deterioration.

Do not use shot in carafes, cruets, or bottles since it is apt to scratch and may even cause the bottom to crack away in a round disklike separation.

To remove the discoloration caused by perfume, wine, vinegar, or other liquids in bottles, cruets, or carafes, put three tablespoons of a mild detergent into the bottle with a small amount of water and allow to stand overnight or longer if the stain is considerable. When the discoloration has been dissolved, empty and rinse with clear water.

Because cut glass is particularly sensitive to extremes of tempera-

PLATE 153

UPPER: *Plates, broken pillar cutting, early Middle Period. These pieces "fogged" and alkaline salts formed on surface. The condition could have been arrested by applications of Glass Wax. (Smithsonian Inst.)* LOWER: *Pitcher, horizontal-prism cutting. Avoid sudden changes of temperature for such old pieces. (Samuel Hawkes)*

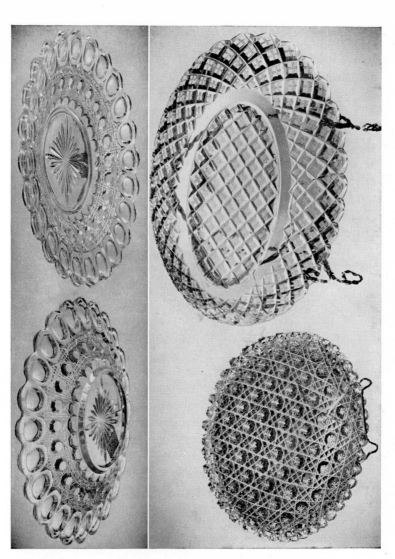

PLATE 154

UPPER: *Plates, deep roundelet and chair-bottom motif. Plates should never be stacked, but displayed on cabinet racks. (Smithsonian Inst.) LOWER, LEFT: Nappy in Harvard pattern variation "pinched" by cabinet door. RIGHT: Bread tray, large block motif, cracked by pressure from heavy piece placed inside. (Author's Collection)*

ture, never place it in a refrigerator, nor subject it to boiling water. Even hot water may cause cracking.

Do not bring pieces of cut class directly to a warm dining room from a cold pantry. Take care that changes in temperature are gradual. Collections should never be stored in rooms where temperatures are likely to be extreme as in unheated storerooms or unventilated attics. Sudden changes may cause the separation of applied handles from the body of old pitchers, cups, drinking vessels, and sugar bowls. Do not put ice cream, cracked ice, or cool drinks in glasses that have come out of a warm kitchen. Do not put electric lights too near cabinet pieces. In other words avoid any extreme change in temperature.

Pressure is also an enemy of cut glass. Store cut glass pieces bottom side up, whenever possible. This minimizes the hazards of stacking which invariably results in split tumblers or cracked bowls. Cups, plates, nappies, and sauce dishes should be stored separately since the pressure of their combined weight when stacked will cause pinching or pressure cracks.

If you happen to have a fine old piece of cut glass which clouds rapidly with an almost iridescent white fog, wash it thoroughly and immediately apply Glass Wax to the surface. Such a piece is called sick glass. The condition is caused by devitrification due to imperfect fusion of the metal or too high an alkaline content in the batch. Frequent applications of the wax will save such a piece, otherwise exposure to the air will cause gradual disintegration. I use Glass Wax on all my old and rare pieces and find that it not only increases the brilliance but keeps pieces brighter longer and protects them from fogging. Since Glass Wax is not practical for articles in daily use, it is suggested that pieces showing surface deterioration be retired to inactive duty in the cabinet so that their beauty can be preserved for posterity.

Your cut glass is the result of man's labor and skill. It will be tomorrow's heirloom. It deserves attentive respect and the care awarded all precious and irreplaceable things.

❖ ❖

ADVICE TO COLLECTORS

1. Read all you can about American glass. No one can appreciate the beauty and value of cut glass or distinguish between what is fine and what is not unless he knows something of the techniques of making and decorating glass.

2. Have a general idea what your collection is to consist of before you start scouting. Will you collect useful, fairly common articles or rare cabinet pieces? If you collect a set for use at party luncheons or formal dinners, you will want to select a pattern that is readily collectible. Of the Early Period this might be Colonial Flute or Block. In the Middle Period a collectible set would be Small Diamond, Nailhead Diamond, or Lincoln Band. The easiest table settings to assemble are those of the Brilliant Period— Strawberry-Diamond and Fan (Plate 156), Kimberly, or Pinwheel. If you prefer a collection of rare pieces, choose them of one kind— goblets, lamps, or cruets—or of one period like the Brilliant, or of one locale, such as Pittsburgh or Wheeling. There should always be unity in a collection. Don't buy just any piece of glass because it looks old or because it is cut. If you do, you will end with an uninteresting assortment that will mean little to you and less to anyone else.

3. Let the nature of your collection be determined by space. If you live in a small apartment or a little house where your collection is to be displayed in a picture window or small fireside cabinet, collect accordingly. Search for wine glasses (Plate 157), small cologne bottles, miniatures, butter patties, toothpick holders, knife holders, salt cups, or small cruets from the different periods, localities, and

[361]

PLATE 155

LEFT: *Toilet-water bottle, 5½ inches high. Clear blown glass, engraved. New England Glass Co., about 1850. (Brooklyn Mus.)* RIGHT: *Claret decanter, flute-cut, grape pattern and coat of arms engraved by A. Jardel. Presented to James Monroe by Benjamin Bakewell in Pittsburgh, 1817. (White House)*

PLATE 156

A few of many pieces available in American Strawberry-Diamond and Fan pattern. UPPER, LEFT TO RIGHT: *Cologne bottle, salt dish, saucedish, butter patty and square nappy.* LOWER: *Candlesticks, rose bowl, and finger bowl.*
(Author's Collection)

PLATE 157

Collectible small articles of cut glass. Rows 1 and 3: Tumblers. Row 2: Sachet powder bottles, mustard pot, smelling salts bottle, toothpick holders, rare miniatures—pitcher and compote—sugar shaker. (Mrs. John M. Feeney) Row 4: Salt dishes, butter patties and butter dish. (Rows 1 and 4, Author's Collection)

glasshouses. If you have a pair of large wall cabinets where small pieces would be lost, look for decanters, compotes, pitchers, candlesticks, punch cups, or goblets.

4. Collect what you can afford. If purse and travel permit, consider the exquisite engraved pieces from the Early American and Middle Periods, but if your budget is limited watch out for cut glass novelties—the hats, boats, slippers, and match holders made of crystal or colored glass. Keep in mind that glass was never cut in mass production. It cannot be collected that way.

5. Memorize the one or two patterns that please you and hunt for these. Familiarize yourself with their every aspect: how they look in goblets, how they appear in nappies, or in plates. Make these *your* patterns. Then later you can, if you wish, add one or two more to your informed repertoire. Don't try to memorize all the cut glass patterns! No one can do this, not even talented glass cutters. Try, however, to familiarize yourself with the basic motifs such as strawberry-diamond, nailhead diamond, block, hobnail, hob-star, pinwheel, bull's-eye, and fringe.

6. Catalogue all cabinet pieces. For this purpose use a box of index cards. Number the cards and paste small stickers on the bottom of each piece of glass with the corresponding number on it. Then write on the card the number, name of piece, dimensions, probable manufacturer, approximate date, locality, pattern, where you acquired it and when, how much you paid for it, and any other interesting bits of information you have concerning it. A typical catalogue card might read:

> 201—Pitcher—6 x 10″
> Probably Bakewell and Page Company
> 1827—Pittsburgh, Penna.
> Strawberry-Diamond (English), with small Bull's-Eye
> Bought from Gailey Wilson, Hickory, Penna.
> August 1, 1947—$35.00
> Condition perfect—rare.

Such a card is useful in many ways. It jogs your memory concerning the piece. If you ever want to sell part or all of your collection, you have a good idea of what investment you have in the

PLATE 158

Part of a service of three decanters, wine glasses, tumblers, and mineral-water glasses believed to be from Greenpoint glassworks, in later year of Middle Period, 1873–1880, during ownership of J. B. Dobelman. Because of age and identification, the wine glass, though chipped, is valuable. (N.-Y. Hist. Soc.)

PLATE 159

Cut glass berry bowl attributed to Kensington Glass Works (Butland Period), Philadelphia, about 1800. Combination of strawberry-diamond with horizontal prism and nailhead or sharp-diamond motifs. Pontil scar has been ground to an oval. (Smithsonian Inst.)

of American cut glass, you may be able to classify the piece as to approximate date and manufacturer. But never be *sure* unless you *know* through exact documentation.

11. Study fine glass wherever you can—in museums, in the homes of friends, in other collections. Almost everyone who owns fine glass, especially family pieces, enjoys showing it to others who appreciate it.

PLATE 160

LEFT: *One of a set of tumblers, South Ferry works, probably 1854–1860. Engraving of The Hermitage, home of Andrew Jackson. (Samuel Hawkes)* UPPER: *Wine glasses, replacements to White House service purchased by Monroe, 1819. First two have teardrops in stems. (White House)* LOWER: *9-inch bowl, Morgan pattern. (Virgil*

PLATE 161

UPPER: *Wine glasses, Boston and Sandwich Glass Co., for the family of Mrs.*
G. W. Mitton. (Photograph, courtesy Charles Messer Stow, New York Sun)
LOWER: *Rare, large, covered compote. Heavy diamond cutting. Believed to be*
from Jersey City Glass Co. of George and P. C. Dummer. Cut about 1850 by
a workman as a presentation piece. (Mrs. Henry R. Rea)

APPENDIX

various pieces. Such a record is necessary for insurance records, and all glass collections should be insured. A record is important, too, in the possible settlement of estates. Many a fine glass collection has been dissipated because all information concerning it was buried with its owner.

7. *Collect American cut glass only.* Or to put it another way, avoid confusing the focus of your collection by including a doubtful or a colorful piece of foreign glass. First, because we are Americans and our glass needs to be recognized and catalogued; second, because American glass will increase greatly in value as the years pass by; third, because in many respects American glass is finer than European, although generally not so elaborate; and finally, because much foreign glass brought to America for sale has been proved to be modern glass made up in the old style to sell as antique.

8. *Buy only sound pieces* unless you are convinced that rarity makes a damaged piece worth owning. If you must buy a chipped, cracked, or broken piece be sure you are aware of its bad condition. Reliable dealers will always point out defects before making a sale. Generally speaking, only sound whole pieces are desirable. Once I bought a Colonial Flute decanter with a cracked neck because its stopper was whole and I hoped that some day I should find a good decanter of the same type in which the stopper might be missing or damaged. Sure enough, in less than a year, the second Colonial Flute decanter came to light and its steeple stopper was split right down the middle. Of course, you may not always have such luck, so it is wise policy to buy only sound pieces.

9. *Before buying examine every piece of glass in a bright light.* Daylight is best. A small magnifying glass is handy for reading trade-marks. Avoid snap judgments. Some late pieces of pressed glass look much like cut when they are polished and well displayed.

10. *Beware of those who know the exact origin* of every piece of glass they sell. By this time it is extremely difficult to identify cut glass according to point of origin. In many cases it is impossible. When you are told that a piece of early cut glass is Waterford, ask that a written guarantee accompany the bill of sale. Be content if a dealer can tell you the approximate locality in which he found the piece of glass. With this information and your general knowledge

PLATE 159

Cut glass berry bowl attributed to Kensington Glass Works (Butland Period), Philadelphia, about 1800. Combination of strawberry-diamond with horizontal prism and nailhead or sharp-diamond motifs. Pontil scar has been ground to an oval. (Smithsonian Inst.)

MOTIF CHART

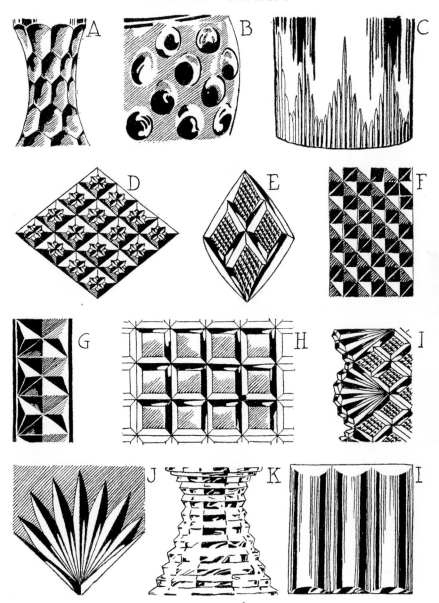

PLATE 162

Motif Chart: (English or Irish names in parentheses) (A.) Saint Louis panel (convex diamond); (B.) Bull's-eye (roundelet, puntie, etc.); (C.) Fringe (blaze); (D.) Strawberry-diamond (cross-cut or chequered diamond); (E.) English strawberry-diamond shown in field of four; (F.) Nailhead diamond (sharp); (G.) Large shallow or relief diamond; (H.) Block; (I.) English strawberry-diamond with fan border; (J.) Fan; (K.) Step or horizontal prismatic cutting; (L.) Pillar (pillar flute).

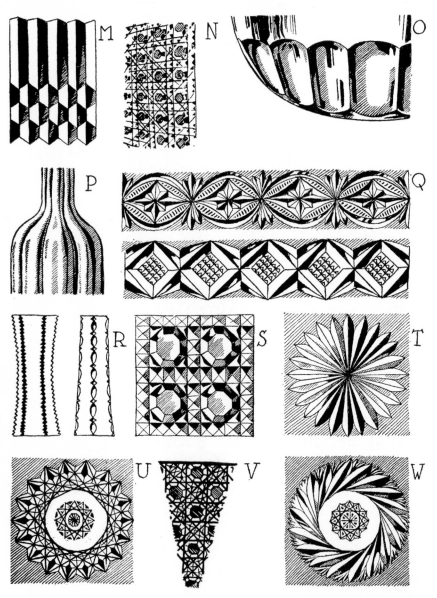

PLATE 163

Motif Chart: (M.) Prism, straight and broken; (N. and V.) Chair-bottom or cane; (O.) Half flute; (P.) Full flute; (Q.) Borders. UPPER: *Vesica.* LOWER: *English strawberry-diamond; (R.) Notched prism; (S.) Hobnail; (T.) Single star; (U.) Modified Hob-star; (W.) Modified pinwheel or buzz.*

◇ ◇

LIST OF KNOWN PATTERNS
(The italicized patterns are classified in detail in this book;
variations are marked with a v.)

Accomac Cut
Acme
Agawan
Alexis
Alice
Allston
Almora
Alsatia
Ambassador v-1
American
Anemone
Angelic Cut
Angulated Ribbon (7)
Apache
Aquilla
Arabesque
Arabesque-X
Argand
Armah
Arrow
Astic
Astor
Atlanta
Aurora
Azalea
Azora

Baker's Gothic (12)
Baltic
Bangor
Bellair
Belmont
Belmont-II
Bergen's White Rose (31)
Beryl
Bethalto
Bird-in-a-Cage v-36
Boise
Bolo
Braidwood
Brainard
Brazilian (15)
Bristol Rose (29)
Brockton
Brunswick v-39
Bull's-Eye (44)
Burbank
Burley
Burton

Calypso
Camellia
Cameron

Canadian Star
Canterbury v-1
Canton
Carlisle
Carlton
Carolyn
Celphas
Champion
Cherries
Chrysanthemum (21)
Chrysanthemum II
Cincinnati
Cinderella
Clark
C. Laurel B.
Cleary
Cleone
Clermont
Cleveland v-1
Club
Cobweb (2)
Colburn
Columbia (27)
Comet (46)
Cordovia
Corinthian (40)
Corinthian-Elmira
Cornell v-4
Cornflower (50)
Corning (32)
Corning-Harvard v-36
Coronet (26)
Cosmos
Crafton
Croesus (33)
Croesus with Russian Field v-33
Creston

Crown Cut
Crosby
Crystal v-8
Crystal City
Cut Buzz v-45

Daisy
Davies Bull's-Eye v-44
Delft v-40
Denrock v-12
Devonshire (11)
Dewey
Diana
Dianthus
Donald
Dorflinger Princess v-35
Double Daisy
Drake
Druid
Duchess
Dunbar
Dunkirk (43)

Earl
Eaton
Eleanor v-27
Elfin
Elmira Corinthian v-40
Emerald
Empress
Estella
Eulalia
Excelsior

Faust
Fedora
Florence (13)

Florentine
Flower Basket
Fortuna
Frances
Fringed Gentian

Gem
Gertrude
Gladys
Golden Wedding (30)
Golf
Good Luck
Gooseberries
Gorham
Gotham v-12
Grand Prize
Grapes
Grecian (9)
Guilford

Haldane
Hampton
Hanover
Harvard (36)
Harvest v-8
Hawkes' Aberdeen (41)
Heron
Highland v-4
Hindoo v-43
Hindoo v-39
Hob-in-Pillar Panel v-10
Hobnail and Fan v-10
Hobnail and Russian v-10
Hobson
Hollywood

Idaho

Imperial (34)
Irernia
Irma
Isabella (28)
Isis

Jefferson
Jersey
Jewel Cut
Jubilee
Julia
Jupiter

Kaiser (49)
Kauwaunee
Kedron
Kenmore
Kensington
Keota
Keystone
Kimberley
Kimberly (23)
Kohinoor v-36

La Konta
Lanark
Lattice v-26
Leighton's Bow-Knot (5)
Lenox
Leo
Leorin
Leroy
Libbey Chrysanthemum v-21
Libbey Harvard v-35
Lilita
Lily-of-the-Valley (47)
Linwood

Lily
Limoge
Lisbon
London
Loretta
Lorimer v-6
Lorraine
Lotus
Lotus II
Louis XIV (14)
Luana
Lucile
Luray

Macbeth (19)
Madison
Manitou
Marcella
Marguerite v-24
Marquise
Marine
Marion v-29
Martindale
Marvel v-45
Mayflower
Mayton
Maximillian (cf. catalogue)
Medora
Merna
Meteor v-32
Mikado
Middlesex (6)
Miller's Maltese Cross v-5
Milky Way
Mineola
Modern White House v-39
Moneta

Montague Cut
Monteith
Monarch
Montauk Cut
Monte Carlo
Moonbeam
Moultrie
Muncy

Nassau
National v-36
Nautilus (37)
Navarre v-44
Navajo
Nebo
Neola
Nevada
New Brilliant
Newport
New York
Niagara
Nile
Norwood
Notched Prism and Bead

Oakland
O'Connor's Princess v-35
Odd
Old-fashioned Hobnail (10)
Oregon
Orela
Orient
Oriental v-32
Othello
Owl
Oxford
Oxford II
Ozella

[378]

Pairpoint Princess v-35
Palace
Palmer's Goblet
Panel v-36
Paragon
Paris
Parisian (3)
Pearl
Pebble v-24
Pekin
Persian v-1
Perth
Petrel
Petunia
Pinwheel (45)
Pinwheel and Star v-45
Pittsburgh Victoria v-42
Plain Flute (48)
Planeta
Plume
Pluto v-39
Plymouth Cut
Poinsettia
Polar Star v-1
Pond Lilies
Portland
Premier
Preston
Prima Donna
Princess (35)
Princeton
Prism (38)
Prism and Bead v-39
Prosperity
Puritana

Queens
Quilt Block v-36

Quincy

Raleigh
Rambler Rose
Rattan (24)
Regal
Regency
Regina
Reo
Rex
Richardson's Pitcher (16)
Richelieu
Rochester Harvard v-36
Roman
Romola
Rookwood
Roseclare
Rose of Sharon v-24
Russian (1)
Russian and Pillar (8)
Russian Swirl v-8
Russian and Leaf v-8

Saint James
Salem
Santa Maria
Satyr
Shalimar
Sheba
Signora
Six Sea Shells (25)
Snowflake
Solano
Sparkler
Special
Spider Web v-1
Stamford
Star v-11

[379]

Stars with Greek Border
Stella
Sterling
Steuben
Strand
Stratford (17)
Strawberries
Strawberry-Diamond and Fan
(18)
Strawberry-Diamond and Prism
v-4
Strawberry-Diamond and Star
(4)
Strawberry-Diamond and
Scallop v-4
Sultana v-6
Sweet Clover

Tasso v-39
Taurus
Temple
Thistle
Thyrza
Tiger Lily
Titus
Tivoli
Tokio v-11
Tolbert
Tosca
Trellis v-36
Tulip
Tunis
Tyrrell
Twenty-Two v-45

Uncatena
Upton

Venetia
Venetian (20)
Venice v-20
Vera
Versailles
Victor
Victoria (42)
Vogue

Waldo
Waldorf
Walker
Wapello
Warden
Washington
Wasp
Watseka
Waverly
Wayne
Wedgemere (22)
Westmond
Wheat v-8
Wheat
Whirlwind v-45
White House (39)
Willow
Wilson
Windsor
Windsor Cut

X-Ray

Yale
Yeddo
Yquem
Yucatan

Zambesi
Zendar v-25

CLASSIFICATION OF STIEGEL'S FOUR-TEEN ENGRAVING PATTERNS,
1771–1774
(from *Stiegel Glass* by Frederick William Hunter)

I. "Alternating figures, ellipse like and diamond-shaped, formed by intersecting arcs of circles. With and without diamond-cut trellis work filling the ellipses and with dots and trefoil ornaments engraved in the angles formed by the intersecting arcs. Usually a single wavy line is engraved as a border above this design, which is the one most used on Stiegel pieces. [For illustration of this and the other patterns, see Plate 37.]

II. "Four segments of circles, filled with diamond-cut trellis work and finished at the top by a straight line engraved around the glass. A decoration of garlands and tassels is added below the circle segments.

III. "Floral design based upon a conventionalization of the tulip. Various treatments all showing diamond-cut trellis work filling the calix of the tulip.

IV. "Alternating pyramids and inverted scrolls; the pyramids being formed by heavy graved lines and filled with diamond-cut trellis work; and the design being elaborately ornamented with dots, trefoils and other devices.

V. "An alternation of perpendicular wavy lines and a floral design.

VI. "A vine border.

VII. "An alternation of inverted foliated designs with double lined semicircles enclosing four dots.

VIII. "Two-handled basket containing plant or flowers. The body of the basket showing basket work done with the diamond point. This design is copied from the Dutch pieces.

IX. "Vignettes of pavilions with flags flying alternating with a circle and a scroll design. The pavilion pillars are cut in with the diamond.

X. "The dove and flower or two love birds and a heart, enclosed in circle with sunburst radiations.

XI. "A beautiful floral design based on a conventionalization of the rose.

XII. "A design formed by the elliptical intersection of two wreaths inclosing four-petalled flowers. The wreath leaves are engraved; their center line is cut with the diamond.

XIII. "A design of pendant wreaths caught up with bowknots. Here again the center line of the wreaths is diamond-cut.

XIV. "Alternating palm leaves and trefoil designs with one straight and one wavy line as a border above and below."

❖ ❖

TRADE-MARKS

DURING the late years of the nineteenth century and the early years of the twentieth some of the leading glass manufacturers adopted the use of trade-marks for identification of their wares. Several hundred such marks were registered. Some of these were insignia etched into the glass, as those of Libbey or Hawkes. Some were pressed into the blanks, like the Heisey H. Others, Dorflinger's for instance, were simply paper stickers attached to each piece. Not all glass manufacturers had a trade-mark and not all of the companies using marks were consistent. At best, the general use of the trade-mark was confined to a comparatively few years of manufacture, 1892–1914. For this reason, while the discovery of a trade-mark is conclusive proof of origin for a specific piece of cut glass, the absence of a trade-mark does not discredit an otherwise fine piece of American cut ware.

J. D. BERGEN CO.,
Meriden, Conn.

EMPIRE CUT GLASS CO.,
Flemington, N. J.

BUFFALO CUT GLASS CO.
Batavia, N. Y.

H. C. FRY GLASS CO.,
Rochester, Pa.

CLARK

T. B. CLARK & CO., INC.,
Honesdale, Pa.

HAWKES
(*New Mark.*)

(*Old Mark.*)

T. G. HAWKES & CO.,
Corning, N. Y.

C. DORFLINGER & SONS, INC.,
White Mills, Pa.

A. H. HEISEY & CO., INC.,
Newark, Ohio.

J. HOARE & CO.,
Corning, N. Y.

PLATE 164

*Trade-Marks on Cut Glass. (Reproduced from the trade-mark files of the
United States Patent Office)*

HOPE GLASS WORKS,
161 Dorrance St., Providence, R. I.

TRADE-MARK.

MERIDEN CUT GLASS CO.,
International Silver Co., Successor,
Meriden, Conn.

(Mount Washington Glass Co.)'

THE PAIRPOINT CORPORATION,
Prospect St., New Bedford, Mass.

THE LIBBEY GLASS MFG. CO.,
Toledo, Ohio.

QUAKER CITY CUT GLASS CO.,
60th St. & Baltimore Ave., Philadelphia, Pa.

LYONS CUT GLASS CO.,
Lyons, N. Y.

H. P. SINCLAIRE & CO.,
Corning, N. Y.

MAPLE CITY GLASS CO.,
Taken Over By
T. B. CLARK & CO., INC.,
Honesdale, Pa.

I. STRAUS & SONS,
42-48 Warren St., New York.

PLATE 165

Trade-Marks on Cut Glass. (Reproduced from the trade-mark files of the United States Patent Office)

◇ ◇

GLASSHOUSE CHART

COLLECTORS and students of American glass agree that identification is always a hazardous proposition if specific records are not available. It is no less risky to accredit definite output to various manufacturers. Especially is this true in the study of cut glass. However, because a start must be made some time if our glass history is ever to become authentically organized, the following chart is offered as a beginning. That it has been compiled with trepidation is an understatement. Over a period of many years known facts, scraps of information, correlative references, and suggested clues have been catalogued and analyzed. Sources include newspaper files, old advertisements, public records, county histories, correspondence, letters, personal reminiscences, old manuscripts, and contemporary observation. These sources often disagree over the exact names of early glasshouses. The chart does not presume to be perfect either with regard to those houses which are included or to those which have been left out; but in the light of present knowledge, may it serve as a guide and signpost for further research and investigation from which will at last evolve a more perfect history of a fine American craft.

Key to source numbers in chart. Names in parenthesis refer to authors listed in Bibliography (see Appendix VII).

1—Old newspapers and advertisements
2—Public documents
3—*Antiques Magazine*
4—Old city and county directories
5—County or other local historical compilations
6—Old invoices

7—Crockery and glass journals
8—Directories of the glass industry
9—Glass catalogues

Following is a listing of manufacturers known or believed to have produced cut glass.

EARLY AMERICAN PERIOD, 1771–1830

1771–1772	Manheim Glass Works	Henry William Stiegel
1772–1774	American Flint Glass Manufactory, Manheim, Penna. (*Hunter*)	Lazarus Isaacs retained as cutter (1773) Flint containing some lead, resonant, thin. Unpolished wheel-engraving patterns of birds, flowers, etc., probable German origin.
1771 (1691?) –1820	Northern Liberties Glass Facture, Philadelphia, Penna. (*Gillingham*)	Little known of proprietors or product
1772–1804	Kensington Glass Works (John Elliott and Co.), Philadelphia, Penna. (*Gillingham*)	John and Samuel Elliott, Isaac Gray High grade English flint; cutting follows Irish and English forms and motifs.
1780–1786	Schuylkill Glass Works, Philadelphia, Penna. (*O'Hara letters*)	Robert Morris and John Nicholson. Peter William Eichbaum found first employment here on coming to America. No documented examples of work, indications that lightweight soda-potash glass was handblown into common shapes such as Rodney decanters and wheel-engraved wine glasses.
1784–1796	New Bremen Glass Works, Frederick-town, Md. (*Enoch Pratt Free Library*)	John Frederick Amelung High grade Bohemian glass, light weight, good color, wheel-engraved.

1795–1819	Pittsburg Glass Works, Pittsburgh, Penna. (*O'Hara, Craig* papers)	Col. James O'Hara. Isaac Craig a partner between 1796 and 1804 Primarily green and window glass, open-pot glasshouse. Experimented with white glass, some cut (1800–1804). Limited commercial output.
1799–1802	Federal Hill Works, Baltimore, Md. (*Stow, Knittle, O'Hara* papers) (1)	Frederick M. Amelung Lightweight Bohemian flint, similar to glass produced by Amelung (father), not as good metal or workmanship.
1800(?)–1810(?)	Johnson Glassworks, Md. (*Stow, O'Hara* papers)	Sometimes spelled Johnston White glass, wheel-decorated, no known examples
1802–1870	Dunbarton Glass Works, Durhamville, N. Y. (*Schoolcraft* papers)	Probably cut glass in the early period. No known pieces
1807–1808	Robinson and Ensell, Pittsburgh, Penna. Firm became Bakewell and Ensell in 1808 (*O'Hara, Craig* papers) (2)	George Robinson and Edward Ensell Lead glass tableware, probably cut by Peter William or Arnold Eichbaum in their cutting shop on a percentage system.
1809–1882	B. Bakewell and Company, Pittsburgh, Penna. (*Bakewell, Pears*) (1, 2, and 3)	Benjamin Bakewell and Benjamin Page. Many changes in firm name —1836 John Palmer Pears joined, firm became Bakewell, Pears and Co., but was locally known as Bakewell's, and remained in control of that family during its entire history. Made fine lead glass tableware—compotes, decanters, tumblers, celery vases, custard cups, champagne glasses.
1809–1811	Pittsburgh Flint Glass Manufactory (or and also George Robinson's Glass House), Pittsburgh, Penna. (1 and 2)	George Robinson Made lightweight handblown tableware which was wheel-engraved. Finally sold out to Bakewell.

1810–1836	Mount Vernon Glass Co., Oneida County, N. Y. (*Schoolcraft* papers)	Lead glass cut in simple motifs; some etched decoration
1810–?	Ontario County Glass Works, Geneva, N. Y. (*Schoolcraft* papers)	Henry Rowe Schoolcraft and W. Beul Hollow ware and lead glass tableware, particularly tumblers
1810–1895	Pennsylvania Flint Glass Works, Pittsburgh, Penna. (1 and 2)	Edward Ensell and Frederick Wendt (both had worked for O'Hara). 1812—Ensell withdrew. Wendt, Beltzhoover, John K. Nickle, and Charles Ihmsen continued company. Lightweight handblown lead glass tableware, often wheel decorated and engraved. Sometimes colored. Frequently called "Birmingham glass."
1812–1818	Trevor and Ensell, Pittsburgh, Penna. (1 and 2)	Edward Ensell, Sr. and J. B. Trevor Lightweight handblown tableware, wheel engraved
1812–1891	South Boston Crown Glass Co., South Boston, Mass. (*Jarves*) (1 and 2)	Thomas Caines started lead glass output here, withdrew from company in 1820 to found Phoenix Glass Works. Flint glass production continued sporadically. Lead glass of good color and quality cut in Irish motifs with crosshatched figures
1813–	Vermont Glass Factory, Lake Dunmore, Salisbury, Vt. (*Schoolcraft* papers)	Henry Rowe Schoolcraft, Epaphras Jones, Samuel Swift, and Milo Cook Made lead glass of good quality with some light-wheel engraving and etched decoration
1814–1855	New Hampshire Glass Factory, Keene, N. H. (*Schoolcraft* papers) (1, 2, and 5)	John Elliott, D. Bradford. Daniel Watson, John Hatch, Nathaniel Sprague, Aaron Appleton, and Timothy Twitchell, shareholders.

[389]

Captain Lawrence Schoolcraft, manager. (John Elliott formerly [1772–1804] at Kensington Works in Philadelphia.)

Good lead glass, some cut in English and Irish patterns

1815–1828 Isaac Duval and Co., Wellsburg, W. Va., formerly Va. (1, 2, and 5)

Isaac Duval

Cobalt blue flint, amber, purple emerald, cut decanters, wines, and vessels

1817–1888 New England Glass Co., Cambridge, Mass. (*Watkins*)

Deming Jarves, agent; Amos Binney, Daniel Hastings, and Edmund Monroe, stockholders. Richard Fisher, superintendent until 1820.

All kinds of white and colored lead glass in heavy quality and fine cutting. Lamp shades, decanters, tumblers, etc.

1820–(?) Baltimore Flint Glass Co., William Whitaker and Christian Keener, Baltimore, Md. (1 and 2)

Certain that they made and cut lead glass, but no known pieces.

1820–1870 Phoenix Glass Works, South Boston, Mass. (1 and 2)

Thomas Caines.

Fine quality cut and engraved white and colored glass.

1820–1874 Union Flint Glass Co., Philadelphia, Penna. (*Gillingham*)

Group of New England Glass Co. workmen

Probably so similar to New England Glass Company output that pieces are indistinguishable.

1820–1840 Bloomingdale Flint Glass Works, New York City (*Hobbes*) (8)

Richard Fisher, John Fisher, and John L. Gilliland

Heavy lead glass tableware of superior quality and deep cutting, much crosshatching, scalloped edges, and relief diamond motifs

1822–1870 Camden County Glass Works (later known as Waterford), Camden, N. J. (1, 2, and 3)

Jonathan Haines

White lead glass probably of the lighter or single-flint width, light engraved decoration

1823–1845	Stourbridge Flint Glass Works, Pittsburgh, Penna. (*personal reminiscences of Robinson descendants*) (1, 2, and 4)	John Robinson (no relation to George, 1807) Heavy double flint of excellent quality cut in finely polished pillar, relief-diamond and crosshatched patterns. Product ranks with Fisher glass as among finest produced in America. Factory destroyed by fire, 1845, never rebuilt
1823–1868	Brooklyn Glass Works (John L. Gilliland and Co.), Brooklyn, N. Y. (*Dorflinger, Gillinder* papers) (1, 2, and 4)	John L. Gilliland Fine quality heavy lead glass cut in diamond, lunar slices, with crosshatching
1824–1860	Jersey City Glass Co., Jersey City, N. J. (*Niles Register, Franklin Journal*)	George Dummer and P. C. Dummer Cut, etched, and engraved including wines, decanters, tumblers, carafes, pitchers, fruit dishes in wide variety of sizes. Heavy lead glass with single star bottoms
1825–1888	Boston and Sandwich Glass Co., Sandwich, Mass. (*Chipman*)	Deming Jarves, Henry Rice, Andrew T. Hall, Edmund Monroe White and colored glass cut and engraved
1827–1873	Fort Pitt Glass Co., Pittsburgh, Penna. (1, 2, 4, and 5)	Robert B. Curling, William Price, (predecessor of Dithridge Glass Co.) Heavy lead glass with flute and panel cutting. May also have made thinner lead glass in handblown shapes with light surface cutting.
1829–1845	Union Flint Glass Works, Pittsburgh, Penna. (1, 2, 4, and 5)	Captain John Hay and William McCully Probably lightweight tableware then in vogue, sketchy unpolished engraving.
1829–1839	Ritchie and Wheat, Wheeling, W. Va. (formerly Va.) (*Jefferson*)	John Ritchie and Jesse Wheat, later became Ritchie and Wilson Fine quality lead, flute and panel cuttings

MIDDLE PERIOD, 1830–1880

1802–1870	Dunbarton Glass Works, Durhamville, N. Y. (6)	Heavy lead glass, flute cutting, inferior quality
1809–1882 (1824) (1836)	B. Bakewell and Co. Bakewell, Page and Bakewell Bakewell, Pears and Co. (*Bakewell, Pears*) (1, 2, 5, and 6)	Benjamin Bakewell, Benjamin Page, Thomas Pears, and other members of the Bakewell family Fine lead glass cut and engraved at beginning of Middle Period. Product declined to a commercial pressed ware toward end of period.
1810–1895	Pennsylvania Flint Glass Works, Pittsburgh (Birmingham district), Penna. (1, 2, 4, and 5)	Ensell and Wendt (1810), Beltzhoover, Wendt and Co. (1812). John K. Nickle and Charles Ihmsen. Whitehead, Ihmsen, Phillips, (1837). Made thin flint glass containing high percentage of lead—handblown, engraved, and cut.
1810–1838	Mount Vernon Glass Co., Oneida County, N. Y. (*Schoolcraft* papers)	Lead glass cut in simple motifs and left unpolished; some panel cutting shows wheel polishing.
1817–1888	New England Glass Company, Cambridge, Mass. (*Watkins*)	Deming Jarves (see Early American chart). One of the leaders in Middle Period engraving and cut decoration. Also made fine colored glass during Middle Period.
1820–1870	Phoenix Glass Works, South Boston, Mass. (4)	Thomas Caines, William Caines, William Johnston Fine flint glass tableware cut and engraved.
1820–1874	Union Flint Glass Co. (*Gillingham*)	Group of New England Glass Co. workmen Fine lead glass, clear and colored, engraved and cut. Similar to New England Glass Co. ware.
1820–1840	Bloomingdale Flint Glass Works, New York City, N. Y. (*Hobbes*) (8)	Richard Fisher, John Fisher Output of factory identified with the Early American Period since it

continued to follow early fashion in panel, diamond, and scallop motifs until end of enterprise.

1822–1870   Camden County Glass Works, Waterford, N. J. (1, 2, and 3)

Jonathan Haines
     Lightweight engraved glassware during early years of Middle Period

1823–1845   Stourbridge Flint Glass Works, Pittsburgh, Penna. (1, 2, and 4)

John Robinson, John Robinson, Jr., Thomas Robinson, Alexander W. Anderson
     Fine quality heavy lead glass. (See Early American Period.)

1823–1868   Brooklyn Glass Works, Brooklyn, N. Y. (South Ferry Works) (*Dorflinger* and *Gillinder* papers) (1, 2, and 4)

John Loftus Gilliland. Amory Houghton bought works in 1864. First quality cut glass, colored and gilt. Forty cutting frames in operation. One of most important producers of Middle Period.

1824–1860   Jersey City Glass Co., Jersey City, N. J. (*Niles Register, Franklin Journal*)

George Dummer and P. C. Dummer
Heavy double flint of superior quality in white and colors; panel cutting.

1825–1888   Boston and Sandwich Glass Co., Sandwich, Mass. (*Chipman*)

Deming Jarves and partners. (See Early American period.)
     White and colored, cut and engraved

1827–1873   Fort Pitt Glass Co., Pittsburgh, Penna. (1, 2, 4, and 5)

R. B. Curling and Co. (William Price) 1831—R. B. Curling and Sons. 1850—Curling, Robertson and Co. Edward Dithridge became proprietor in 1863. Predecessor of Dithridge Glass Co.
     Much fancy colored and clear cut glass, flute, panel cutting, and etching

1829–1839   Ritchie and Wheat, Wheeling, W. Va. (*Jefferson*)

John and Craig Ritchie, Jesse Wheat
     Fine quality lead glass in flute and panel cutting

[393]

1831–1867	M. and R. H. Sweeney and Co., Wheeling, W. Va. (*Jefferson*)	Michael, Thomas, and R. H. Sweeney Fine quality heavy lead glass
1831–1851	Redford Factory, Plattsburg, N. Y. (2 and 5)	Charles Corning and Gersham Cook, owners; John S. Foster, superintendent. White glass of simple cutting
1832–1860	O'Leary, Mulvaney and Co., Pittsburgh, Penna. (1, 2, 5, and 6)	William O'Leary and Patrick Mulvaney, 1847; Mulvaney and Ledlie (James Ledlie), 1850; Ulam and Ihmsen joined firm. Made double lead glass of high quality, colored and clear. Cut, engraved, cased, and flashed decoration.
1832–1854	Millville Glass Works, Millville, N. J. (1, 4, and 5)	Frederick Schetter, founder, Whitall Brothers, successor. Good quality cut glass tableware; large cutting shop 1840–1854.
1833–1880	Phoenix Glass Works, Pittsburgh, Penna. (1, 2, 4, and 5)	William McCully (see Union Flint Glass Works). Thomas Wightman, Frederick Lorenz, and A. W. Buchanan. During Middle Period firm made some of the finest cut and colored double flint glass in America.
1833–1860	Redwood Glass Works, Alexandria Bay, N. Y. (1 and 6)	Schmauss and Co., Gerlack and Co., De Zing and Co., owners. Made glass for small cutting shops in New York City and Brooklyn. Commercial quality metal and standard shapes.
1834–1877	S. McKee and Brothers, Pittsburgh, Penna. (1 and 4)	McKee and Ihmsen families Cut glass of commercial quality prior to 1850 when they converted to pressed lime glass.

1834–1883	Temperanceville Glass Works, Lewisville, N. J. (2 and 5)	Daniel Miller, Lewis and Jacob Stanger Record of a few flint glass dishes, light cutting
1837–1870	Joseph Stouvenel and Co., New York City (1 and 2)	Joseph Stouvenel One of the most important cutting shops of the period. Stouvenel, a master glass cutter, won awards in 1837, 1841, 1843, 1853 for fine glass. Operated small factory. Also bought blanks from Gilliland, Fisher, and others.
1837–1894	Mount Washington Glass Co., South Boston, Mass. (*Watkins and Thomas A. Tripp*)	Deming Jarves organized company for his son, George. In 1850 Jarves and Commerais. 1860 Wm. L. Libbey and Timothy Howe. 1869 Libbey moved business to New Bedford, Mass. 1870 Libbey sold Mount Washington Glass Works. 1876 independent management. 1894 became part of Pairpoint Corporation. Lead glass lamps, bottles, lamp shades and small tableware. Much indistinguishable from New England Glass Co. glass of same period.
1837–1898	Williamsburg Flint Glass Works, Williamsburg (Brooklyn), N. Y. (*Gillinder*)	Walther Co. (Dannehoffer continued company after death of Walther family.) Family owned and operated house that made exquisitely fine cut glass in French tradition with rock-crystal surface cutting.
1839–1891	Plunkett and Miller, Wheeling, W. Va. (*Jefferson*) (1 and 2)	1845 Hobbs, Barnes and Co. (John L. Hobbs, James B. Barnes, John H. Hobbs, James F. Barnes.) 1863 Hobbs, Brockunier and Co. John H. Hobbs and Charles Brockunier. William Leighton, Sr. became superintendent same year.

Fine white and colored glass, much panel cutting and wheel engraving before 1863

1840–1870	Phillips, Best and Co., Pittsburgh, Penna. (*Col. Harry Fry*) (1 and 2)	William Phillips Fine quality cut tableware
1840–1923	Medford Glass House, Medford, N. J. (4 and 6)	1860 Cockran's Glass Factory. 1899 Star Glass Works Fine cut tableware
1841–1857	Excelsior Glass Works, Camden, N. J. (1, 2, and 4)	John and James Capewell and John Bamford Fine flint glass of excellent quality. Nine expert blowers, cutters, and engravers employed.
1842–1890	Saint Louis Flint Glass Works, Saint Louis, Mo. (7 and 8)	James B. Eads. 1857 G. W. Scooly Fine cut glass through period
1842–1858	American Flint Glass Works, South Boston, Mass. (7 and 8)	Continuation of the old South Boston Glass Co. Cut lamps and cologne bottles
1845–1862	Suffolk Glass Works, Boston, Mass. (7 and 8)	Joshua Jenkins Cut tableware and lamp shades
1848–1891	O'Hara Glass Works, Pittsburgh, Penna. (1 and 4)	James B. Lyon, formerly Wallace, Lyon and Co. Good quality lead glass, clear and colored until 1860, then converted to pressed lime ware
1848–1852	American Flint Glass Works, Wheeling, W. Va. (5 and 8)	D. Southwick and Co., Edward Anderson, William Anderson, Franklin Anderson (1852) became part of Hobbs, Barnes Co. Fine colored and clear cut glass
1849–1867	Boston Flint Glass Works, Boston, Mass. (4 and 8)	Thomas Leighton, Sr., John H. Leighton Fine quality colored and clear cut and engraved glass
1849–1864	Maryland Glass Works, Baltimore, Md. (4)	Continuation of the Baltimore Flint Glass Co. Commercial quality cut and engraved tableware

1850–1905	E. V. Houghwout and Co., New York City (9)	Cutting shop only. Bought blanks from Dummer and Gilliland. Fine line cuttings.
1850–1855	Hope Glass Works, Pittsburgh, Penna. (4 and 9)	L. Harcum Mineral water bottles, hock, claret, and wine glasses
1850–1890	J. and F. McKee Glass Co., Pittsburgh, Penna. (1, 7, and 8)	Frederick and James McKee. Later James Bryce joined firm. Colored cut and engraved glass made before 1860 is of high quality.
1851–1924	Union Glass Co., Somerville, Mass. (*Dorflinger* and *Gillinder* papers) (4, 8, and 9)	Amory Houghton, Francis Houghton until 1864. Exhibited lamps and shades at Centennial in Philadelphia, 1876. One of eight companies cutting in 1865. Fine cut and colored glass in all varieties
1851–1891	Adams, Macklin and Co. (4 and 8)	John Adams, Godfried Miller, A. A. Adams, W. Adams, James Dalzell, George F. Easton Cut glass and opal ware
1852–1905	Empire Glass Co., Cleveland, N. Y. (8 and 9)	Operated by Stevens, Crandall and Co. Later sold to J. Hoare and Co. Commercial quality cut glass
1852–1863	Long Island Flint Glassworks (Concord Street Glasshouse), Brooklyn, N. Y. (*Dorflinger* and *Gillinder* papers)	1854 Christian Dorflinger built Plymouth St. Works. 1860 Christian Dorflinger built Greenpoint Flint Glass Works. 1863 sold Plymouth St. Works to J. S. Hibbler. 1863 Greenpoint Flint Glass Works sold to Hoare, Burns and Dailey. 1873 Greenpoint Flint Glass Works sold to J. B. Dobelmann. Fine lead glass, colored, cased, cut and engraved
1852–1880	Suffolk Glass Works, Boston, Mass. (8)	Joshua Jenkins and G. S. Laselle Made lamps, shades, and heavy cut ware
1852–1877	Bay State Glass Co., Boston, Mass. (8)	Commercial quality cut glass.

1854–1910	Hoare, Burns and Dailey, Brooklyn, N. Y. (*Samuel Hawkes-J. Hoare*) (9)	Later J. Hoare and Co. In 1873 moved to Corning, N. Y. Usually identified as a cutting shop, manufactured some glass before 1873 in Brooklyn. Fine quality cut glass in all varieties
1857–1910	Empire State Flint Glass Works, Brooklyn, N. Y. (7, 8)	Francis Thill Lead glass, cut, colored, and engraved
1858–1869	Cape Cod Glass Works, Sandwich, Mass. (7)	Deming Jarves, founder; Nehemiah Packwood, John Jones, designers Lead glass and cut ware similar to Boston and Sandwich Glass Co. output.
1861–1905	Jersey City Flint Glass Works, Jersey City, N. J. (*Dorflinger*) (7 and 9)	H. O'Neil Colored glass, cut tableware, fish globes, bar room accessories, and lamps
1861–1930	Franklin Flint Glass Works, Philadelphia, Penna. (*James Gillinder and J. Fletcher Gillinder*)	William T. Gillinder, founder. In 1863 Edwin Bennett became a partner. In 1867 James and Frederick Gillinder bought Bennett's interest, becoming Gillinder and Sons. Pressed ware subsidiary in Greensburg, Penna. in 1888; became part of U. S. Glass Co., 1891. In 1912 three sons of James Gillinder moved to Port Jervis, N. Y. to operate as Gillinder Brothers. Only Philadelphia plant (Franklin Flint Glass Works) made fine cut tableware. Excellent quality cut glass, colored and engraved; chandeliers
1861–1939	Pairpoint Corporation, New Bedford, Mass. (*Thomas A. Tripp*)	Thomas A. Tripp, Pres. Merged with Mount Washington Glass Co. in 1873. Chandeliers and tableware.

1862–1893	J. S. Hibbler and Co., Brooklyn, N. Y.	Continuation of the old Dorflinger Plymouth Street Works; engraved glass and lamps.
1863–1890	Central Glass Co., Wheeling, W. Va. (7)	Group of workers from Hobbs, Brockunier and Co., cooperative Made and exported much fine cut and colored glass.
1865–1895	Lafayette Flint Glass Works, Brooklyn, N. Y. (8 and 9)	1880, East River Flint Glass Works, P. Schneider's Sons. 1882, Francis Storm Fine cut glass of French design with rock-crystal cutting
1865–1900	Constitution Flint Glass Works, Brooklyn, N. Y. (7 and 8)	Augustine Thiery and Co. Fine lead glass perfume bottles, cut and colored
1866–1891	Richards and Hartley Flint Glass Co., Tarentum, Penna. (*Col. Harry Fry*)	Lightweight tableware
1866–1891	Ripley and Co., Pittsburgh, Penna. (7)	D. C. Ripley and George Duncan, Augustus H. Heisey, James E. Duncan Fine cut glass early in their organization. 1870 converted to pressed lime glass.
1866–1891	William Doyle and Associates, Pittsburgh, Penna. (7 and 8)	Fine tableware in small quantity, engraved and cut
1866–1905	Ditheridge and Co., Pittsburgh, Penna. (Monaca, Penna.) (7 and 9)	A continuation of old Fort Pitt Glass Co. 1900 moved to Monaca. Good quality lead glass, cut and engraved
1868–1964	Corning Glass Works, Corning, N. Y. (7 and 8)	Amory Houghton, Sr. 1852 operated Union Glass Works, Somerville, Mass. 1864 Amory Houghton, Sr. bought the John Gilliland South Ferry Glassworks in Brooklyn, N. Y. 1868 moved to Cor-

ning, N. Y. and established Corning Flint Glass Works.

Made much glass for other cutting shops and designers. Did not cut glass after 1873.

1869–1880   Scott and Rapp, Greenbank, N. J. (8)   Fine small ware, wine glasses, engraved glass and buttons

1870–1874   Plymouth Street Works, Brooklyn, N. Y. (8)   Fowler Crampton and Co.

Fine cut glass. Shop had 35 frames.

1872–1900   Rochester Tumbler Co., Rochester, Penna. (*Col. Harry Fry*)   H. C. Fry, Pres.

Cut glass tumblers

1873–1898   Greenpoint Flint Glass Works, Brooklyn, N. Y. (7 and 8)   J. B. Dobelmann, cutter for Hoare, Burns and Daily. 1884 E. P. Gleason. Cut glass of superior quality. After Gleason bought factory he converted to engraved bottles and lamp shades almost exclusively.

1874–1893   Long Island Flint Glass Works, Brooklyn, N. Y. (*Dorflinger, Gillinder* papers)   John N. Huwer, may have been one of the Dannehoffer partners who continued the Williamsburg glasshouse after death of Walther family.

Fine cut glass

1876–1905   Meriden Britannia Co., Meriden, Conn. (7 and 8)   Horace Wilcox, Pres.

Lead glass with 35 cutters to make pickle dishes, castor bottles, etc.

1879–1891   Agnew and Co., Pittsburgh, Penna. (8)   John Agnew

Clear and golden amber perfume bottles, bitters and medicine bottles of good metal and cut decoration

BRILLIANT PERIOD, 1880–1905

(Because of the large number of glasshouses and cutting shops operating at approximately the same time during the Brilliant Period, an *alphabetical* arrangement of the more important companies seems more convenient than a chronological one.)

Adams and Co., Pittsburgh, Penna. (2 and 8)
: Became part of United States Glass Co. in 1891.
    Fine cut glass in addition to cheaper commercial ware

C. G. Alford and Co., 192 Broadway, N. Y. (8)
: Cutting shop only, standard patterns

Allentown Glass Co., Allentown, Penna. (4, 7, and 8)
: Baker, proprietor, had been partner of J. S. Edsall in Tunkhannock Glass Co.
    Standard cut patterns on glass of intermediate quality

Bawo and Dotter, 26 Barclay Street, N. Y. (7 and 8)
: Importers, glass merchants, also maintained small factory for making and cutting glass to order.
    Cut glass of original design and exquisite quality

A. J. Beatty and Sons, Tiffin, O. (9)
: Became participating company in United States Glass Co. in 1891.
    Commercial grade glass in standard patterns

Bellaire Goblet Co., Findlay, O. (8 and 9)
: One of participating companies in United States Glass Co. in 1891
    Fine lead glass cut and engraved goblets

J. D. Bergen Co., Meriden, Conn. (1, 7, 8, and 9)
: Bergen himself a manufacturer, designer, and cutter prominent for workmanship during Middle Period. Carried traditions into new glass designs.
    Fine glass of good design and sharp cutting

George Borgefeldt and Co., 16th and Irving Place, N. Y. (8)
: Cutting shop only

Bryce Brothers, Mt. Pleasant, Penna. (8)	Became one of the participating companies of U. S. Glass Co., 1891. Commercial cut and pressed tableware, some few exhibition pieces of fine cut glass. Cutting glass today.
Buffalo Cut Glass Co., Batavia, N. Y. (8)	Cutting shop only
Burley and Tyrrell Co., 720 Wabash Avenue, Chicago, Ill. (8)	Cutting shop only
Central Glass Co., Wheeling, W. Va. (7)	U. S. Glass Co. participant after 1891 (See Middle Period chart.)
Challinoir, Taylor and Co., Tarentum, Penna. (8)	U. S. Glass Co. participant after 1891 Made some fine ware of unusual design, only average metal
T. B. Clark and Co., Inc., Honesdale, Penna. (7, 8, and 9)	Fine glass, well designed and cut
Columbia Glass Co., Findlay, O. (9)	U. S. Glass Co. participant after 1891 Commercial ware
Conlow-Dorworth Co. Palmyra, N. J. (8)	Cutting shop only
Crown Cut Glass Co., Inc., Hancock, N. Y. (8)	Cutting shop only
Crystal Cut Glass Co., Chicago, Ill. (8)	Cutting shop only
Deidrick Glass Co., Monaca, Penna. (2, 7, 8, and 9)	Made cut glass and a patented silvered glass called "Silvart."
Diamond Cut Glass Works, N. Y. (8)	Cutting shop only.
C. Dorflinger and Sons, Inc., White Mills, Penna. (*Dorflinger* papers)	(See Middle Period chart.) Fine cut glass in all shapes, colors and patterns
Doyle and Co., Pittsburgh, Penna. (9)	U. S. Glass Co. participant after 1891 Commercial ware

George Drake Cut Glass Co., Corning, N. Y. (8 and 9)

Cutting shop which used Corning Glass Co. blanks.

Duncan and Dithridge, 25 West Broadway, N. Y. (7 and 8)

Fine intaglio cuttings. Lead glass cut in flower motifs.

George Dungan and Sons, Pittsburgh, Penna. (8)

U. S. Glass Co. participant after 1891.
Some few pieces of fine cut ware as exhibition pieces.

O. F. Egginton Co., Corning, N. Y. (2 and 9)

Cutting shop using Corning Glass Co. blanks.

Elmira Glass Co., Elmira, N. Y. (9)

Cutting shop using Corning Glass Company blanks. Became subsidiary of J. Hoare and Co.

Empire Cut Glass Co., Flemington, N. J. (7)

Cut glass in standard patterns.

Eska Manufacturing Co., 311 West Redwood Street, Baltimore, Md. (8)

Cutting shop only

Flemington Cut Glass Co., Flemington, N. J. (8)

Cutting shop only

H. C. Fry Co., Rochester, Penna. (*Col. Harry Fry*)

Organized by H. C. Fry, former pres. of Rochester Tumbler Co. and National Glass Co.
Some of finest lead glass produced in America made here. Fine color, high lead content, sharp cutting.

Gillinder and Sons, Philadelphia, Penna. (*James Gillinder* and *J. Fletcher Gillinder*)

(See Middle Period chart.)
Fine cut tableware, exquisite engraving, colored and cased glass, and intaglio cutting

Gray and Hemingway, Cincinnati, O. (8)

Tumblers, decanters, and other lightweight glass with surface cutting

Greenpoint Flint Glass Works, Brooklyn, N. Y. (1, 2, and 8)

Founded by Christian Dorflinger in 1860 (see Middle Period). Operated by J. B. Dobelmann in 1873.

Became the E. P. Gleason Manufacturing Co. in 1884.

Fine cut glass engraved bottles, vases, and chimneys

T. G. Hawkes Glass Co., Corning, N. Y. (*Samuel Hawkes*)

One of foremost glasshouses in America. Founded by T. G. Hawkes in 1880. Steuben Glass Works built as a subsidiary in 1903.

First quality glass, good metal, original design, and sharp cutting

A. H. Heisey and Co., Inc., Newark, O. (8 and 9)

Fine cut glass of simple design

J. S. Hibbler, also known as Hibbler and Rauch and Hibbler & Co., Brooklyn, N. Y. (7 and 8)

Continuation of Plymouth Street Works founded by Christian Dorflinger

Fine cut glass of all varieties. Also engraved glass.

L. Hinsberger Cut Glass Co., New York City (8)

Cutting shop only

J. Hoare and Co., Corning, N. Y. (*Samuel Hawkes*) (9)

Hoare, Burns and Dailey originally cut glass at the South Ferry Works in N. Y., moving to the Greenpoint Flint Glass Works in 1863. Moved to Corning, N. Y. in 1873 to cut on Corning Glass Co. blanks. Became one of the largest glass cutting shops in the world.

Hobbs Glass Co., Wheeling, W. Va. (8 and 9)

Became one of the participants of the United States Glass Co. in 1891. (See Middle Period, Hobbs, Brockunier Co.)

H. P. Hitchcock Co., 319 S. Saline Street, Syracuse, N. Y. (8)

Cutting shop only

Honesdale Decorating Co., Honesdale, Penna. (7 and 8)

Cutting shop which also used much gilt decoration

Hope Glass Works, 161 Dorrance Street, Providence, R. I. (8)	Cutting shop only
Hunt Glass Co., Corning, N. Y. (8)	Cutting shop using Corning Glass Co. blanks
Imperial Glass Co., Bellaire, O. (*Col. Harry Fry*) (7, 8, and 9)	Used pressed blanks for their commercial clear glass, but did make some very fine colored cut glass and a high grade white glass with colored flashing. Still cutting.
Irving Cut Glass Co., Inc., Park Street, Honesdale, Penna. (7)	Cutting shop only
Jewel Cut Glass Co., 200 Fifth Avenue, New York City (8)	Cutting shop only
Keystone Cut Glass Co., (George W. Murphy), Hawley, Penna. (8)	Cutting shop only
Kiefer Brothers (place and date unknown) (6 and 9)	Cutting shop only
King Glass Co., Pittsburgh, Penna. (8)	U. S. Glass Co. participant in 1891
Kings County Rich Cut Glass Works, 174 North Fourth Street, Brooklyn, N. Y. (8 and 9)	Cut many interesting and well designed patterns on blanks of good quality.
Koch Cut Glass Co., Elgin, Ill. (2 and 9)	Some cut glass but bulk of output cut over pressed blanks, sold under patent name "Koch-Kut."
Krantz, Smith and Co., Inc., Honesdale, Penna. (8)	Cutting shop only
Lafayette Flint Glass Works (East River Flint Glass Works) Brooklyn, N. Y. (8 and 9)	(See Middle Period chart.) Fine cut glass bottles for perfume and cosmetics; intaglio cuttings.

Libbey Glass Co., Toledo, O. (*C. U. Fauster*) (2, 5, 7, 8, and 9)

Continuation of New England Glass Co.
Fine cut glass of good metal and superior design and cutting

Liberty Cut Glass Works, Egg Harbor City, N. J. (9)

Cutting shop only

Joseph Locke and Sons, Locke Art Glassware Co., Mount Oliver, Penna. (Pittsburgh) (*Dr. Alexander Silverman*)

Joseph Locke has been associate of E. D. Libbey in New England Glass Co. Inventor of amberina, pomona.
Fine engraving and etching

Long Island Flint Glass Works, Brooklyn, N. Y. (7 and 8)

Huwer and Dannehoffer (See Middle Period chart.)
Fine grade cut and engraved glass

Lowell Cut Glass Co., 148 Warren Street, Lowell, Mass. (8)

Cutting shop only

William Lum and Son, 508 Broome Street, N. Y. (8)

Cutting shop only

Luzerne Cut Glass Co., Pittston, Penna. (8)

Cutting shop only

Lyons Cut Glass Co., Lyons, N. Y. (8)

Cutting shop only

McKanna Cut Glass Co., Honesdale, Penna. (8)

Cutting shop only

Maple City Glass Co., Honesdale, Penna. (7, 8, and 9)

T. B. Clark and Co. bought company in 1904.
Cut glass in standard patterns

Medford Glass House (Star Glass Works), Medford, N. J. (8)

Cut glass in standard patterns

Meriden Britannia Co., Meriden, Conn. (7 and 8)

Horace Wilcox, Pres.
Cut glass for silver frames, epergnes, candlesticks, bowls, etc.

Meriden Cut Glass Co. (International Silver Co.), Meriden, Conn. (7 and 8)	Cut glass for silver mountings
Michigan Cut Glass Co., Lansing, Mich. (7 and 8)	Cutting shop only
C. F. Monroe Co., Meriden, Conn. (2, 7, and 8)	Cut glass, also pressed blank patented as "Kelva-cut."
Moses, Swan and McLewee Co., Trenton, N. J. (8)	Cutting shop
Richard Murr, San Francisco, Calif. (*Col. Harry Fry*)	Protégé of H. C. Fry Some fine cut glass. Also patented blanks pressed with Kohinoor cut.
S. F. Myers Co., New York City (8)	Cutting shop only
National Glass Co., Rochester and Pittsburgh, Penna. (7)	A syndicate in 1899. Capitalization $4,000,000. Participating companies: Rochester Tumbler Co., McKee Brothers, Crystal Glass Co., Canton Glass Co., Indiana Tumbler and Goblet Co., Model Flint Glass Co., Seneca Glass Co., West Virginia Glass Co., Cumberland Glass Co., Greensburg Glass Co. Various types of cut glass
Newark Cut Glass Co., Arlington St., Newark, N. J. (9)	Mail order glass distributor. Cut poor grade of glass in commercial quantities.
Nickle Plate Glass Co., Fostoria, O. (9)	Participating company in United States Glass Co. in 1891. Commercial ware
A. E. O'Connor, Goshen, N. Y. (7 and 8)	Cutting shop. Very good glass cut to order in excellent patterns.
J. S. O'Connor, Hawley Penna. (7 and 8)	Formerly designer for C. Dorflinger Cut fine glass in well-organized patterns

O'Hara Glass Co. (James Lyon Glass Co.), Pittsburgh, Penna. (8)

Became participant in U. S. Glass Co. in 1891.

Fine quality cut and engraved glass, also large commercial output

Ohio Cut Glass Co., New York City (8)

Cutting shop

Ottawa Cut Glass Co., Ottawa, Ontario, Canada (8)

Cutting shop

Pairpoint Corporation, Prospect St., New Bedford, Mass. (*T. A. Tripp*)

(See Middle Period chart.)

Made and cut fine glass for many years.

F. X. Parsche and Son Co., Chicago, Ill. (2 and 8)

Cutting shop. Designed and cut fine pieces to order.

Peerless Cut Glass Co., (Kelley and Steinman), Deposit, N. Y. (8)

Cutting shop only

Pitkin and Brooks, 8 East Lake Street., Chicago, Ill. (8)

Cutting shop

Quaker City Cut Glass Co., 60 St. and Baltimore Ave., Philadelphia, Penna. (8)

Cutting shop

Richards and Hartley Co., Tarentum, Penna. (8)

Became a participating company in United States Glass Co. in 1891.

Cut glass in standard patterns

Paul Richter Co., Inc., 159 North State Street, Chicago, Ill. (8)

Cutting shop only

Ripley and Co., Pittsburgh, Penna. (8)

Became a participating company in United States Glass Co. in 1891.

Cut glass in standard patterns

Rochester Tumbler Co., Rochester, Penna. (*Col. Harry Fry*)

Largest tumbler manufacturing company in the world. Cut glass tumblers, star bottom, cut and plain. Shipped to all ports of the world.

Roden Brothers, Ltd., 345 Carlow Avenue, Toronto, Ontario, Canada (8)

Cutting shop only

Saint Louis Flint Glass Works, Saint Louis, Mo. (7 and 8)

James B. Eads and G. W. Scooly
   Cut glass of fair quality sold mostly in Middle West

Seattle Cut Glass Co., 813 Second Avenue, Seattle, Wash. (8)

Cutting shop

H. P. Sinclaire and Co., Corning, N. Y. (8 and 9)

Cutting shop. Used Corning Glass Co. blanks.

Standard Cut Glass Co., New York City (8)

Cutting shop

Sterling Glass Co., Sterling Place, Cincinnati, O. (8)

No record of product

L. Straus and Sons, 42-48 Warren St., New York City (7 and 8)

Company also listed as I. Straus and Sons at same address. Large cutting shop and small manufactory. Made to order glass of high quality. Much sold in Europe.

Taylor Brothers Co., Inc., Philadelphia, Penna. (8)

No record of product

Thatcher Brothers, Falmouth, Mass. (8)

Cutting shop

Francis Thill Sons and Co., (Empire State Flint Glass Works) Brooklyn, N. Y. (7 and 8)

Fine lead glass, clear, colored, engraved, and cut

Tunkahannock Glass Co., Tunkahannock, Penna. (7 and 8)

J. S. Edsall, owner, sold in 1898 to Benjamin Franklin Crawford who moved to Pittston, Penna.
   Much fine line cutting of good quality

[409]

Tuthill Cut Glass Co., Middletown, N. Y. (8)	Cutting shop
Unger Brothers, Newark, N. J. (8)	Cutting shop
Union Glass Co., Somerville, Mass. (7 and 8)	Formerly owned by Amory Houghton. Exhibited lamps and shades at Centennial Exhibition in 1876. Julian de Cordova made fine cut glass here in 1890.
Union Salt Castor Co., 38 Vesey St., New York, N. Y. (7)	Cut glass castors with chain tops
United States Glass Co., S. 9th and Bingham Streets, Pittsburgh, Penna. (*Frank Bryant*) (7, 8, and 9)	Organized July 1, 1891, with the following companies participating: Adams & Co.; Bryce Brothers; Challinoir, Taylor & Co.; George Dungan & Sons; Richards and Hartley; Ripley & Co.; Gillinder & Sons (Greensburg, Penna.); Hobbs Glass Co.; Columbia Glass Co.; King Glass Co.; O'Hara Glass Co.; Bellaire Goblet Co.; Nickle Plate Glass Co.; Central Glass Co.; Doyle & Co.; A. J. Beatty & Sons (Tiffin, O.); A. J. Beatty & Sons (Steubenville, O.); Novelty Glass Co. (leased only).
E. J. S. Van Houten, 290 Broadway, New York City (8)	Cutting shop
Whitall-Tatum Co., Millville, N. J. (7 and 8)	Continuation of old Millville Glass Works. Cut glass bottles of all shapes, colors.
Wright Rich Cut Glass Co., Anderson, Ind. (8)	Made cut glass of intermediate quality

IRISH EXPORT CHART

YEARLY SHIPMENTS OF CUT GLASS FROM IRELAND TO AMERICA, 1784–1793

(Figures taken from M. S. Dudley Westropp: *Irish Glass,* but shillings and pence dropped from valuation in pounds)

| Date | Number of drinking glasses shipped to | | | | Other glass imports Value in £ |
	Penna.	N. Y.	New England	Other Places	
				(from Dublin)	
1784	1,200	..	..	5,136	..
1785	..	..	..	..	£204
1786	..	..	..	..	
				Waterford	215
				Other	28
1787	..	1,200	..	..	12
1788	..	8,240	..	..	28
1789	..	..	4,416	..	8
1790	21,928	10,693	..	..	1,614
1791	17,508	14,207	19,604	..	998
1792	3,000	26,200	21,881	..	1,755
1793	45,048	36,000	20,970	..	2,015
TOTAL	88,684	86,540	66,871	5,136	£6,877

YEARLY SHIPMENTS OF CUT GLASS FROM IRELAND TO AMERICA, 1794–1803

| Date | Number of drinking glasses shipped to | | | | Other glass imports Value in £ |
	Penna.	N. Y.	New England	Other Places	
1794	24,250	..	146,832	10,080	£837
1795	3,384	33,800	78,920	..	
1796	77,556	95,240	24,290	..	2,176
1797	..	265,786	231,384	80,000	1,155
1798	..	32,028		..	1,668
1799	..	40,000	14,400	..	150
1800	6,000	7,920	19,560	6,960	276
1801	..	38,183	..	13,104	850
1802	57,740	74,479	3,900	96,304	702
1803	..	113,616		..	..
TOTAL	168,930	699,972	519,286	206,448	£6,978

CUT AND ENGRAVED GLASS

YEARLY SHIPMENTS OF CUT GLASS FROM IRELAND TO AMERICA, 1804–1811

Date	Number of drinking glasses shipped to				Other glass imports Value in £
	Penna.	N. Y.	New England	Other Places	
1804	46,080	9,648	..	..	£1,624
1805	3,600	101,562	17,280	2,771	1,098
1806	82,080	8,544	..	..	
1807	..	62,820	..	11,800	3,647
1808	..	12,276	..	3,726	
1809	Non-Intercourse Act prohibited trade with England and Ireland				
1810	..	205,200	..	164,574	4,932
1811	16,608	32,256	..	83,256	8,357
TOTAL	148,368	435,306	100,536	186,872	£20,099

YEARLY SHIPMENTS OF CUT GLASS FROM IRELAND TO AMERICA, 1812–1822

"After about the year 1812, the number of drinking glasses exported seems to have decreased, but a large number of bottles and other glassware was sent from Dublin, Cork, Waterford, and Belfast to the same places as enumerated in the foregoing lists."— M. S. Dudley Westropp, *Irish Glass,* p. 157. (In addition to Pennsylvania, New York, New England, Maryland, Carolina, and Virginia, the following figures include: Barbados, Jamaica, Hudson's Bay, Newfoundland, "West Indies," Denmark, Portugal, Spain, Antigua, St. Kitts, Spain, Madeira, Africa, "Straits," Guernsey, Trinidad, France, and Montserrat.)

Date	Number of drinking glasses shipped	Other glass imports Value in £
1812	4,800	£4,196
1813	None	8,672
1814	1,954	5,918
1815	577	7,774
1816	4,320	27,962
1817	1,600	22,991
1818	Bottles exported from Ireland— no drinking glasses	20,651
1819	" " "	9,692
1820	" " "	11,128
1821	" " "	7,200
1822	" " "	6,098
TOTAL		£132,000

◇ ◇

GLOSSARY

Age Marks. Scratches on bottom of glass vessels indicating repeated use.

Air-Twist. Spiral thread of air imprisoned in glass stem.

Amberina. A red and amber art glass patented by Joseph Locke.

Annealing. The process of cooling glass slowly under controlled reduction of heat.

Arsenic. A metallic element sometimes used as clarifying agent in manufacture of glass.

Baluster. A pillarlike stem, as a stair balustrade.

Barilla. Salts from calcined plants native to Spain.

Batch. The component parts of a single melting, comparable to a "batch of dough."

Best Metal. Glassmaker's term for lead glass of superior quality.

Blank. An uncut glass vessel originally designed for decoration.

Blaze. Fringe decoration made with miter splits.

Block. Wooden tool used as hand mold to give symmetry to offhand pieces.

Blown. Glass that is gathered on pipe and blown into shape by workman.

Blowpipe. Long, hollow, iron tube used for original gather and subsequent glowings.

Bobêche. A saucer-shaped disk to catch candle drippings.

Bohemian Flint. High-grade potash glass in which one ingredient is calcined vegetation.

[413]

Bull's-Eye. American term for concave, round-ball motif, same as roundelet, kugel, printie, puntie.

Button. A flat horizontal knop or knob.

Buzz. Whirling figure in which radiants are tangent to center, same as pinwheel.

Calcine. To reduce to a powder by the action of heat.

Cameo. Cased glass on which top layer is sculptured leaving figure in relief on background of another color.

Carry-in Boy. Apprentice who carries glass from chair to annealing lehr.

Cased. Glass in which one or more layers is encased in an outer shell of one, two, or more layers of glass of other colors.

Chair. Bench with extended arms in which blower sits while working glass. Also term used to designate a unit of workmen, usually four or five—the blower or gaffer, the gatherer, servitor, carry-in boy, and if necessary, footmaker.

Copper-Wheel Engraving. (See engraving)

Craigleith. A fine stone from Scotland used for smoothing first cutting and for intricate cutting.

Crystal. Natural crystalline quartz or rock crystal; also fine glass of high lead content.

Cullet. Broken glass used as an ingredient of a batch.

Cut. Glass decorated by application to a moving wheel.

Diamond-cut. Surface scratched with a diamond point in a decorative pattern; used by Amelung and Stiegel.

English Flint. Usually designates heavy glass of lead content. May also mean early English nonlead glass made with sand containing flint rock.

Engraving. Decoration by application to a series of small copper wheels. Design is usually unpolished.

Etching. Decoration applied through corroding action of either hydrofluoric acid or its fumes, not by cutting.

Finger Tumbler. A short wide-bottomed, 6-ounce whisky tumbler.

Fire-finished Blank. A blank intended for cutting on which the first deep incisions have been pressed and the refractory surface re-established by heat.

Fire Polishing. Erasing defects such as nicks or scars, by reheating vessel on pontil in glory-hole.

Firing Glass. Short, heavy-stemmed goblet originally designed for Freemasons, who, in response to a toast, rapped the table with sufficient vigor to sound like a volley of gunfire.

Flashing. Coating of one color with a thin layer of another. Frequently outside color is cut through to show a pattern against a contrasting background.

Flint Glass. Properly any glass of which flint-bearing sand is an essential ingredient. See Bohemian Flint, English Flint, Lead Flint.

Flute. A vertical panel cutting usually used without other decoration. Also called Colonial flute.

Flux. An alkaline or metallic substance used to assist in vitrification of silica.

Fly. Explosion of glass caused by inner stress due to improper annealing.

Foot maker. Glass worker who makes feet, handles, tops, etc.

Founding. Glass making from assembly of ingredients to delivery of molten glass to blowers.

Free-blown. Glass blown without the aid of mold or press, offhand.

Gadrooning. Molded and occasionally pincered ornament around the base of a bowl or on the foot.

Gaffer. Master blower, head of shop or chair; sometimes used to designate foreman of several shops or chairs.

Gather. Blob of molten metal which clings to end of blowpipe ready for blowing.

Gatherer. Man who makes the gather for the gaffer—second ranking man on chair.

German Flint. Much the same as Bohemian flint, varying only in source of ingredients more than in chemical properties.

Girandole. An ornamental branched candle-holder whose principal decoration is pendent prisms.

Glass. "A substance, the principal and essential constituents of which are silica and an alkali. It may be considered as consisting of one or more salts, which are silicates with bases of potash, soda, lime, oxide of iron, aluminum, or lead, in any of which compounds. One of these bases may be substituted for another, provided that one alkaline base be left." (Ure's *Dictionary of Chemistry, Art, Glass*)

Glassmaker's Soap. Black oxide of manganese which, added to the batch, washes out the yellow or green tint of iron in the sand used in batch.

Glory Hole. A small furnace used for the frequent reheating necessary in working offhand glass.

Glyptic. Pertaining to carving or engraving.

Green Glass. Also called bottle glass. Common metal made of sands which have high iron content. Such metal contains simplest and cheapest ingredients—sand, pearlash, soda.

Hand Blown. Free blown or offhand glass blown without the use of a mold.

Hatched. Chased or engraved with parallel or crossed lines.

Herring-bone Fringe. See Blaze.

High Color. A pink, blue, or violet tinct noticeable in crystal glass, caused by an excess of decolorizer (i.e. manganese) usually in connection with lead glass.

Hobnail. A six-sided, flat-topped motif resembling the hobnail of a heavy boot.

Hob-Star. A star of so many points that the intersection forms a motif resembling hobnail.

Knop. A protuberance in the stem of a vessel, a knob.

Kugel (n.). Bull's-eye motif (German).

Lapidary cutting. Sharp angular cutting associated with cutting of diamonds and precious stones.

Lead Glass (Lead flint). Metal fused with an oxide of lead. Usually used in connection with glass of high lead content in which there are approximately 60 pounds of lead to 100 pounds of sand.

Lehr (or Leer). An annealing furnace, arch, or oven.

Lime Glass. Metal in which lime is the principal ingredient with silica.

Low Color. Green or yellowish green tinct noticeable in crystal glass, caused by presence of iron in the batch.

Manganese. Glassmaker's soap used to counteract the presence of iron in batch.

Marver. Metal slab on which gather of metal is rolled after it is taken from furnace and before it is given to the gaffer to be blown.

Metal. The essential fabric of glass.

Miter. Stone most commonly used in cutting. Also used to describe the deep incisions made with miter wheel, as miter cutting.

Mold Blown. Glass blown by hand into an undecorated paste mold suspended in a tub of water.

Motif. One of several figures used in glass patterns.

Muddy (or Bad Color). White or crystal glass that shows yellowish or brownish tinct caused by carbon.

Mushets. Engravers' and cutters' tools made of highspeed steel containing tungsten.

Nail-Head Diamond. Sharp pointed diamond formed by four pyramidal sides.

Needle Etching. Process in which design to be etched with hydrofluoric acid is drawn through wax resist by a needle point.

Offhand. Fashioned freehand without the use of either press or mold.

Opal (Opaque). Nontransparent glass—may be white or colored. White opal is commonly called milk glass.

Open Pot. Clay pot resembling wash tub used to melt glass, usually for nonlead metals.

Overlay. Process in which small pieces of colored or opal glass are placed upon the outside of molten glass and worked out to form a colored or opal coating of contrasting color.

Panel Cutting. Long scooped-out indentations, concave flutes.

Pantagraph Etching. Acid etching process in which needles transmitting design follow a perforated plate or stencil.

Paste Mold. A mold of wood or iron lined with a paste made of beeswax, rosin, and other ingredients. This mold is suspended in a tub of water and the vessel blown hot into it.

Pattern. The repetitious use of one or more motifs to form a design in cut glass decoration.

Pattern Glass. Same as pressed.

Pendeloque. Pear-shaped pendant on glass chandelier.

Pillar. Prism that has been smoothed down to a rounded or convex surface.

Pontil. Long solid rod (occasionally hollow), used to hold vessel while it is still hot and being finished by the gaffer or foot maker.

Pontil Mark. Scar left by the pontil on the vessel after it has been cracked off.

Potash. An ingredient sometimes used in place of soda ash; acts as flux.

Pressed Blank. A lead glass vessel intended for cutting on which the first deep incisions have been pressed while glass was still molten.

Pressed Glass. Molten glass dropped into a pressing mold where it is pressed by means of a plunger into the pattern previously cut into the sides of the mold or the plunger.

Prince Rupert Drop. A small piece of hot glass which on being dropped into a tub of water, cools quickly into a clear cold piece of glass like a teardrop. The heavy end can be pounded with a mallet but if the capillary end is snapped off the whole piece will fly into powder.

Printie. Irish version of kugel, Bull's-Eye, roundelet, etc.

Prism. A long cut figure in which two or more miter-cut sides form a ridge or bar.

Puntie. See Printie; also a common term for pontil.

Resist. Wax coating to protect glass from action of acid in etching bath.

Rock Crystal. Natural quartz rock; also a trade name for fine lead crystal, commonly cut and polished in shallow French Baccarat motifs.

Rougher. Glass cutter who puts the first heavy incisions in glass with an iron wheel.

Roundelet. English version of kugel or bull's-eye.

Saint Louis Neck. Concave hexagonal diamond cutting of the earlier English period; used extensively on Early American cruets and castor bottles.

Serrated. Saw-tooth edge.

Shop. Same as chair.

Sick Glass. Condition caused by separation of small crystals, devitrification, or by too high alkaline content.

Silica. Sand, essential ingredient of glass.

Smalt. A deep blue glass colored with cobalt oxide.

Soda Ash. Sodium carbonate used as flux to start melting of batch; also furnishes part of alkali necessary for making glass.

Soda Barilla. One of the types of Bohemian flint glass made in America in the eighteenth century. Formula used calcined seaweeds and river sand. Such glass is light in weight, slightly resonant. American pieces usually show some low color.

Split. An acute-angled cut made with grinding wheel.

Splitter. The grinding wheel used to make splits.

Standard. The original unified arrangement of cut glass motifs patented or produced under a specified name.

Strawberry-Diamond. Square diamond-shaped figure made with deep cuttings on four sides. The top of figure is flat and cut with only one cross in the American motif. See Motif Chart (Appendix VI) for English strawberry-diamond.

Striae. Cords or wavy lines sometimes in lead glass of early period due to unwise choice of raw materials, unsatisfactory batch mixing, unsuitable melting conditions, accidental inclusion of outside materials, or corrosion of the pots.

Sweetmeat Dishes. Eighteenth-century term for dessert dishes.

Tear. Bubble of air imprisoned in glass either accidentally or by the deliberate nicking of the glass while molten.

Trailing. Rope of looped threads of glass applied to outer surface of vessel while molten.

Variation. Any deviation of motif arrangement which does not essentially alter a standard design.

Vesica. Literally, a bladder; in design, a pointed oval.

Waterford. Glass made in Waterford, Ireland, only.

Wheel Engraving. Usually copper-wheel engraving, a process by which surface of glass is decorated by application to any one of a number of copper wheels of varying sizes.

White Glass. Sometimes called crystal. Clear transparent metal in which no coloring agent has been used; to be differentiated from milk-white glass, green glass, and bottle glass. White glass may be lead glass, potash-glass, soda-glass, or lime-glass, depending on ingredients and formula used.

◇ ◇

BIBLIOGRAPHY

Note: An exhaustive bibliography cannot be included in this volume. The following is limited to the principal sources consulted by the author.

MANUSCRIPTS

Letters of James O'Hara, 1790–1819 Denny papers, Historical Society of Western Pennsylvania, Pittsburgh, Penna.
Letters of Isaac Craig 1790–1804 Craig Papers, Carnegie Library, Pittsburgh, Penna.
Vitreology or the Art of Smelting, Henry Rowe Schoolcraft, (1812) Library of Congress, Washington, D. C.
Notes on Glass, Thomas Gaffield, Massachusetts Institute of Technology, Cambridge, Mass.

CONTEMPORANEOUS SOURCES

Amelung, John Frederick, "Remarks on Manufactures, Principally on the New Established Glass House near Frederick-town, in the state of Maryland 1787."
Hamilton, Alexander, "Report on Manufactures" and "Correspondence," 1791.
Jarves, Deming, *Reminiscences of Glass-Making,* New York, 1865.
Johnston, William G., *Life and Reminiscences,* Pittsburgh, 1901.
Kern, William, "Reminiscences of the Boston and Sandwich Fac-

tory," speech delivered before the American Association of Flint and Lime Glass Manufacturers at Atlantic City, N. J., July 20, 1906.

Parke, John E., "Recollections of Seventy Years and Historical Gleanings of Allegheny, Penna." Boston, 1886.

Prime, Alfred Coxe, "The Arts and Crafts in Philadelphia, Maryland and South Carolina," Series One, 1721–1785, Series Two, 1786–1800, The Walpole Society, 1932.

HISTORIES AND DIRECTORIES

Bishop, J. Leander, "A History of American Manufacturers from 1608–1860," Philadelphia 1864.

Boucher, John Newton, "A Century and a Half of Pittsburgh and Her People," vols. I and II, 1909.

Clark, Victor Selden, "History of Manufacturing in the U. S.," 2 vols. 1916.

Craig, Neville B., "History of Pittsburgh," 1851.

Cramer's *Almanack,* Pittsburgh, 1809.

Donehos, "Pennsylvania, A History."

Durant, Samuel W., "History of Allegheny County, Penna.," Everts Publishing Co., Pittsburgh, 1876.

Fahnestock's "Pittsburgh Directory," 1850.

Harris, Isaac, *Pittsburgh Business Directory,* 1837.

Jones, Samuel, "Pittsburgh in 1826, Containing Sketches Topographical, together with A Directory of the City and a View of its Various Manufactures," 1826.

Leonard, John William, "Pittsburgh and Allegheny Illustrated," 1889.

Newton, Nichols and Sprangle, "History of the Pan-Handle," Wheeling, 1879.

Riddle and Murray, *Directory for Pittsburgh for 1819.*

"Story of Maumee Valley, Toledo and Sandusky Regions," Chicago, 1929.

Thurston, George H., "Pittsburgh's Progress, Industries and Resources," 1886.

Warner, A., "History of Allegheny County," Chicago, 1889.

White's *History of Invention,* "Origin and History of Glass."

Williams, Thomas J. C., "History of Frederick County, Maryland," vol. 1, page 268, 1910.

Wilson, Erasmus, "Standard History of Pittsburgh," Pittsburgh, 1898.

SECONDARY SOURCES

Bakewell, Benjamin Gifford, "Family Book of Bakewell, Page, Campbell," Pittsburgh, 1896.

Barber, Edwin, *American Glassware Old and New,* Philadelphia, 1900.

Barstow, Harry, *Glass.*

Bate, Percy H., *English Table Glass,* N. Y., 1905.

Bining, William, "The Glass Industry of Western Pennsylvania, 1797–1857," presented as a thesis for a master's degree, University of Pittsburgh, 1936.

Buckley, Francis, *History of Old English Glass,* London, 1925.

Buckley, Wilfred, *The Art of Glass,* London, 1939. *Wolff and the Glasses that He Engraved,* London, 1935.

Cambridge Glass Company, "The Art of Making Fine Glassware," 1945.

Chipman, Frank W., "The Romance of Old Sandwich Glass," Sandwich, Mass., 1932.

Dillon, Edward, *Glass,* London, 1907.

Dorflinger, William, "The Development of the Cut-Glass Business in the United States," paper read before the American Association of Flint and Lime Glass Manufacturers at Atlantic City, July 25, 1902.

Edwards, Richard, "Industries of Pittsburgh," Pittsburgh, 1879.

Fettke, Charles Reinhard, "Glass Manufacture and the Glass Sand Industry of Pennsylvania," Harrisburg, 1919.

Gessner, Frank, *Glassmaker's Handbook,* Pittsburgh, 1891.

Gillinder, James, "American Glass Interests," from *One Hundred Years of American Commerce,* 1895.

Gillinder, James, *Industrial Chemistry,* edited by Allen Rogers, 2 vols. Excellent technical source for manufacture.

Gillinder, William, "Treatise on the Art of Glass Making containing 272 Practical Receipts," Birmingham, England, 1854.

Gregg, Arthur B., "Old Heldebergh," Altamont, N. Y., 1936.

Harding, William G., "Glass Manufacture in Berkshires," Berkshire Historical and Scientific Society, vol. 2, pp. 24-27, Pittsfield, Mass., 1894.

Hartshorne, Albert, *Old English Glasses,* London and New York, 1897.

Heller, Ralph W., "Edward Drummond Libbey," a thesis for U. of Toledo (1948).

Hower, Harry S., "Some Scientific and Technological Contributions to the Glass Industry in the Pittsburgh District," 1935.

Hunter, Frederick William, *Stiegel Glass,* Boston, Mass., 1914.

Irwin, Frederick T., *The Story of Sandwich Glass,* Boston, 1926.

Janneau, Guillaume, *Modern Glass,* New York.

Jefferson, Josephine, *Wheeling Glass,* Mount Vernon, Ohio, 1947.

Kirch, T. E., "A classified list of the United States Patents on glass."

Knittle, Rhea Mansfield, *Early American Glass,* New York, 1927.

Kramer, Le Roy, "Johann Baltasar Kramer, Pioneer American Glass Blower," 1939.

Kummel, Henry Barnhard and R. B. Gage, "Glass sand industry of New Jersey," 1907 (very technical).

Lee, Ruth Webb, *Antique Fakes and Reproductions,* 1938. *Early American Pressed Glass,* 1931.

Lehmann, Helen Mary and Beulah Elfreth Kennard, *Glass and Glassware,* New York, 1922.

Lewis, J. Sydney, *Old Glass and How to Collect it,* London, 1925.

Macbeth-Evans, "Fifty Years of Glass-Making," Pittsburgh, 1919.

MacFarlane, John F., "Manufacturing in Philadelphia, 1683–1912."

MacManus, Theodore F., "A Century of Glass Manufacture, 1818–1918," Libbey Glass Company, 1918.

Marson, Percival, *Glass and Glass Manufacturing,* London, 1920.

McKearin, George S. and Helen, *American Glass,* N. Y., 1946.

[423]

Moore, N. Hudson, *Old Glass,* New York, 1924.

Pellatt, Apsley, *Curiosities of Glass Making,* London, 1849.

Percival, Maciver, *The Glass Collector,* London, 1919.

Phillips, C. J., *Glass, the Miracle Maker,* 1941.

Porter, George Richardson, "A treatise on the origin, progressive improvement and present state of the manufacturing of porcelain and glass," Philadelphia, 1846.

Powell, Harry, *Glass-making in England,* Cambridge, 1923.

Quattlebaum, W. Dan, "Early American Glass, Informal Sketches with Special Notes on Amelung."

Rackham, Bernard, *A Key to Pottery and Glass,* London, 1940.

Rogers, Frances, *5,000 Years of Glass,* 1937.

Sausay, Alexandre, *Marvels of glass-making in all ages,* London, 1869.

Scoville, Warren Candler, "Revolution in Glassmaking," The Story of E. D. Libbey and M. J. Owens, 1948.

Setzer, Dorothea, "The Sandwich Historical Society and Its Glass," 1936.

Skelly, Leloise Davis, *Modern Fine Glass,* 1937.

Stannus, Mrs. Graydon, *Old Irish Glass,* 1920.

Stanwood, Edward, "American Tariff Controversies," 1903.

Swan, Frank Herbert, "Portland Glass Company," 1939.

Swisher, Idella Gwatkin, "An Introduction to the Study of Tariff," 1931.

Thorpe, W. A., *A History of English and Irish Glass,* London, 1927.

Thurston, George H., "Allegheny County's Hundred Years," 1888. "Pittsburgh's Progress, Industries and Resources."

Watkins, Lura Woodside, *Cambridge Glass,* Boston, 1930. *The Development of American Glass-making,* 1935.

Waugh, Sidney, *The Art of Glass Making,* 1938.

Weeks, Joseph Dane, "Report on the Manufacture of Glass," Washington, 1883. United States Census Reports, Tenth Census, (1880).

Westropp, M. S. Dudley, *Irish Glass,* London, 1921.

Wilson, Simon N., *The Glass Industry in Ohio,* 1938.

Yoxall, J. H., *Collecting Old Glass,* 1916.

DOCUMENTS AND PUBLIC RECORDS

"Pennsylvania is Nation's Leading Manufacturer of Glass Products," Commonwealth of Pennsylvania, Department of Internal Affairs Bulletin, May 1936.

Register of Pennsylvania, S. Hazard (editor), devoted to the Preservation of Facts and Documents and Every Other Kind of Useful Information Respecting the State of Pennsylvania, I-XVI, Philadelphia, 1828–1833.

Tariff Acts passed by the Congress of the United States 1789–1909, compiled under the Joint Committee of Printing, Government Printing Office, 1909.

United States Census Reports, Sixth Census, 1840; "General Statistics on Manufactures," 1870; Thirteenth Census, "General Statistics on Glass Industry."

United States Duties by the Several Acts of 1816, 1824, 1828, and 1932.

United States Foreign and Domestic Commerce Bureau, "The Glass Industry," 1917.

MAGAZINES AND PERIODICALS (Technical)

"Art of Cutting Glass," *Harper's Weekly,* January 25, 1890.

"Berkshire Crystal," *Hours at Home,* October, 1870.

"Manufacture of Incised or Cut Glass," *Scientific American,* April 30, 1904.

"A New Means of Using Compressed Air in the Manufacture of Glassware," *Scientific American,* May 10, 1902.

"New Sand for Glass Making," *Franklin Journal,* 1926.

Pellatt, Apsley, "On the Manufacture of Flint Glass," *Railway Magazine,* December, 1840.

Powell, Harry J., "Cut Glass," *Journal Society of Arts,* vol. 54, London, 1906.

Riley-Pearson, W. H., "Glassmaking: the Art and the Trade," *World's Work,* London, 1904.

Silverman, Alexander, "Some Recent Developments in American Glass Manufacture," *Bulletin of the American Ceramic Society,* November 15, 1947.

Tatum, C. A., "One Hundred Years of Achievement in American Glass Manufacture," *Scientific American Supplement,* April 21, 1900.

Willey, Day Allen, "The Process of Cutting Glass Dishes," *Scientific American Supplement,* June 28, 1902.

EARLY AMERICAN PERIOD

Bakewell, Mary E., "The Bakewell Glass Factory," *Carnegie Magazine,* July, 1947.

"Fresh Reflections on American Glass," *Antiques Magazine,* February, 1938.

Gest, N. C. and Park G. Smith, "The Glassmaking Kramers," *Antiques Magazine,* March, 1939.

Gillingham, H. E., "Pottery, China, and Glass Making in Philadelphia," *Pennsylvania Magazine of History and Biography,* vol. 54, 1930.

Innes, Lowell, "Glass Cut at Pittsburgh," *Carnegie Magazine,* June, 1946.

Jarves, Deming, "American Glass," letter to *Niles' Register,* July 3, 1819.

Keyes, Homer Eaton, "Safe Clues in the Amelung Quest," *Antiques Magazine,* September, 1934.

Knittle, Rhea Mansfield, "Concerning William Peter Eichbaum and the Bakewells," *Antiques Magazine,* March, 1927. "Glassmaking in Wheeling, West Virginia," *Antiques Magazine,* August, 1933.

McCready, Jessie and Delphine, "The Ihmsen Family," *Antiques Magazine,* August, 1938.

McKearin, George S., "Wistarberg and South Jersey Glass," *Antiques Magazine,* October, 1926.

"Notice of the Glass Blowing, Cutting and Porcelain Manufacture at Jersey City," by the editor, *Franklin Journal and American Mechanic's Magazine,* October, 1826.

Ormsbee, Thomas H. and Florence Cragin Allen, "Glassmaking at Lake Dunmore, Vermont," *American Collector*, August and September, 1937.

Pears, Thomas C. Jr., "The First Successful Flint Glass Factory in America," *Antiques Magazine*, March, 1927. Visit of Layfayette to the Old Glass Works of Bakewell, Pears and Co.," *Western Pennsylvania Historical Magazine*, October, 1925.

Sicard, Hortense F., "Glassmaker to Two Presidents," *Antiques Magazine*, July, 1935.

Stow, Charles Messer, "Amelung and Contemporary Maryland Glassblowers," *Antiquarian*, December, 1930.

Susswein, Rita, "Early 19th Century New York Produced Fine Glass," January 23, 1934, *American Collector*.

Swan, Mabel M., "Deming Jarves and His Glass Factory Village," *Antiques Magazine*, January, 1938.

Watkins, Lura Woodside, "Deming Jarves and the Pressing of Glass," *Antiques Magazine*, October, 1931.

White, Harry Hall, "New York State Glass Houses," *Antiques Magazine*, July, 1929-Part I; September, 1929-II; November, 1929-III. "Albany Glass Works," *Antiques Magazine*, July, 1936. "Henry Rowe Schoolcraft, Glassmaker," *Antiques Magazine*, December, 1938-Part I; February, 1938-II; April, 1939-III. "Early Pittsburgh Glass-Houses," *Antiques Magazine*, November, 1926.

MIDDLE PERIOD

"Dyott's Improvement in Melting and Fusing Glass," *Franklin Institute Journal*, December, 1828.

Newton, Janet Foster, "Dorflinger Glass," *Antiques Magazine*, January, 1944.

McKearin, Helen, "Glass at World's Fairs," *Antiques Magazine*, Part I, August, 1939; Part II, September, 1939.

Rolfe, Richard Carman, "Bar Glass," *Magazine of Old Glass*, February, 1940. "Our Nineteenth Century Glass Industry," *Magazine of Old Glass*, May, 1939.

Seymour, Henry James, "Glass and Glass-Makers," *Magazine of Western History,* vol. 3, February, 1886.

Silverman, Alexander, "Sandwich Glass," I-II-III-IV-V, *The Glass Industry,* February, March, April, May, and June, 1939.

"Story of Cut and Engraved Glass," *Brush and Pencil,* vol. 18.

BRILLIANT PERIOD

"American Cut-Glass Unrivaled," *Brush and Pencil,* vol. 10, 1902.

Edwards, Harriet, "Present Fashions in Glass," *Harper's Bazaar,* November 3, 1900.

Herrick, Christine Terhune, "New Cut Glass and China," *Harper's Bazaar,* February, 1904.

Powell, Harry J., "Cut Glass," *Journal Society of Arts,* vol. 54, pp. 776-781, London, 1906. "Table Glass," *American Architect,* vol. 81, page 35, August 1, 1903.

Silverman, Alexander, "Frederick Carder, Artist and Glass Technologist," *American Ceramic Society Bulletin,* September, 1939. "Joseph Locke, Artist," *The Glass Industry,* August, 1936.

ENGLISH AND IRISH GLASS

Hughes, G. Bernard, "English Rummers and Firing Glasses," *Antiques Magazine,* February, 1931.

O'Fallon, J. M., "Glass Engraving as an Art," *The Art Journal,* 1885.

Thorpe, W. A., "The Development of Cut Glass in England and Ireland," II—Period from 1780 to 1851, *Antiques Magazine,* November, 1930. "The Beginnings of English Cut Glass," *Connoisseur,* October, 1930. "The Rise of English Cut Glass," *Connoisseur,* November, 1930.

Westropp, M. S. Dudley, "Irish Cut Glass," *Antiques Magazine,* June, 1928.

CATALOGUES

Bakewell, Page, Bakewell catalogue, (ca. 1860) courtesy Carnegie Library, Pittsburgh, Penna.

Gillinder and Sons, Inc., catalogue (Philadelphia), courtesy of New York Public Library.

Glass Factory Year Book and Directory, 1904.

J. Hoare and Company catalogue and scrap book, courtesy, Mr. Samuel Hawkes, Corning, New York.

Illustrated catalogue of the Philadelphia Centennial Exhibition, 1876, vol. I.

Libbey Glass Company catalogue, courtesy Libbey Glass Company, Toledo, Ohio.

Maple City Glass Co. catalogue, (Hawley, Penna. ca. 1900) courtesy Bella Landauer Collection, New York Historical Society, New York.

Newark Cut Glass Company catalogue, Newark, New Jersey, (ca. 1905) courtesy C. W. Meredith, Rochester, Penna.

"Pottery and Glass Trade Handbook," London, 1933.

"Steuben Glass," with an introduction by Sidney Waugh.

United States Glass Company catalogue, 1900, courtesy Mr. Frank Bryant, Tiffin, Ohio.

John Wanamaker catalogue, Philadelphia, Summer 1887, courtesy Bella Landauer Collection, New York Historical Society.

MISCELLANEOUS

Scrapbooks of the Bella Landauer Collection, New York Historical Society, including many old invoices, advertisements and "notices."

Scrapbooks on "Glass," New York Public Library.

Scrapbooks on "Glass," Toledo Public Library.

Picture files of the Thomas G. Hawkes Glass Company, Corning, New York.

Scrapbooks of Advertisements and 'Notices' of the Libbey Glass Company, Toledo, Ohio.

INDEX

INDEX

INDEX

INDEX

INDEX